The
Sense
Of
Humor

Let Humor Fast Track You to Healthier, Happier Living

Elk Lake Publishing

The Sense of Humor

Copyright © 2016 by Max Elliott Anderson

Requests for information should be addressed to:
Elk Lake Publishing, Atlanta, GA 30024
ISBN-13 978-1-942513-97-1

Interior Format: Anna M. O'Brien

Editor: Deb Haggerty

The
Sense
Of
Humor

Let Humor Fast Track You to Healthier, Happier Living

Max Elliot Anderson

Dedication

To the memory of my dad, *Ken Anderson*, who brightened the lives of so many people around the world through his gifted use of humor and laughter.

Table of Contents

Introduction

During these uncertain times, what people need most is a good laugh. Imagine what would happen if we understood there is an untapped force contained within us that has the positive power to totally change our lives. And what if we discovered all we had to do in order to unlock this secret was simply to start using it?

So it is with humor.

The Sense of Humor is designed to demonstrate the *sense* humor can make in the life of anyone who is willing to use it.

The basic premise of *The Sense of Humor* is this: Humor and a sense of humor are unique gifts from God intended to enable people to enjoy a more positive life while at the same time brightening the corner where they are.

In other words, humor will deliver direct benefits to the user. Outside of this primary benefit, humor will touch the lives of everyone around the user in positive ways.

Personally, I've used humor extensively in my film and video production work as well as in the middle grade mysteries and adventures I write for young readers.

In its early stages, this project began as a simple joke book. However, as discussions progressed, I was exposed to the relationships between humor and the medical profession. As a professional video producer, my projects for medical clients opened the door to the potential benefits of humor and laughter in medicine. The same had occurred with some of my industrial clients.

My father, Ken Anderson, and I began to explore various areas of life where humor had also been cited as beneficial: education, families, and others. Before the book was finished, my father died at the age of eighty-eight. I continued developing the concept, gathering research material, selecting appropriate jokes and humorous stories and shaping the final manuscript.

Because of our earlier collaboration, you will find the words "we" and "our" occasionally used. It's a way of letting my father's legacy live on through this project.

We interviewed people in the medical field and in education. We've cited research from authorities on the subject of humor and its benefits.

Each person arrives at the same understanding. Including humor in all facets of our lives will improve our lives.

The effects of humor are most dramatic in medicine. We cite scientific studies and their findings to reveal humor aids in the healing process. And a personal sense of humor helps combat stress and depression.

I believe if you allow these concepts to take hold in your life, you'll find positive results throughout many of your personal relationships.

The Bible tells us in Proverbs 17:22, *A merry heart does good like a medicine.*

One—

An Introduction to The <u>Sense</u> of Humor

A good laugh is a mighty good thing and rather scarce a thing.
—Herman Melville

When was the last time you enjoyed such a hearty laugh you felt good all over? Have you wondered if laughter had any real purpose, or did you simply relegate the experience to such mysteries as the sonic blast from a sneeze or the reason why we have mosquitoes? This "good all over" feeling has, in recent years, become the object of much research in Western Europe and, more recently, here in North America. In his book, *Laughter and Health,* Dr. James Walsh writes, "Laughter provides the inner organs of the body with beneficial massage. Stomach, lungs, heart gain significant benefit."

April in America introduces National Humor Month, which is fitting since this month is kicked off with April Fool's Day. But the idea laughter is the best medicine is getting some scientific credence from studies that show laughter can lower blood pressure, increase blood circulation, improve alertness, increase tolerance to pain, and have positive influence on the body's immune system.

For the purpose of observing humor in this book, let's consider the following:

1. Humor was designed by our Creator in the same manner and purpose as such emotions as joy, pleasure, and anger.
2. Humor may well be intended to serve us as the foremost of our emotions.
3. The Evil One endeavors to impair the humor emotion by means of neglect and perversion.

Learning Objective:

As you put into practice the teachings of this book, your communication skills will improve. You will develop a positive attitude and be a better friend, associate and person. You will create an environment where life becomes more enjoyable within your own circle of influence, learning that humor is like love; the more you give, the more it comes back to bless you.

We will explore claims of health benefits when tested techniques are used.

Educators report that humor increases retention of facts in the classroom, facilitating an environment where students enjoy learning. Positivity increases on the job, in industry, and at the office when humor is present.

PLEASE NOTE:

We do not pretend to be masters of the subject. Nor do we think of this book as a definitive statement on humor. Like you, we will continue to search and, hopefully, discover how humor can be beneficial to the world in which we live. A couple of weeks after the destruction of the

The Sense of Humor

World Trade Center in New York City and the bombing of the Pentagon in our nation's capital, a reporter asked one of the late night TV talk show hosts how he had handled humor on his program the previous night, his first telecast since the tragedy.

"People need humor," replied the entertainer, "It's part of their healing. We've got to use our smarts, however, and carefully wean them back to their previous levels of tolerance."

Subsequently, playing it safe, this same host televised several shows using neither gags nor one-liners, relying only on interviews with prominent personalities from the entertainment community.

The aggressively satirical magazine, *The Onion,* which followed the death of Mother Teresa with the headline, "Mother Teresa Dispatched to Hell in Wacky Afterlife Mix-up," ducked possible censure by temporarily suspending publication.

Will Rogers had it right when he said, "Everything is funny as long as it's happening to somebody else."

Except for Pearl Harbor, past wars—involving aircraft and sophisticated combat equipment—have always been fought on somebody else's turf. Unlike Europe and Asia, Americans died by droves on the "Killing Fields" while their personal property, secure behind the boundaries of their home country, remained unscathed.

Not so this time.

We were victims! The blood of Americans stained American soil. Who so much as thought of joking about those Twin Tower heroes? Off limits, each and every one!

A new, untested President, who had been consistently lambasted by comedy writers and the press, emerged now with courage, strength, and leadership by which to capture the affection of an entire nation. You could no more make jokes about the President than you could about motherhood.

Then the same president, George W. Bush, turned the world's attention onto a desert millionaire by the name of Osama bin Laden as the architect of terror. The US wanted him, declared Bush, "dead or alive."

Comedians were sure they had their man!

One standup comic in a New York night spot told his audience he had to cut short his act because he was flying to LA. "You can't fly direct anymore," he said. "My plane goes by way of the Empire State Building."

Angry jeers came from the audience. So severe was their protest, the comic bowed out and left the stage.

Humor floundered. Gag writers would sit and stare at blank sheets of paper for hours.

No off-color joke ever told could possibly equal the disgust engendered by that scene found on a videotape in Afghanistan and released by the US Government to millions of viewers all over the world. The most sought after fugitive of all time laughed as he spoke of the many people killed in the Twin Towers and how results exceeded expectations. His most ill-timed humor seemed reserved for the moment when he told of his amusement at learning the men on the suicide mission had boarded the hijacked airliners, which, a short time later, crashed into the Towers, the Pentagon and in a field in Pennsylvania.

Not until their deadly mission was underway did most of the hijackers learn this was the actual event that would require they sacrifice their lives!

By contrast, September 11th produced a multitude of serious-thinking Americans who, in the wake of that terrible terrorist strike, developed new vocabularies, as strongly religious implications became the predominant mood of an entire nation.

World War II proved to be the watershed of the largely unnoticed but significant episodes you will come upon in this book. Don't be surprised if what you find on these pages is new information. Our research intensified a desire to help others discover and utilize the material we have uncovered.

The Sense of Humor

Let me give you a background of present day *laughology*, as we've coined the word. First, however, allow me to set the stage with some personal experiences.

Shortly after the close of World War II, my father, author and filmmaker Ken Anderson, spent several weeks in China with the founder of World Vision International. Their schedule sent them via Tokyo. Both on their approach to Tokyo's Haneda Airport, and as they took off and headed toward China, they looked down on a burned out city. "It appeared like a giant honeycomb," my father told us. "Firebombs had been dropped onto Tokyo, consuming the tinderbox buildings and leaving only rock foundations."

An hour out of Tokyo, the captain informed the passengers in six minutes they would pass over the city of Hiroshima. A vast area of that city had been swept away as if by a giant hand.

"An awesome sight!" he said.

I had a similar experience. Only two months after completing my military service in the US Army during the Vietnam era, I found myself on a film production assignment to Hong Kong, Taiwan, Japan, Korea, and of all places, Vietnam. Switching off my military brain and turning on my civilian brain was difficult. As we approached the airport in Saigon, I was shocked to see all the bomb blast craters that littered the countryside. I could only imagine the pain and agony felt by all who lived down there.

The earlier trip to China was my father's first introduction to the discovery of what a shock war is to any culture. However, his most revealing experience was to be in Western Europe. He made a survey trip through post-war Germany, visiting the devastated cities of Berlin, Dusseldorf, Cologne, and Stuttgart. "Devastation was everywhere," he said. "It was plain enough to see why German spirits lagged."

Meanwhile, back in the US, champagne corks were popping. An

15

entire nation celebrated the lifting of restraints as multitudes fled away from the church to investigate a carnal world's lifestyles.

Serious-minded European youth began reading again the writings of Schopenhauer, the pessimist, and Sartre, the existentialist. Student tours ventured both west and east: west to America and its libertine ways; east to the Orient's unhallowed teachings.

A group of undergrads, reportedly from the University of Heidelberg, ventured east to the Himalayan foothills of India, spending several weeks in an ashram near the holy city of Hardwar. Here they had many sittings at the feet of such men as Swami Nairansingh, one of India's touted gurus.

One morning, taking a stroll along a footpath leading away from their ashram, the students approached a temple from which they reported hearing a cacophony of laughter. Curious, they jogged the remaining distance, there to look upon an unprecedented spectacle. Inside the temple, a dozen holy men danced about the interior calling out sordid mantras, at times in classic dance movements, occasionally with obscene gestures.

All the time they laughed at the top of their voices.

Being decent, well-bred youth, some of the group demanded an immediate return to the ashram. But older students decided to remain.

One of the holy men came to the Germans and, English being the second language of educated people in both India and Germany, agreed to answer questions for a few buckshees of Indian currency.

Lively interchange resulted.

"Laughter is one of the sweetest gifts from the gods," the holy man began, "By laughing and dancing, we energize our bodies so we become receptive to important truths which would otherwise evade us."

These young German students displayed nothing but curiosity about this man's elaborate claims of religious truth obtainable through the rite of mirth. Several of the Germans were medical students and they became fascinated when the informant reported the use of laughter in physical healing, in the overcoming of such problems as stress and negative emotions. He suggested an array of claimed benefits for the procedure.

Returning to their autumn studies, the medical undergraduates reported their findings to faculty and classmates.

Student allegations from India spread from campus to campus throughout Germany. In several universities *laughology* was first looked upon as a novelty, something to laugh at rather than to learn from.

"Have you sung a mantra to your favorite god this morning?" one student might ask.

"Nein," replies another. "Spreicken mit der Furher's geist."

However, as word spread of universities like Heidelberg supposedly considering research, more and more of Germany's students took notice. Reports surfaced of interest and even experimentation among others such as those in behavioral studies and psychology, industry, and business.

Scandinavian educators plunged into the *laughology* potential with abounding interest. European countries such as Holland, Belgium, Britain, Switzerland, and others followed.

The Swedes took to *laughology* with high enthusiasm. During the last November of the old century, the International Laughter Club was established in Kalmar, a small city on the coastline of Sweden. Mane Scoeg Brendin was named first president. Dr. Madan Katara from Umbi, India, spent several months in Kalmar where he developed a method called "Laugh for No Reason." Kalmar became the center of humor activity, featuring experiments and demonstrations. Leaders came from all over Scandinavia and beyond to study under Dr. Katara.

From the Swedes, reputedly, came the anecdote about the Laughter

Luncheon Club to which a member brought a friend one noon, explaining, "We don't really tell jokes anymore; we don't need to. We've told them all and everybody remembers, so now we just give the jokes a number. You'll see."

Sure enough, as soon as the luncheon began, one member stood and called out loudly, "Fifty-two." Following this, a small ripple of laughter occurred. Another member stood and called out, "Eighty-six," after which a roar of laughter permeated the room. This continued throughout the luncheon. Numbers called, mild to robust reactions following.

"I don't quite understand," the visitor said, as he and the club member left the luncheon site. "All you do is call out numbers. Some cause heavy laughter while others are only given a few chuckles."

"Oh," explained the club member, "you know how it is with jokes. Some people can tell them; others can't."

CEOs, plant managers, and the like also came to learn from Dr. Katara how to incorporate humor into the workplace, thus enhancing morale and assuring productivity. Many Swedish products merchandised in the US, with brand names such as *Husqvarna, Bracking, Saab, and Volvo,* are manufactured in a corporate culture where humor is implemented.

Meanwhile, more and more college level people—faculty and students—came to Sweden and Germany to verify reports they had heard about laughter research. Sooner or later, inevitably, word reached the UCLA campus. A team from UCLA flew to Germany, returning with enthusiastic reports of their findings.

First, the primary benefactor was Mattel Children's Hospital, specialists in cancer research, stress, and related ailments of childhood. Dr. Lanie Zeltzer, director of the Pediatric Pain Program at Mattel, led the way. With the drive of a UCLA running back, Zeltzer plunged into the program. He organized the research study known as "RX Laughter."

The Sense of Humor

Dr. Zeltzer praised the effect of cartoons and family comedies, saying, "We're getting a pretty good handle on how laughter can have a strong impact on a child's mental well-being. We are also getting an in-depth look at the possible physiological links between health, having a good sense of humor, and the act of laughter itself. We are going to be studying the impact humor can have on the immune system as well as muteism, plus pain transmission and control."

Several people left places of prestige and higher pay to join the research teams.

The ball was rolling!

A five-year study pursued at UCLA speaks with optimism about the potentially positive effects in children suffering from life-threatening, often terminal, illnesses such as cancer and AIDS.

Research verified the suspicion laughter could significantly alter stress hormone levels known to weaken the immune system, also directly boosting the body's natural defenses. Slowly, word spread across the United States to New England. Hospitals, especially children's floors, initially became the most active. But now, there is considerable emphasis on the medical needs of all ages.

Not only is humor seen as an aid to healing, but also as a boon to studies of physiological and psychological therapy.

Dr. Patrick Dickson, British physician and author, says, "Laughter is a powerful way to reduce tension and stress, creating a sense of well-being, increasing contentment, and alertness. Happiness places the problems and difficulties of life into understandable context."

Students engaged in *laughology* research offer their own documentation:

"Whenever I'm studying for a test, or needing to decide on a creative approach for some project, I try to get three or four of my dorm buddies together for a half hour laugh session."

19

Says another, "Humor gives me an escape hatch, so I can bail out of problems and get on with my studies."

And another, "I need a perspective of what's going on in my life."

"Laughter gives me feelings of happiness and joy," one coed claims. "Instead of feeling all gloomy and frustrated because there is no perceived solution, laughter lifts me out of my pool of problems and gives me new insight."

Let us recognize humor for its intended place in our world and in our lives. As previously stated, we personally believe humor was designed by the Creator to very likely function as the most important of all our emotions.

A professor at Connecticut State University, studying uses of humor similar to our approach in this book, is reported to have said, "Humor is a way to relieve stress. Some things are so tragic that we have to laugh." And, there has always been a thin line between comedy and tragedy.

As one comedian puts it, "If you can find humor in a situation you can survive it."

My parents' family physician, Gary Pitts, MD, spent nearly an hour at their first consultation. At the conclusion, he reached for their hands, forming a circle. He also fits the *laughology* model. He expressed interest in the research for this book.

A large portion of Gary's practice involves obstetrics. Adept at using humor to help a mother in labor stay in a cooperative mood, he also specializes in being the first person to cause a newborn to smile.

Gary applies *laughology* to many areas of his vocation. He goes about those heavily laden days with a smile flickering up out of both corners of his mouth.

"I use humor a lot," he says, "would you believe especially with terminal patients? I first make sure of the dying person's relationship to God. Then I use little touches of humor. You should see the looks in the eyes of a terminal friend, as I step up to the bed each morning with a yarn like the one about the poor guy who had one of his legs amputated. The doctor came to see him next morning and said, 'I've got good news and bad news. The bad news is the surgeon made a mistake and cut off the wrong leg. The good news is the bad leg is getting better and won't need amputation.'

"When a man lies dying," Dr. Pitts says, "especially if he's sure of his relationship to the Lord, he isn't interested in talking about his own aches and pains. Truly, many times such a person wants laughter. At a time when it's almost unthinkable for him to laugh, he wants to be hit with the funniest thing you can think of to tell him."

Dr. Pitts is an example of a person using humor without first discovering the benefits by the process we are now evaluating.

Back in the later years of the last century, the book, *Anatomy of an Illness*, by Norman Cousins, was published. The book startled the medical world. Cousins was only a layman, but his ideas found wide acceptance by the medical profession. People wrote to ask him if he truly laughed his way out of a crippling disease doctors believed to be irreversible.

Albert Schweitzer reportedly believed the best medicine for any illness included a good sense of humor.

Our purpose with this book is to launch the concept, moving you out from the pages here to your own exploration into the role of humor in your life.

In Chapter Four, "Humor As a Tool of Ministry," for example, you will see numerous stories of people who find humor a valuable service to others. Because we want to be honest, we will also give you some examples of the kind of approach to humor we ourselves cannot accept. Likewise, we will see humor functioning in the home, at school, the shop, and the office in such ways that laughter's role strikes us as being uniquely strategic.

We will also discover, whereas many theologians have declared the

Bible to be a humorless book, God's Word offers us some interesting examples of mirth in human experience.

Admittedly, we are in the early stages of our North American investigation, testing, and development of such a potential tool. Our research has been mostly a matter of data gleaned from others. In addition, we have interviewed humor experts as well as other professionals who use humor effectively. What we have done, as you will see, is to hopefully introduce enough material to whet your interest for further study and implementation.

The New Age movement has long incorporated laughter into its yoga and meditation rituals, and touted the benefits. We want to state, up front, our belief God intended humor and laughter as benefits to His followers, the church, and the more you understand them, the better your life and relationships will be.

We live in difficult a time of economic distress, social changes, and political upheaval worldwide. Your only hope of getting through may lie in your sense of humor.

If we can convince you something new and wonderful really is happening with humor, we will have succeeded in our primary objective!

One should take good care not to grow too wise for so great a pleasure of life as laughter.

—Joseph Addison

Two—

Is Laughter Really the Best Medicine?

The more serious the illness, the more important it is to fight back, mobilizing all your resources: spiritual, emotional, intellectual, physical.
—Norman Cousins

The prestigious Mayo Clinic has published numerous articles concerning the relationship between humor, laughter, and well-being. Articles include, "Laughter and Humor, The Best Medicine?" "Laughter and Humor in Critical Care," "Why We Need Humor in Health Care," "Stress Relief From Laughter? It's No Joke," and many others.

Humor is more than simple joke telling or a bout of laughter for that matter. You will begin to discover, in order to be most effective, a healthy sense of humor must become part of the very fiber of your personality. When this happens, the use of humor, the enjoyment of humor, and the beneficial effects will become more of an attitude of conditioning in your life.

There isn't anything funny about being sick. When one part of your body hurts, your entire being suffers. The same condition exists with the church as we are instructed in the Bible. If one person is suffering, we have a responsibility to reach out and try to help. Illness and the prevention of illness both provide a perfect lab experiment as we learn how humor works. Interestingly, this was the subject where available research material seemed almost endless at times. And, the debate goes on.

But what if we were to discover our Creator had designed us in such a way as to protect us from disease, or to restore us to health more quickly, through the use of humor principles?

In my own life, I've always had a sense of humor ranging anywhere from healthy to over active. As I researched the subject of humor and health, I encountered numerous references indicating people with a healthy sense of humor were either sick less often, or they managed to bounce back more quickly. I began to think of myself and realized I am seldom ill.

That's not to say I've come through my sixty-plus years unscathed. At the age of three, I was the first member of my family to receive the diagnosis, "It's polio." The doctor went on to tell my mother I might never walk again. Yet, I believe my healing, and that of my sister and brother, were nothing short of God's miraculous touch—a subject for another time. I began to look back over my life and realized I rarely missed a day of school or work due to illness. When my own children were small, they managed to bring home every kind of sickness from school or Sunday school. Still, those didn't touch me for the most part.

Then, several years ago, I went to New Guinea to shoot a film project in the jungle. Life was primitive at best, for us as well as our subjects. While living in this isolated location, we encountered a horrendous, all night torrential thunderstorm followed by a flood that had me out looking for Noah the next day. Our campsite was quickly inundated by water. That's when we understood why the villagers lived in huts set on platforms built high up on stilts. We'd slogged around in the deep waters and mud for days, as I shot the scenes we still needed. Who knows what was in that water, but when I came home, I developed an open ulcer on one of my ankles.

So I went to my doctor. He knew what part of the world I had just visited because he also had the privilege of giving me a battery of shots before I left. I remember clearly how he wouldn't touch my skin. He leaned down slowly and started sniffing at the wound. "Does it smell?" he asked. I didn't think so, but also reminded him the head of a person six-foot-four-inches tall is a long way from his ankle. "It's kind of like a giraffe drinking water," I told him. Naturally we both had a good laugh at the image.

He prescribed some antibiotics but didn't think they would help. He sent me home and asked me to return in a week so he could see the wound. About four days after my first visit, I called to tell him the ulcer was healing nicely. He was greatly amazed. I firmly believe now, with some of the new information I am learning, my sense of humor could be what has protected me all these years, without my knowing the effects.

I have also concluded the same God, who can heal such a catastrophic illness as polio in the body of a three-year-old back in the 1940s, might also be dispensing smaller prescriptions, in the form of humor and laughter, to help His children fight some of the lesser day-to-day maladies that attack our minds and bodies.

Then, after a lifetime of good health, I've undergone several surgeries in the past few years. One was for a ruptured appendix—I know, my kids enjoyed reminding me that's usually reserved for much younger people—the repairs to four hernia areas during one operation, and a couple of others. In each case, during the post-op phases, my surgeons were literally stunned by my rapid recovery and quick healing.

The benefits of laughter and health came into national prominence through the motion picture, *Patch Adams*. Dr. Adams is a physician whose groundbreaking work in the field of humor's positive effects in healthcare led him to establish the Gesundheit Institute. This health facility has treated thousands of people at no charge. Dr. Adams honed his humor skills as a street performer and then incorporated that knowledge into his medical practice. He said, "I interpret my experience in life as being happy. I want, as a doctor, to say being happy does matter to your health. Happiness may be the most important health factor in your life." If you have yet to see the film *Patch Adams*, I would highly recommend the movie as you continue your own search in the field of medical humor.

Dr. Steve Allen Jr, son of the famous comedian, not only runs a thriving medical practice, he is also sought after nationally as a humorist. He came to speak at a medical convention in Rockford, Illinois, where I live. I enjoyed listening as he suggested medical staff should smile more often with their patients. He reminded the audience they needed to lighten up and reduce or relieve their own stress simply because of the stressful conditions under which they work. Dr. Allen encouraged medical personnel to practice silliness, which he described as follows:

"The word silly comes from the word, *selig*—Middle English and German—it means four things: Blessed, Prosperous, Healthy, and Happy."

He concluded by saying, "We want ourselves, our colleagues, and our families to feel those same things."

I made a point of meeting him after his presentation because I was interested in his insights relative to this chapter. I found him to be supportive and quite interested in the project. After we talked, he gave me his card and asked for a copy of the book. His late father is quoted as saying, "My natural way of approaching stress in my own life was to use humor ... Even at some rather dark and depressing moments, jokes would occur to me and I'd find myself laughing at them. I became convinced each of us has that gift. Everyone taps the well of their laughter and playfulness throughout life."

A study by the University of Maryland Medical Center included one hundred fifty people who had heart disease and one hundred fifty who didn't. Their findings showed those who had heart disease were less likely to laugh in stressful circumstances.

Ancient history records the relationship between the words *humor* and *health*. The word humor comes from the Latin word, *umor*, which means fluid or liquid; to be moist. The practice of Greek and Chinese medicines saw the body linked to the cosmos. They believed the earth's elements were converted during digestion into three fluids or humors. Later, Hippocrates distilled the idea even further until Galen, a physician in the second century AD, suggested there were four humors, and they were related to the elements and seasons. They further believed these contributed to temperament and disposition.

But Norman Cousins, as mentioned in chapter one, knew from the research of Carol Simonton negative emotions affected the body in negative outcomes. Cousins reasoned positive emotions must have the opposite effect. Alert purists might allege a touch of New Age philosophy here, but after you read further, you will likely form a different opinion.

Gelotolgy, the actual study linking humor and health, got started in the United States during the 1930s. Today, humor is becoming serious business in America. The effects are being studied both in the psychological as well as the physiological realms. Some studies indicate simple laughter increases the level of immunoglobulin A (IgA) which can be found in saliva. This is the body's first line of defense against organisms in our respiratory tract. Patients with a better sense of humor tended to have higher levels of IgA. Laughter also increases the number of killer cells to attack cancerous cells and viruses.

Laughter increases a person's intake of oxygen, further cleansing the body from within. According to an old Jewish proverb, "What soap is to the body, laughter is to the soul."

Stress is known to cause negative physiological changes in the body, contributing to high blood pressure, muscle tension, immunosuppression, and others. Studies now report laughter does the exact opposite, providing a natural antidote to stress. One study has concluded, if you have a strong commitment to yourself and your work, you believe you are in control of the choices in your life; and if you see change as a challenge, not a threat, then you will likely cope with stress successfully. Another report indicates while we rarely have control over the events that happen to us, we do have control over our response. Stress is not the event itself but, rather, our reaction to that event.

At a recent concert, the lead singer told of his bout with leukemia, and how he had lasted longer than his doctors expected. He attributed this to his faith, of course, but also in large part to the use of humor in his life. Interesting, don't you think?

There seems no end to the number of people who complain of a list of symptoms and then the medical community comes up with a name and diagnosis. In recent years, something called Seasonal Adjustment Disorder, or SAD, has been identified. SAD comes from those dark-gray fall and winter days when there isn't enough sunlight. Doctors tell us the remedy for this condition includes two hours in light, exercise, spending time outdoors, and … laughter.

Humor has been said to be the most underrated elixir for good health. In fact, in some medical circles, the idea continues to be shunned or discouraged. Still, humor is a prescription that can be accessed at any time, by anyone, anywhere, and laughter is free.

Hmmm, is there a connection here?

The Sense of Humor

According to French writer and philosopher, Voltaire, "The art of medicine consists of keeping the patient amused while nature heals the disease." And the New England Journal of Medicine estimated eighty-five percent of all human illnesses are curable by the body's own healing system. Recent data suggests the more positive input we can include in our lives—the more we are supporting our body's ability to tap into its natural healing processes.

I'm not a person given to depression, and I sympathize with people whose battles in this area appear to be connected to chemical imbalances and the like. But, like everyone else, I have my bad days too. I've come to believe Satan is the deceiver. He wants to tear us down, get us discouraged, and yes, possibly even depressed. When we are in this state, we are rendered useless to anything God would have us to do. Whenever I feel this way, I remind myself confusion, attack, and negativity couldn't possibly come from God. He is a God of order, hope, and optimism. At these times, I stop what I'm doing, literally change my thought patterns, and chart a new course.

Often the turnabout begins with a simple prayer, "Lord, these feelings I'm having couldn't possibly come from you. Please remove them, and help me replace them with what you would have me think." From there, I begin remembering all the good things God has done in my life in the past. I thank him for the positive people and events that come to mind. This is followed with a little dose of positive self-talk. If I'm alone, I talk right out loud. What follows next is an overwhelming sense of joy, hope, and a more positive attitude and outlook that allows a different perspective, so I can move forward again, positively.

Conversely, my video production work has included its share of medical programs. By far, the most brutal I have ever covered are seen in orthopedic procedures. I recently learned a young orthopedic surgeon had quit his practice due to an emotional breakdown. This caught my attention because, several years ago, I interviewed him along with several other physicians who were new to the area. Looking back, I recalled how this surgeon appeared to have little or no sense of humor at all during our interview. From what I know now about humor in health and medicine, and from the nature of his particular line of work, one can only wonder about the correlation.

Experts tell us there is no longer any doubt your daily frame of mind makes a significant contribution to your health, especially when your attitude persists day in and day out, year after year. Whatever you can do to include a more positive, upbeat frame of mind in facing the daily onslaught of problems in your life will contribute to your better health. Your own sense of humor is one of the most powerful weapons you have to make sure your mood supports good health every day.

My dentist, Dr. Larry Bargren, has treated my family for over twenty-five years. Yet, only recently did I notice he incorporated four special techniques in the course of his practice. He uses touch, eye contact, an explanation of what he is doing at all times, and humor. Recently, I was in the chair for the second of three crowns I was having done. I wondered, as we talked prior to his grinding away on my tooth, if he and I enjoyed humor together simply because we knew each other so well—we originally met in the same Sunday school class at church—or if he used humor with everyone. "It's interesting you would ask that question," he said, "because I never really thought about it before."

So we arranged for an interview session where I could explore the subject more deeply. I had always heard the dentistry profession had one of the highest percentages of suicides, and I wanted to know more about the subject.

While suicide within the dental profession is a problem, statistics indicate the rate is no higher than in other medical professions or the field of law. Still, according to the American Dental Association (ADA), the

The Sense of Humor

practice of dentistry has its share of stress, and stress is a leading factor contributing to suicide in general. Because the stress factors related to dentistry aren't going away any time soon, the ADA is interested in a better understanding of the subject. Their surveys indicate that very few dentists are doing anything to increase their defenses to combat stress.

"I'm not a confrontational person," Larry began. "I find if I use humor, that allows me to come across to any of our patients in a less threatening way. I feel the worst thing we can do is take someone who is coming through the doors, probably crawling across the parking lot, their blood pressure already high, and then just send them in to see the dentist, which adds even more to their stress. I tell my staff to look for something good to say to each patient, even a joke no matter how small, just to help lighten their load."

Dr. Bargren had some advice for dentists who don't already regularly inject humor into their daily practice. "I think humor is the best medicine for *my* benefit, more than anything else. When we remember the treatment we've rendered for that particular patient we may, and I know I do, I'm able to recall some type of a pun I made or the patient made about what's happening to them today. That is somewhat of a crutch I use to distract myself from that connection of myself to their problem."

Always tuning in to his patients, Larry observed, "I've noticed every once in a while when I'm in another treatment room, I can hear a patient who was first brought in to the adjoining room where they are talking louder than normal. I especially notice they always want to try to laugh, and they laugh real loud, too. The first couple of times, I didn't think anything of it. I thought the person was just in a very good mood. But I found out over time they were using laughter as some kind of a defensive mechanism. These patients tended to be the most afraid and the most tense."

Dr. Bargren recently moved to Arizona, but he enjoyed a thriving practice here, especially with first time children's visits. "If you're going to establish a relationship with a child, one of the best things to do is to include some laughter. But if they don't laugh, I know they aren't quite ready yet, so we'll end the appointment right there and reschedule another time for them to come back. I like for the child's first visit to be not with me because then I can hear them with one of my assistants down the hall. The assistant tries to get them to laugh. If I hear the laughter, then I know I'm coming in for the exam. If I don't hear the laughter, and especially if the room is *real* quiet, I might not even go in during that visit. So laughter, I would say, is a good yardstick as to when I can take the exam to the next level."

Occasionally Larry encounters a patient who is completely without humor. "We have a number of patients who have no sense of humor at all. I find that the treatment room becomes very quiet. In retrospect, from the patients we've seen within the past couple of months, who have no sense of humor, I know it's harder, treatment wise, much harder on the staff and on myself as well, and I know harder on the patient because of the increased tension in the room. When we sense a patient doesn't have a lighter side, our treatment strategy is tougher."

Dr. Bargren is exemplary because he was already employing a number of humor techniques without even realizing it. His mentor is Dr. Marvin Berman, a pediatric dentist specializing in the treatment of children who had previously undergone their dental procedures with the use of IV sedation or had been admitted into a hospital setting for dental treatment. "Dr. Berman has used the highest level I've ever seen," Larry said, "of including humor as a distraction to where the child doesn't even know he's gotten the inoculation, taking the child's mind off of what is happening."

Doctors have known for many years that stress weakens the immune system. Yet, not until the mid-1980s did research begin to study the impact of humor and laughter on stress. The best evidence came from measurements taken before and after subjects viewed a humorous video. Watching a comedy video for one hour also increased the level of T-cells (the body's natural killer cells), which seek out and destroy tumor cells as well as helping the body fight cold, flu, and other viruses. The evidence is clear there is something about the way humor and laughter cause the immune system to kick in, metabolically, to become more effective in doing what it was designed for—the fighting of external threats to our health. Experts suggest we should look for more opportunities to find humor in our everyday lives and to laugh more. Groucho Marx may have been right when he said, "A clown is like an aspirin, only he works twice as fast."

The debate continues whether or not endorphins are released into the bloodstream as a result of laughter. But laughter does aid in muscle relaxation, which reduces tension. Even if this relaxation is brief, such relaxation has been shown to reduce pain in clinical tests. Laughter provides an excellent source for cardiovascular exercise. The heart will continue to race fifteen to twenty seconds after a good belly laugh, and the heart rate will remain elevated for three to five minutes after. Some have referred to laughter as internal jogging, which gives the heart a good work out just by laughing several times a day. For patients who are bedridden, laughter can still offer good exercise for better cardiac conditioning.

Laughter helps people who do not practice deep breathing exercises. Deep breathing allows the individual to expel more air from the lungs. If this isn't done, residual air remains in the lungs and thereby in the system. Under stress, breathing becomes more rapid and shallow. This form of breathing leaves water vapor and carbon dioxide in the lungs while allowing in less oxygen. Retaining higher levels of water in the system presents a health risk to people with respiratory difficulties creating a more favorable environment for pulmonary infection and bacterial growth. Laughter helps force these gases out and increases the level of oxygen taken in.

Looking at a sense of humor as a deterrent to colds and flu, one study found the mothers of newborn infants, who actively used a sense of humor to cope with stress had fewer upper respiratory infections. Their infants also had fewer such infections. The studies seemed to indicate these mothers had higher levels of immunoglobulin A in their breast milk. By contrast, mothers with lower levels of IgA in their systems had babies with more illnesses during the first six months after the children were born.

Another study found people who suffered from heart disease also had a forty to forty-five percent reduced likelihood of laughing in response to social situations. Whether forcing yourself to laugh when you're angry has some of the same positive effects as regular laughter is not clear, and this aspect continues to be studied. Anger and stress release chemicals from the cells lining our blood vessels causing them to constrict. Laughing does release chemicals into the bloodstream like nitric oxide that help to dilate blood vessels. This chemical, related to nitrous oxide (laughing gas), is sometimes used to relax dental patients.

When you feel stress taking over in your life, reframing your thinking is important. Purposely put humor in strategic places in your life. Include signs, funny calendars, cartoons, or make sure to tell jokes several times throughout your day. Look for humor all around you. Read something funny, watch a comedy TV show, or read a humorous book. Get out, have fun, exercise, and change your attitude. Think back. When was the last time you felt good? What were you doing? Who were you with? Where were you? Mentally go back and put yourself into that situation, picture how your felt, dwell on your emotions. When you do these things, you'll be amazed how humor has changed your entire perspective in life, helping you to cope with stressful situations more easily.

Children are the most fun to study because they don't have any of the preconceived ideas adults have perfected to an art form in some cases. One study monitored children's reactions to a harmless painful task, which involved the child placing a hand into cold water. Researchers set a limit of three minutes for the test. The average time a child could stand the cold lasted thirty seconds. But the average duration jumped to a little over two minutes when a funny video was played while the child's hand was in the cold water.

This principle is also used with children who are suffering with AIDS and cancer. Stress is reduced, which reduces fear before and during procedures like chemotherapy, which leads to less time spent in recovery. Researchers recorded the most laughs when they showed slapstick videos. Most of the children had never seen such performers as Abbott and Costello or Laurel and Hardy, but these videos generated hearty belly laughs.

When used with their patients or people in nursing homes, humor allows health workers to provide better care because it forms a bond between them and those they serve. Humor has a direct result in the overall quality of life for nursing home residents whether a joke followed with laughter or just a simple smile, a touch, or a playful exchange. Even though the aging process changes the way we look at and respond to humor, age doesn't end one's capacity for and enjoyment of humor.

Everyone has heard someone say, "I almost died laughing," though likely no one has actually died. Still, the role of humor in health is rarely discussed by doctors. One of the world's most potent health aids is available without a prescription and is completely free. There is no research that says laughter will cure your illnesses, but a number of studies point to humor as a health benefit. Medicine continues to look for the "magic pill" to cure our ills. God may have already placed that remedy deep within each of us!

Why do adults laugh fewer than ten times a day compared with children who tend to laugh over four hundred times per day? In recent years, I've enjoyed observing this in my little granddaughters. Think about what you might be missing as an adult if you fail to include humor in your daily routine. Sense of humor is like the wind. We can't see or touch the wind and yet the wind's power is unmistakable.

Humor is much the same as the wind. Being one of our emotions, we can't see humor or touch laughter, but we know they're real. As important as the wind in nature, humor is available to help us in nurture: to cope with stress, fight illness, and aid in the healing process. Once we understand how to harness humor for ourselves, we are provided a pathway to a better, healthier, happier, more productive life for us and for those in our circle of influence.

Nobody ever died of laughter.

—Max Beerbohm

Three—

Funny Families

Our five senses are incomplete without the sixth—a sense of humor.
—Source Unknown

Thinking back to my childhood and family, I remember enjoying humor a lot. Of course, I was one of seven children. That alone made humor a requirement, not a luxury, if you hoped to survive. Our family was a little different. Our entire family made a camping trip across the United States in a 1953 Ford station wagon. At night, we all stayed together in a big tent. Talk about a circus! Often humor needed to be used to defuse a sticky situation. This was an era of pre-air conditioning in most cars. As we traveled through the desert out west, we put wet washcloths over our faces to keep cool. We looked more like a family in the witness protection program than one on vacation. My siblings may not have appreciated me at all times, but I know I often made use of humor in those days.

We used to play a joke on our parents. After we'd made a "pit stop" at a gas station, or one of those famous Route 66 roadside attractions, one of us would crouch down and hide in the car. After all, who could possibly keep track of that many little people? About a mile down the road, someone would say, "Hey, where's?" and say one of our names. When the person finally popped up and screamed, "Here I am!" everybody roared.

One night we happened to be traveling long after dark. Following one of those gas station stops, we piled into the car and off we went into the night. About an hour down the road, someone woke up and asked, "Hey, where's Donn?" We all looked around, and everyone thought the usual prank was being pulled. But the question persisted until our parents said, "Okay, that's enough, Donn, now come on out."

"No, really," was the response, "He's not here." He had been left back at the gas station. Police had been notified and alerted to be on the lookout for a '53 Ford station wagon full of kids. After we were reunited, and our parents given a stern lecture from the police, we were again on our way. If the same thing happened today, I'm sure my parents would be thrown in jail. And who knows what would have happened to the rest of us?

Especially funny was when our large family stopped at one of those roadside gift shops—the kind with shelves and shelves of things made out of nothing but glass. My parents, along with my brothers and sisters, all filed out of the car and into the shop like circus performers exiting one of the clown cars. Shopkeepers made a point to follow us around very closely. I'm not sure if they thought we might steal them blind or simply smash everything in the place. One particularly protective proprietor asked, "Are all these children yours?"

To which my dad replied, "As far as we know."

We often told funny stories. One of our favorites was *Willie The*

The Sense of Humor

Ghost, which was always told at night in a dark room. Our dad traveled a lot, but we always knew when he was back home because we had nothing but fun, fun, fun.

My children learned very early home was a safe place where they could come and not be attacked or hurt. Along with this absolute, there was a considerable helping of humor. No one ever ran crying from the dinner table because of a mean, vicious, or cutting remark. Instead, there was a lot of give and take along with giggles and laughter.

I incorporated a sense of fun as I raised my children and have continued that tradition with our grandchildren. After all, what better place is there for establishing a solid sense of humor early in the life of a child than in the context of family? Humor plays an important part in many facets of our lives including our relationships inside and outside the family, in our work, our ministries, and in education.

In my family, we used a mixture of humor. Since each person enjoyed different forms of humor, play to all of these was important. With one child, I could be more slapstick, and with another, less silly. One might have enjoyed an intricate joke, while another preferred a funny story or a good punch line.

Their favorite activity, which both kids enjoyed, happened on the nights when I told *Harv and Marv, The Dumb Guy Detective* stories. Harv and Marv weren't really dumb, they just made the crooks think they were so they could catch the bad guys. One summer, I was unable to go with my wife and children to visit their Grammie in Florida for two weeks. A couple days after they left, I recorded two Harv and Marv stories complete with music clips, scary background music in just the right places, and sound effects from an effects library. I sent the tape containing both stories down to them. One of the stories was about the "Alligator in the Lake." Since Grammie lived on a lake and, in years past we had seen alligators, the story took on added significance. Even though I couldn't make the trip with them, I was with them, in a sense, My wife told me they nearly wore out the tape playing the stories over and over, especially at bed time. A key component in any Harv and Marv story was a healthy helping of humor.

I began using humor very early with my granddaughters, Grace and Olivia. One thing I did whenever one of them tripped and fell and I knew they weren't hurt, was to loudly call out, "Kaboomskie." Or "Kapowie," if they ran into something or were hit in some way by a toy or something else. Then, instead of collapsing into tears, they'd laugh back at me. One is three and the other soon will be. I recently found out they do the same thing when I'm not around. I'm already getting smiles from granddaughter number three, Abby, who is only two months old. We'll work on laughter a little later.

If parents fail to understand the critically important role humor can play in their homes, much personal growth, development, and understanding may be lost. Humor promotes team building and a family should be a team. Humor helps people feel connected and lets them know they belong to something important.

Humor has the ability to strengthen families. Humor relieves tension and reduces anger and aggression. The use of humor simply makes life more fun. At times, humor is the only way to get at the truth because there are things that can be said or done in a humorous way that cannot happen in any other context. Balance should be actively sought between the things truly important and serious, including good discipline, and the lighter side of life.

For example, a parent might notice that the child's room is a disaster *again*, and choose to scream, "Can't you do anything right? Now go clean up that mess in your room." Or, "How many times do I have to tell you?" or, "Why can't you keep your room nice like your sister?"

The Sense of Humor

A better approach might be, "Hey, I just went past your room and I'm sure the closet blew up. Before you go outside to play, take a couple minutes to clean up the mess so the fallout doesn't affect the rest of the house." Other personality traits can be pointed out and corrected using this humorous method as well.

A key element to the success of any family is found in achieving happiness. Our children enjoy imitating us. Why else does a daughter like to play dress up, or house, and why does a son put a tie around his neck and pretend to shave? If we as parents exhibit negativity, lack of humor, and create a tense environment, our children are likely to do the same. But just think of what can happen if we create a climate of laughter, fun, play, and humor. Our children will likely adopt these traits too.

Our homes today are marked by multiple TVs boasting hundreds of cable and satellite channels, smart phones, individual computers, and other electronic devices for each family member. These seem almost designed to fragment the family, keeping us from spending time together—either quality or quantity. Family bonds can still be created and even strengthened in this environment with the use of humor.

Road trips can offer special challenges for a family. Of course, children today have their own personal entertainment and sound systems in the car just to keep them entertained—how sad. Almost like in-flight movies on an airplane, kids now have video screens in front of them to keep the "little darlings" entertained. They're able to shut out anyone or anything around them as they travel down the road.

When we had to take a long road trip, we brought along games, lots of picture books, and fun. My children's favorite was something I usually kept under the front seat until we'd driven a long way and they started to get bored. And, keep in mind, these trips were pre-video and electronic revolution. However, the concept will still work today, and I hope you'll give it a try on one of your next family road trips.

I created scavenger hunts for the road. Often the list was three typewritten pages long, listing just about everything they might see along the way. Their lists were slightly different so they didn't have exactly the same things to find. Some items were designed to be impossible to locate like a three-legged-cow, a barn on fire, a monkey hanging from a tree eating a banana, and so on. But the squeals of excitement, laughter, and enjoyment I heard coming from the back seat, I still remember.

As a parent, your job is to make family life as comfortable as possible. With that in mind, think about your home. Is home a fun place? Is there laughter? Is your family happy? And one day, when you're gone, what would you like your children to remember most about you—how much money you made, how important you were at work, or church, how clean the house was? Not likely.

Humor in a family isn't only for the kids. Parents benefit too and home should also be a safe place for parents. Our jobs and responsibilities away from our families provide enough stress. There isn't any reason to bring that burden home and dump the stress on our spouse. We are better prepared to face challenges if our home life is tranquil and light. Obviously, circumstances will come up that test us all, and our responses may be anything but light and funny, and that's okay. The important thing is to strive for an environment that, on balance, is far more fun than sad.

Parents can fall into the trap of thinking they have to be perfect or at least that their children think they are. A parent may believe he or she will lose the respect of their children if they admit mistakes. But if we admit our goofs, and especially if we do so with humor, the opposite happens. Besides, when they get a little older there will be no doubt in our children's minds we aren't at all perfect. This is especially evident when they enter their teen years. Sometimes I think humor was invented by God specifically to help our teenagers and us survive this phase and

The Sense of Humor

live on to maturity.

Humor can be used to teach your children important concepts they need to know. Telling funny stories about your childhood or things you remember your parents told from theirs will help children connect with their own family heritage. My father told lots of stories about a few of the characters from his little farming community in Iowa. Some of these people became real and vivid to us and we remember them even today.

There were times when I needed to discipline or punish my children. I always explained why I was doing what was about to happen. Then after the punishment, I spent far more time assuring them of my love. Humor was often used in the after time.

Many times children come home from a difficult day at school, a hard exam, or a loss in a sporting event. Injecting humor at these times demonstrates that life goes on and they will get through it. I remember when my children were in their teens. Their lives centered around their high school and what went on there. To them, school seemed like the most important place and time on this earth. Whatever the difficulty, I would say, "Believe it or not, there is life after high school." They didn't like hearing the truism, but it helped put things into perspective.

You'll be able to get a good measure of the kinds of friends your children are choosing by testing their sense of humor. Parents need to keep a watchful eye in this area. If you feel that things aren't right, you can point to a fact like, "Did you notice how David never smiles or laughs? How are things at his house?" This isn't prying, but just shows you are aware of the differences and is another way to help your children to decide who they should spend their time with. Even more important than the sense of humor in their friends, you will be able to watch for any changes in your children's own senses of humor.

A dad told me recently, "Now that you've told me about your humor project, I remembered something. Our son was in medical school but decided to drop out. When he went away to school, he was a real jokester. He loved telling jokes and hearing them as well. He always smiled and had a great sense of humor. But when he came home, all of that was gone. Looking back now, I think he was suffering from depression and we didn't even recognize what was wrong."

As parents, we are constantly concerned about our children, making sure they don't fall prey to drugs, sexual activity, or anything else harmful. If you notice one of your children suddenly pulling away from the family, if they no longer express a positive healthy sense of humor as they did in the past, you need to assume something has seriously changed. This is where you need to step in, do some probing, use humor if fitting and help them stay on the right track. Experts tell us when teenagers feel safe, they want to be with you.

Probably no more important a place for laughter, and by far the most difficult, can be found than in the single parent home. There are already many forces at work adding to stress, pressure, and anxiety. In this environment, anything funny will help lighten the load. Remember your children mimic you. At the same time, they are sent off each day into a world that already poses difficult choices for them. Whatever you can do to help them develop their unique sense of humor is armor they desperately need. Here again, if your children are happier and better adjusted, you will benefit from reduced friction in your own home.

A family has the luxury of developing its own inside jokes and personal punch lines. They get to remember the antics of crazy old Aunt Mildred, the uncle who backed out of the garage—without opening the door first—or any one of a number of other funny things unique to the family. Taking funny pictures at birthdays or while on a trip, provide immense enjoyment and great memories as you look back.

One of our family funny favorites involves an uncle who shall remain nameless for the purpose of this illustration. Remember humor is

The Sense of Humor

not supposed to hurt or embarrass people—especially family. We were shooting a film where a burning house became the pivotal, dramatic point of the story. We had taken over the entire street of the small town where this film was being made. An elaborate scene had been carefully choreographed involving cars, people, and a fire truck. In a perfect world, what was supposed to happen was a pickup truck driven by a relative was to pass through the frame just after the fire truck pulled out of the firehouse, siren blaring and lights blazing, roaring off to fight the fire.

We rehearsed and rehearsed the movement several times, making sure everyone understood the intricate timing. Then came the time to shoot the scene for real.

"Roll sound," the director announced.

"Rolling," the soundman barked.

"Roll camera," was the next command.

"Speed," I said.

"Action!" came the shout so everyone knew the scene was supposed to start *now*! Unfortunately, our relative jumped the gun and hit the gas way too early. Instead of arriving just after the fire truck moved away, he drove his pickup right into the path of the fire truck rumbling out of the station. The fire truck T-boned the smaller truck, pushing it to within about a foot from the camera before it stopped. We got the whole scene on film including my shadow and that of the camera on the side of his truck. His truck came that close. This family story still brings a chuckle to us after several years.

Look for your own family stories that can be passed down to the next generation. If you journal, make a point of keeping a separate "funny book" reserved just for the fun things that happen in your family.

I used to ask my children how things went in school, or at work. Their usual answer might begin with how terrible the work was. Invariably I'd

45

ask, "And what, if anything, good happened?" There was a sudden mind shift where they would then remember a funny thing that was said or done by someone.

Moms especially need to access as much humor as possible because the truth is, the entire rest of the family dumps everything imaginable on them. With all the cooking, cleaning, work outside the home, carpooling, laundry, etc., etc., etc., humor can make or break the way they view themselves and their place of importance in the family. There is an old saying, "If Mamma ain't happy, ain't nobody happy." Husbands need to be aware of the need for a lighter way of looking at things coupled with a lot of family fun.

A good practice would be watching funny movies together as a family. These can be more contemporary or any of the classics. Often you'll see a marathon of certain programs on one of the cable channels where you can load up your DVR. Our family favorites continue to be "The Andy Griffin Show" and "Leave It To Beaver." Beyond these, I love the old Laurel and Hardy movies, but you'll discover your own personal and family favorites.

Look for other families that enjoy laughing together and having a good time. When our children were smaller and we attended church picnics, or family dinners, our table was the place to be for fun. If you wanted to lose weight, you came to our table because we did so much laughing, eating at the same time was too difficult, almost too dangerous. When you have the ability to choose, why would you want to seek out people who are bitter, negative, and not having any fun?

Take care to teach the importance of appropriate humor within your family. There is no better place to learn these guidelines than in the family structure. Here we make sure to laugh *with* not *at* one another. We also learn how things like "retard" jokes, racist humor, sexual humor, and the like have no place in our lives. Once you view your family as the training ground for the successful lives of your children, these restrictions take on added significance.

If the statement joy is the absence of sorrow and the presence of God, then humor in the family serves to help our children draw closer in their relationship with their Creator. We often spend so much time teaching "Look both ways before you cross the street," "Be careful, the stove is hot," and "Don't go with strangers." Do you notice these are all negative lessons? Important, but negative. I wonder if those lessons would be more memorable if we used humor to teach them. "Be sure and look both ways before you cross the street—you don't want to be flattened like a pancake."

We guide them spiritually. We teach economics, social skills, career paths, all with an eye toward their future. Why not start today to move humor to the head of the list of instruction? If you do that, everything else that matters will fall into place.

Treasure the smiles and laughter of your children and make sure they enjoy yours. May it be said by our children, "I laugh more at home than any place else." As my children have matured, we have so much fun being with them, enjoying their different senses of humor. Now that my wife and I have become grandparents, I'm enjoying a new level of humor as I watch my children raise their own.

Grandparents can play an important role with humor, connecting and bonding one generation to another. Family humor can be a strong and enduring legacy preserved and passed down from generation to generation. Humor may be the strongest glue to hold families together and it doesn't cost a thing.

Expose your children to all sorts of jokes, riddles, stories, and puns. Read humor books and let your children pick out their favorites. Explain funny sayings so they have a better understanding of humor. Read funny bumper stickers, or signs. Funny signs are everywhere, like the one that says, "No trespassing during daylight hours." Does that mean it's all right to trespass after dark? You'll find these everywhere if you look for them.

Read comics together in the newspaper. Explain humor when your children don't "get it." Don't expect them to understand all the nuances of culture and language. Sometimes just the look of something will be funny. No punch line, no funny words, just the picture will cause laughter. Ask your children what they think is funny, and observe them when they are being silly. Try to bring humor of some kind into every day so your children will be saturated with it.

Humor takes many different forms, but within the family, humor's effects are universal. A sense of overall well-being is felt. There is a process of give and take among family members. Even when mistakes are made, by children or parents, they can be looked at in a humorous, non-threatening way, and profound learning will take place as a direct result.

Psychologists, sociologists, and counselors agree, humor must be factored into any healing strategy for the family. Humor shouldn't just be tolerated; humor must be welcomed and embraced.

Family jokes...are the bond that keeps most families alive.

—Stella Benson

Four—

You Are What Makes You Laugh

True humor springs not more from the head than from the heart. It is not contempt; its essence is love. It issues not in laughter, but in still smiles, which lie far deeper.

—*Thomas Carlyle*

Have you ever asked yourself, "Hey, if laughing is so good for me, then how come I can't tickle myself?" That little mystery, along with the fact that you can't lick your own elbow either, and a few other questions will just have to wait till we get to Heaven to find out. One thing we do know is people don't necessarily laugh at the same things. Take a look at the full color comics section in your next Sunday paper and do a little experiment. Read a few of them. Not just your favorites. Try to analyze the different forms of humor you find there. Which ones are more aligned with your own sense of humor? At the same time, see if you can gain a little understanding of the people who create each of those strips.

My all-time favorite comic strip was, is, and always will be "The Far Side." Unfortunately, the comic ceased publishing a few years ago. Still, I continued to get a "The Far Side" calendar for a few years. When I heard the strip wouldn't be published anymore, I began cutting the cartoon out of my daily paper. These I stuffed into an envelope so I could enjoy them later on. They've already turned yellow and the edges are a little ragged. My favorite style of humor involves either things that are visual or things you have to think about in order to get.

But, back to "The Far Side" for a moment. One of my favorites goes like this: You see two guys standing in the morgue. Each has a shirt with the words "Morgue Staff" emblazoned across the front. There are at least five dead bodies laid out around the room. One of the staff guys is holding a ticket he just found on a dead man.

He holds it up, looks at it, and says, "Oh man! Look, Ernie. This guy has the winning lottery ticket in his pocket!"

The other worker, who doesn't look all that bright, thinks to himself, *Lucky stiff.*

Now, if you ask me, that's funny.

As people come in all shapes and sizes, so humor presents itself to us in many different forms. Have you ever wondered what the world would be like if everyone thought just like you do? At first you might say, "Great." But after you think about it, the world would be a pretty dull and boring place if we didn't have variations on the things we like and dislike. This is especially the case with humor.

Did you know?

1. A baby's first smile comes within just a few days of birth, usually after a feeding? This smile is a signal of well-being and contentment.

2. Even though humor is a universal human trait, not everyone agrees on what's funny.

The Sense of Humor

3. Animals don't have a sense of humor, only people.

4. Your sense of humor is partly genetic and partly acquired.

5. Humor comes in several forms.

6. Everyone has a sense of humor, even though it is more active and obvious in some; less active and obscured in others.

7. Your life's experience coupled with your education and maturity all help to determine what you think is funny.

What exactly is humor? How does humor work? What purpose does humor have in our lives? Like love, hope, faith, or anger, humor is a concept that cannot be clearly defined. Humor is a word whose meaning is as diverse as each individual's perception.

I know in my own life, humor has always played an important role. As I was growing up, I never had a fight with another person. I came close a few times, but somehow I was always able to defuse the situation in some way or another, using humor.

I remember one time in particular when I had offended one of the "boys" during my senior year of high school. The "boys" were known as the bad guys and what they knew best was drinking and fighting. I had said something I shouldn't have to one of them, and he threatened, "Meet me at your locker after last period and we'll settle this."

I'm sure my voice trembled as I said, "Okay, sure."

Actually, I was pretty nervous the whole rest of the day because this was a really big guy, and I was a six-foot-four-inch rail. Well, I still am. Anyway, last period came to an end, and I went to my locker and began to collect the books and things I needed for the weekend. From behind me came a thundering voice, "Anderson!" then my locker door slammed shut just as I pulled my hands out. When I turned around, there he was, standing way too far inside my comfort zone. We stood eye to eye for what seemed like an eternity and, I can't explain why, I just started laughing. I laughed so hard and so loudly my eyes began to water.

51

Everyone in the hall stopped dead still to see how brutally I was going to be pulverized, including several of this guy's friends. But instead, he didn't know what to do. So he stood there for a few more seconds. Then one of his black leather-jacketed buddies said, "Come on. Let's go. It ain't worth it," and they left.

That reminds me of an interview I read in American Profile where actor/comedian Tim Allen said he had once avoided a would-be aggressor in prison by talking like the cartoon character, Elmer Fudd. I can picture that and it's something I'd probably try too. Although the only times I've seen inside of prisons or jails have been on film and video production assignments.

Humor helped me countless times during my military service. After all, I was drafted during the Vietnam War era. A strong sense of humor was required just to survive the rigors of Basic Training and the several military posts where I served. I remember doing more than my share of pushups for something I'd said, but usually what I'd said *was* funny. Invariably the other guys laughed, and humor was a great stress reducer. One particular time, I even made my drill sergeant laugh—something that *never* happens. Given all the benefits of humor at the time, those pushups were worth it.

Throughout my college years and on into the work world, I have often used humor to cement relationships or defuse difficult situations.

I'm not a great joke teller, but I love hearing them when they're told well. However, I most enjoy what I would call humor of the moment, where I can see something funny in what a person has just said or in something I've just seen happen. Seinfeld was one of my favorite TV programs because of its style of humor. This is an area of humor where timing is everything, and something that might be funny right now, at this moment, may not be funny at all if the humorous line is delivered late. I also enjoy visualized humor where, in the case of a joke, I can see the situation unfold, rather than simply depending on a punch line.

A few years ago, I had the opportunity to collaborate with an advertising agency from Washington, DC. They were working with a candidate in my city who was running for the state senate for the first time. The candidate was a total newcomer and unknown within the community or the political structure. He was running against a ten-year incumbent who was a grandmotherly figure. I was brought in on the creative team and I also shot and directed a dozen commercials for the campaign. We decided to use humor because who would directly attack a grandmother? The end result caused an unknown to go from total obscurity to seventy-five percent name recognition virtually overnight.

In the first commercial, my candidate sat in a studio and delivered the following:

CANDIDATE: "I'll never forget the response I got when I first told people a decent ordinary guy like me could win the state senate."

VISUAL: We cut to old black and white footage from the 50s of an audience laughing

CANDIDATE: "Then I told people I could actually win by running a positive, issues-oriented campaign, instead of viciously attacking my opponent."

VISUAL: Another, wider shot of the 50s audience laughing

CANDIDATE: "But when I gave them a copy of my issues platform with ways to keep taxes down, improve schools, and create new jobs, people stopped laughing."

VISUAL: The same 50s audience is now clapping and cheering wildly

CANDIDATE: "After all, our future is no laughing matter."

In the second commercial, we had our candidate walking the neighborhoods; meeting people door-to-door. Along the way, he encountered obstacles including an automatic lawn sprinkler that suddenly came on, a skateboard in the driveway of one home, and a dog that chased him.

The dog presented an interesting opportunity to debate whether the ad would be funnier if we saw the dog or if we didn't. I thought the funniest scenario would be to hear a large barking dog, but never see him, so that's what we did. The candidate races through the picture and throws his campaign literature into the air as he runs for his life. The viewer has to visualize the ferocious animal purely from the sounds, along with the reaction of the terrified candidate running away.

Even though this campaign was many years ago, people still talk about the commercials because they were so different from any that had been done in this market. Our candidate won the election by a huge margin and is still in office after many elections.

Humor is often used in the movies. The styles to look for as you determine what makes you laugh include:

Slapstick: This uses broad, aggressive, physical action including harmless cruelty, violence, horseplay, and sight gags. Here you might see the classic pie-in-the-face or falling into the backyard swimming pool.

Deadpan: The best example of this form of humor can be seen in some of the silent films with Buster Keaton or Charlie Chaplain.

Verbal Comedy: Much of this brand of humor was done using cruel verbal wit while cutting down another character or group.

Screwball: These comedies usually include romantic stories focusing on the battle of the sexes. They contain a lot of visual humor, exaggerated characters, a rapid pace, and wise cracks or punch lines.

Dark Comedy: This is a sarcastic approach toward subjects including war, death or illness, pessimism, etc.

Parody and Spoof: A serious film or subject is attacked using a more humorous approach.

The Sense of Humor

What about you? Do you enjoy slapstick or is yours a more subtle humor? Maybe you prefer a good punch line or the ability to perfectly produce puns at a moment's notice. Others like the practical joke. A man's idea of what is funny can be completely different from a woman's perception of humor. Even though laughter is universal, those things that prompt us to laugh are not.

First, we need to recognize that humor is not the same as laughter. Laughter is a physiological response to humor. Laughter has two components. There are the body movements or gestures and the sound we make. Our brain signals us to do both of these activities at the same time.

Some have said that laughter and crying are not opposites, but rather they are a continuum. They report once you understand this, you will see laughter doesn't come from happiness. Laughter and crying are seen as being side-by-side. We don't laugh because we're happy; we become happy because we laugh.

The scientific explanation of our laughter tells us that fifteen facial muscles contract while the main muscle that lifts the upper lip is stimulated. While this is happening, our respiratory system is stimulated, shrinking the larynx so the air intake becomes irregular. This makes you gasp. In some cases, the tear ducts are activated. As the mouth is opening and closing, struggling for more oxygen, the face gets red and moist. The sounds range from very controlled to an all-out belly-whopping laugh.

Laughter usually occurs during a pause in speech or at the end of a phrase or sentence. This seems to indicate the brain knows where and when to insert the laughter during language.

One study showed how all laughter is formed by short, vowel-like notes repeated every 210 milliseconds. Laughter can come out as "ha-ha" or "ho-ho," but never a mixture of the two sounds. We also have other circuits in the brain that generate more laughter. This is why laughter is contagious.

There is a song where the performer does nothing but laugh. And the more you hear the laughter, the more you want to laugh with him. This can be experienced if you are in the presence of someone who laughs uncontrollably. Sooner or later, others will likely join in. There are a couple children's toys and other novelty items that use laughter. If you've ever seen them, you know how they can cause people to laugh, or at least smile, when they hear the recorded sound.

People are thirty times more likely to laugh in social settings than when they are alone. Years ago, television program producers figured out this concept. At first, many of the television comedy programs were simply adaptations of the same radio shows. Most of the early programs were performed before a live audience. As production techniques became more sophisticated, the live audience was not always used. Producers introduced something called the laugh track. Each time something was supposed to be funny, a laughing sound effect would be inserted. Viewers would hear the laughter and were encouraged to think it was funny. The concept of a perceived social setting was supposed to help. Even in live shows or those recorded before a live audience, people are still instructed to clap, cheer, and yes, even to laugh on cue. In case you might think this has only happened in modern times, the Greek playwrights often stacked their audiences. The Roman Emperor, Nero, ordered thousands of his soldiers to attend his acting performances and to applaud.

A further examination into what makes us laugh might take you back to the early days of a television program like "America's Funniest Home Videos." Did you find yourself picking the one you thought was funniest, only to see that clip not even make the top three? Or if yours went that far, did it always win? Mine didn't. Here again, the viewer, the studio audience, and the judges all had different opinions as to what made them laugh.

There are three theories on humor; incongruity, aggression, relief/ liberation.

With incongruity, the listener expects one thing but is cleverly switched to another. When a joke begins, we might already be expecting what's going to happen and anticipating the ending. This is logic coupled with our emotions and is conditioned by experiences we have had in the past. With these thoughts in our mind, the joke goes in a different direction, so our thoughts and emotions have to make a quick adjustment. Now we have new emotions coupled with different thoughts. All at once we have conflicting sets of both thoughts and emotional expectations. This conflict, between different elements of the joke, makes us laugh.

In the aggression, or superiority model, Aristotle and Plato believed we laughed out of a feeling of superiority to or at the flaws of others. Young children seem to start at this level. Here we laugh at someone else for their mistakes, stupidity, or misfortune. We feel superior to the object in the joke, thinking we could never be so dumb. As we disconnect from the situation, we are able to laugh.

Relief and liberation supposes since we live under a system of reality and logic, humor frees us from reality. Freud and others held this view of humor. This humor form can be seen in films where the director builds up the level of tension to an almost unbearable point, then defuses the situation with humor. Good story telling, or joke telling, are done in the same way. In each, the story is built up until there has to be an emotional release. The release comes with something funny, generating laughter.

The primary differences in our laughter appear to be based on age. Infants and children are consumed with new discoveries all around them. Much of what they see makes no sense and they laugh. When they get a little older, children respond to short, simple concepts like knock-knock jokes. Children also like cruel humor because they feel better about themselves and they like humor about bodily functions. Again, this is a time of early discovery. Much has been written about how unkind children are to others, especially when physical or emotional flaws can be obviously seen and picked on.

The awkward stages of pre-teen and teenage are filled with rebellion. At this stage, young people like pretty much everything that shocks their parents. Humor centers around food, sex, people in authority, and antisocial subjects. This is seen as a defensive reaction to their insecurity and tension.

As people get a little older, there are differences in their sense of humor based on maturity. The more we learn, the more we are able to understand increasingly complex jokes. A five-year-old couldn't be expected to understand the nuances of political or social humor, but with age and experience, *we* are able to get the joke. With more of life's experiences behind us, we've likely experienced our share of sadness, disappointments, successes, joy, and failures. Our level of experience determines the maturity of our sense of humor. Someone living in a rural area might not get the point of a Dilbert joke since life in a high rise office cubicle is far removed from small town America. But an office worker would find hilarity in a film like *Office Space*.

We tend to find the most humor from jokes and stories that are closest to our life and experience.

Sense of humor is also a cultural phenomenon. Have you ever laughed at a joke or story and then realized it was funny because of where your relatives are from or because the joke contained information specific to your own heritage or family traditions? People in Spain probably wouldn't find much humor in a Yugoslavian joke. Or what would a person in Brazil find funny in a story from Alaska? Humor is not always international nor universal. In addition to the cultural aspects, humor is regional. Much of this is changing as a result of the Internet. Years ago, a person would have to go to the local bookstore or library to pick up the latest joke book. Now jokes and funny stories travel at lightning speed by e-mail across the Internet. Also, because so many American films and television programs are exported, people in other countries are better informed about what is funny here and may better understand American humor.

Analyzing what makes you laugh is interesting. Once you understand this, you can begin looking for these things in your life. If you have certain fears, try making fun of them. Often the use of humor allows us to take control of a situation. A person who is deathly afraid of heights, for example, may not be able to completely overcome this fear with humor, but it's worth a try.

Laughter has many faces. Every mood, emotion, and feeling can be expressed in laughter. There are some things that are so horrible, frightening, or tragic; we can only laugh in our helplessness. Notice the humor and jokes that have finally emerged since the events of 9/11. These are found on the Internet, the late night TV talk shows, and in your own circle of family and friends. But there are other situations that are so positive that the laughter causes tears of joy. Our moods can be measured by the quality of our laughter, and in the case of 9/11, an entire nation has emerged stronger including our sense of humor as a people. Laughter is one of the most powerful tools we have for coping with the serious issues in our lives. It's been said that we, too, must keep our faith even in the face of this world's terrorism, disasters, and economic difficulties. To be aware and fully alive in this world requires a deep sense of humor; the kind of humor which has a close affinity with faith.

Even though there are the darker ethnic jokes, ones that aim to hurt another group, there is a less mean-spirited variety found in the Sven and Ole or Pat and Mike jokes. These jokes often are told within the culture where they originate. A Norwegian will tell the joke so the Swede looks dumb, and the Swede might tell the same joke, but with the opposite outcome. This humor is done in good fun, and would not be considered malicious.

The practical joke can be simple or elaborate. Usually they are designed to catch another person off guard or to embarrass them. In the well-executed practical joke, the subject is supposed to be led toward thinking or believing one thing, while there is always a surprise ending. You've probably seen the TV show where celebrities get "punked." This form of humor has its dangers. If it is played on a person who doesn't appreciate such humor, or who is unable to comfortably laugh at himself, then the joke can hurt. There is also the possibility the one who has been the target of the joke will do their best to get even, often including pranks that might become increasingly dangerous.

In some instances, playing practical jokes can be fatal. A doctor reported, "We had a patient come in DOA, who had called EMS earlier in the day for chest pain and shortness of breath. When the Rescue Squad arrived, the man decided he was okay and did not wish to go to the hospital. His wife went out shopping that afternoon and when she returned home, she found her husband lying on the kitchen floor. She was unable to wake him but since he 'always plays practical jokes' decided not to do anything. She went upstairs and took a nap. When she wandered back down a few hours later, she found him in the same spot, in the same position. She decided to then call EMS, but her husband was, of course, pronounced dead at the scene!"

You might like to take a little self-assessment test to measure your own sense of humor. Answer the following questions and statements to see where you fit in. This list is not intended to be exhaustive on the subject, and you may think of other questions, but these will help to get you started.

The Sense of Humor

1. If someone makes a joke about you:
   a. Do you laugh?
   b. Do you feel embarrassed?
   c. Do you get angry?
   d. Do you get even?
2. Do you make jokes about others that might hurt, embarrass, or put them down?
   a. Do you enjoy ethnic jokes that make others look stupid?
   b. Do you enjoy racial jokes that degrade others?
   c. Do you use sarcasm and biting humor?
3. Are you able to laugh at yourself when you are with others?
4. Do you enjoy listening to and/or telling dirty jokes?
5. Is your humor good natured, aimed at building people up, and bringing them together?
6. Do you use humor to put people at ease?
7. Do you enjoy slapstick comedy?
8. Do you like visual comedy?
9. Do you enjoy puns and punch lines?
10. Do you look for humor in your own surroundings?

Probably you will find, like most people, that your own sense of humor is the product of a combination of factors. However, if you see yourself at the darker end of the humor spectrum in the humor you dish out or enjoy, then changes are in order.

This list of questions is good for your self-examination and can also be useful as you listen to the humor of others around you. Armed with this information, you will automatically know if your own humor, or that of your associates, family, and friends, is positive or negative.

Remember, humor that hurts, belittles, puts down, or embarrasses is a perversion of the gift God has given us. Determine to alter your sense of humor if you find yourself at the wrong end of the scale.

If we are physically the product of what we eat, and mentally a product of what we think, then it stands to reason that our overall sense of humor is a product from years of input of that which makes us laugh. Analyze it, and if needed, make some positive changes.

Laughter is, after speech, the chief thing that holds society together.

—Max Eastman

Five—

Education—The Lighter Side of Teaching and Learning

Tell a joke in your classroom and you'll make 'em laugh for minutes. Teach them how to enjoy humor and learning, and you'll equip them for a lifetime.

—Max Elliot Anderson

In some ways, the research for this chapter was some of the most difficult. I suspect the reason for this is the use of humor and laughter in the classroom, though studied for several years, has yet to actually find a way into the mainstream. Still, I believe if this is allowed to change, an entire generation will be better off.

As part of my preparation for the effects of humor in education, I began to think back over my classroom experiences to see if any teachers had used humor. Rummaging through my memory bank, I concluded no teachers had used humor in kindergarten, nor in grade school, junior high, high school, and not even in college. What I do remember is a bunch of very serious people to whom teaching seemed to be an equally serious subject. My early classroom experiences may have been more traumatic than some and less than others. But I remember one teacher who cried all the time and ran from the classroom.

Another teacher acted more like one of my army drill sergeants. She was quite large, had a loud voice and a disposition to match. Her method for restoring order and discipline in her class was to walk quietly up behind the perpetrator of any problem or commotion and haul off and smack them in the center of their back with the palm of her hand. Since I often said or did things to make other students laugh, I had the wind knocked out of me on several occasions. Stories abound concerning students who attended parochial schools where the teacher rapping them across their knuckles with a ruler was not uncommon.

I've believed I am responsible for my own actions, never looking to blame someone else for my troubles or lack of performance. But now, I'm questioning something I didn't think much about before. I always hated school; an opinion I held dear until I squeaked into college. There I majored in psychology, hit my stride, made good grades and enjoyed learning for the first time in my life. I sometimes wonder how my earlier attitude might have changed if there had been laughter and humor in some of those early classrooms.

Thinking mine might be an isolated experience, I decided to ask other family and friends. Most cannot remember a teacher who was fun, funny, told jokes, or used humor, yet I know they must be out there, and I hope this book will bring them out of the shadows. I would love nothing more than to receive stacks of letters from students and teachers telling of their positive experiences in this area.

My son, Jim, went to a private Christian school until the ninth grade where he tested for an accelerated, college prep academic program in

The Sense of Humor

the public school system in our city. From there, he attended and graduated from a prestigious, Ivy League university. So I posed the question to him.

"There was only one teacher I can remember in all those years who used humor," he told me, "and that was my economics professor. Other than that there weren't any others." Since Economics was Jim's major, this professor's adept use of humor was probably a welcome relief in an otherwise stressful environment.

Next, I asked my daughter. I was particularly interested in her response for a couple of reasons. Sarah attended Christian schools all the way through high school. Not only did we pay taxes for our public schools, we paid extra for her private school tuition. If ever there were a place where the best techniques of teaching should be used today, it is in our private Christian schools. Yet, Sarah can't recall one teacher who used humor on a regular basis. She has taught in public schools for the past several years now, and not only did she not encounter humor in her university classes, she is unaware if humor is being taught in the curriculum.

Why should this matter you might ask? Simple. Sarah studied to become a teacher. She enrolled in the College of Education, Early Childhood Program, at a well-known university specializing in preparing teachers. Her school ranked in the top five schools nationally for teacher training in the country.

As we attended orientation before she began her freshman year, we were told, "Teachers who graduate from this university are sought after around the country because of our strong program."

Clearly we have a lot to learn about the positive, powerful benefits researchers tell us can be found when humor is included in the learning process.

Research also shows laughter and play encourage learning. Humor leads to an increase in attention span and can help both the students as

65

well as the teacher. The study of humor in the classroom is finding its way onto more and more college and university campuses with such course names as "Tips for Teaching the YouTube Generation," "Using Humor in the College Classroom to Enhance Teaching Effectiveness in 'Dread Courses'," and "Ten Specific Techniques for Developing Humor in the Classroom." Countless research projects continue to study humor and its value in the learning process. The conclusions are consistent in their findings that a strong positive link is formed between a teacher who uses humor, the evaluations their students give of the teacher's performance, and the statistics measuring students' learning.

Student measurement raises a serious issue. If students are not challenged to learn up to their capacity, then our future leaders will be potentially under-prepared. In our city, a number of the public schools have been on a state academic watch list because of poor performance on standardized tests. Our school board began meeting behind closed doors when an issue of promoting failing students to the next grade emerged. An additional study into the probable lack of humor in the affected classrooms might reveal some interesting results.

No one is taking a shot at teachers; quite the opposite. As we have already learned in earlier chapters, the use of laughter and humor has a profound effect on numerous functions of the brain and body. If equal or greater strides could be expected in learning, then we as a society should jump at the chance.

Studies reveal that humor appears to encourage students to learn by increasing their motivation. These students insist humor just makes learning that much more fun. Boredom is reduced in an environment that, almost by its very structure, tends to be tedious. Humor can reduce stress and tension in class, thereby helping students cope with difficult learning situations.

The Sense of Humor

As with the use of humor in other areas of life, we aren't talking about a teacher who stands before the class cracking jokes all day long. Even though an occasional joke might be fine, a teacher can relate a funny story or experience that will help students get the point or remember an obscure fact. A teacher with a natural good sense of humor can simply brighten their students' day by being light from time to time.

Think about your own years in school. Can you remember one or more teachers who were funny, and, because they used humor, you not only remember them years later, but you also can see how they helped you learn in their classes? Or was your educational experience more like what we have been finding where people say they never had a teacher who was fun?

Are you a teacher? Do you regularly use humor in your class or not? Why if you do and why not if you don't?

An important benefit, beyond the ability to enhance learning and increase attention span, is the fact humor has been shown to alter the chemical makeup of the brain so a child's ability to focus and retain information is increased. Beyond these benefits, humor enhances creativity and imaginative thinking so children can try new things in a fun way. This allows students to avoid habitual thinking that is limited and stifling to education and creativity. Students appreciate a teacher who understands the use of humor as a lighter side of learning. Laughing stimulates both sides of the brain. People get the message quicker and remember it longer.

As one expert said, "Humor helps people to relax and makes them more receptive to new thoughts. The barriers go down, and people experience real learning."

"I often teach seminars," said another, "and my motto is, if you can't have fun, why bother?"

"I use humor to assure my students they are safe and that I have a positive regard for them," reports another teacher.

Sarcasm, however, has no place in the classroom. Likewise, the use of negative humor should be avoided. Under no circumstances should a student be singled out and embarrassed by the use of humor on the part of the teacher. Teachers must also guard against other students leveling this brand of humor upon their classmates. Students are already vulnerable. They come to class with stress, uncertainty, and anxieties. Humor can help to relieve these areas if done right and done well.

In one Christian school, the class period was customarily to be either opened or closed in prayer by a student called upon by the teacher. There was a student who was well known for falling asleep during most class periods.

One day, while he was in a deep sleep right in the middle of the hour as the instructor was teaching, another student poked him in the ribs and said, "Hey, Dan, the teacher just asked you to pray."

Without thinking, Dan jumped to his feet and began, "Dear Lord, we thank you for this beautiful day ..."

Immediately, the entire class erupted into laughter and the student was completely embarrassed. Depending on his sense of humor and his ability, or lack thereof, to laugh at himself, this kind of humor in the classroom can be disastrous. The teacher quickly took control of the situation so no additional damage was done.

Teachers must learn to laugh with, not at their students. By making yourself, the authority figure, the object of a joke, rather than making fun of your less powerful students, you help to pull the group together where certain barriers can fall. This use of humor can encourage a bonding between the teacher and students, even making a better connection between students and their subject matter. Laughter not only makes students feel better, it can be a major tool for insight.

The Sense of Humor

One teacher reported, "I find the use of humor vital to the classroom and learning environments. I will often flash a cartoon on the overhead. I usually put a cartoon on my exams and I know humor enhances learning for my students."

Admonishing a group of prospective teachers, a speaker said, "I would like all teacher candidates to be aware of using humor as a direct instructional technique. What we do in life is important, but I think we take ourselves far too seriously. I love watching young children having a good time. When you watch them in a class where the teacher is aloof and distant, you see some very defensive students. If the teacher is having a good time, however, the children are having a good time."

Suppose the subject is history. The mere mention of the "H" word might strike terror in some students. But what if a teacher used humor from a particular era in history to make a point? Here is a joke from the 1920s. Notice how the main character is a tramp.

Today we refer to these people as homeless. Who were the tramps? How did they get around? Why were so many people out of work in this period of time in American history? Notice, too, how today's animal-rights-advocates and the politically correct would find what happened to the dog to be offensive.

The tramp was sitting with his back to a hedge by the wayside, munching at some scraps wrapped in a newspaper. A lady out walking her pet Pomeranian strolled past. The little dog ran to the tramp and tried to guzzle the food. The tramp smiled expansively at the lady.

"Shall I throw the leetle dog a bit, mum?" he asked.

The lady was gratified by this appearance of kindly interest in her pet and murmured an assent. The tramp caught the dog by the nape of the neck and tossed the animal over the hedge, remarking: "And if he comes back, mum, I might throw him a bit more."

Another example comes from a period in time where the joke might set the stage for students to have a better understanding of what was going on during the Franco-German war.

During the siege of Paris in the war when everybody was starving, one aristocratic family had their pet dog served for dinner. The master of the house, when the meal was ended, surveyed the platter through tear-dimmed eyes and spoke sadly:

"How Fido would have enjoyed those bones!"

Studying the humor of the era from whichthe story came increases a student's understanding of the life and times of the people and a new dimension of learning takes place.

An entire study of humor in history could completely open a subject for students that otherwise might have seemed stuffy and unapproachable. Each decade in American history has particular jokes reflecting what was going on in that era. A better understanding of previous periods in history would point out stereotypes of the time, attitudes toward government, the economic climate, and social change would be seen in the humor. Books containing humor from years past, or ones that list funny stories by subject, can yield additional material. Humor might also be helpful in teaching science, sociology, math, or other subjects.

Our culture often teaches a myth that humor and laughter are a waste of time. "Don't be silly," a child may be told in class, or, "Why don't you grow up?" "Can't you be serious?" another might ask, or, "Act your age."

Laughter aids in communication. Even when people don't speak the same language, laughter is still universal. Laughter also helps to break the ice in a new group. Humor's one form of communication everyone can relate to. The better adjusted students are, the more likely they will respond to humor, jokes, and fun. These students won't take themselves too seriously, and their sense of humor will spill over and affect other students around them. Again, this isn't to suggest simple joke telling. We are talking about the natural use of humor in everyday circumstances. Bringing this positive

The Sense of Humor

trait into a classroom setting where humor is encouraged, can only enhance the learning process for everyone involved.

Used properly by a teacher, humor can help to make students feel more accepted and less serious about the less-than-perfect aspects of their lives, abilities, or personalities. Once a teacher, using humor, demonstrates that no one person has all the answers to every question, that a teacher can make mistakes and can laugh at those mistakes, then everyone in the room is more comfortable.

Within the subject of learning styles is the specific area identified as The Multiple Intelligence Approach. There are seven intelligences within this theory. They include:

1. Body or physical
2. Interpersonal
3. Intra-personal
4. Logical
5. Musical
6. Verbal
7. Visual intelligence.

The verbal/linguistic intelligence is related to our words and language in both the spoken and written word. This form is dominant in Western educational systems. V/L intelligence is unlocked by the spoken word, by reading the thoughts of another person, through poetry as well as jokes, twists, and plays on words in the language. Capacities involved in this area are:

1. Understanding order and meaning of words
2. Convincing someone of a course of action
3. Explaining, teaching, and learning
4. Humor
5. Memory and recall
6. Linguistic analysis

Notice how the use of humor fits into these categories as they relate to language and learning. Humor is found in none of the other six categories.

Still, the use of humor can be a tricky subject. Teachers need to take into account the age of their students, their culture, gender, and other factors that may contribute to students' perceptions of humor.

Sometimes teachers completely exclude humor from their curriculum because they consider their work too serious for humor. They are concerned that their students might perceive them as irreverent, offensive, unprofessional, or inappropriate. In fact, in response to one of my questions to a medical professional on the subject of humor, I was told, "Of all my patients, the ones I see who consistently exhibit no sense of humor at all are teachers."

Again, I want to say I know you funny teachers are out there, and your work is to be applauded. Let this be an encouragement to you so you will begin to exert your positive attitude within your circle of influence so that in a few years, teachers employing humor in the classroom will be the majority, not the exception. Your students will appreciate you, and you will be further insulated from burn-out in your critically important work of preparing the next generation.

Both mind and heart have to work together in order for effective learning to take place. As a teacher, you have the most power and influence to shape your students' attitudes toward learning; not just in your class, but for the rest of their lives. The more our society has been directed toward left-brained activities—the things logical and linear— we have lost sight of the fun and excitement in learning. To combat this, one teacher carried a 'teaching toolbox' around with him filled with different items he used to represent elements that were essential to learning. The wilder the image, the more likely his students were to remember the concept or fact he wanted them to know.

The Sense of Humor

Primarily experts outside the field of education have been those who championed the use of humor and its effects within their professions, noting the direct correlation between the physiological and psychological benefits that are believed to be associated with humor and laughter. And yet, all of these professions have their roots in the educational process.

Relating humor in the classroom is not so much an issue of what to teach, but rather how to teach. Humor should only be one of many tools used by the teacher. Students are more likely to listen to a teacher they find fun and interesting. They are more likely to feel comfortable in asking questions. Your students will want to make it to your classes because of your style.

As one expert put it, "There is a direct connection between 'Ha-Ha,' and 'Aha.' And besides, students can't laugh and snore at the same time."

Since good teachers who have a sense of humor have shown through research they are able to use humor effectively as part of their teaching methods, they find humor used correctly is a powerful addition to any classroom experience.

Start by saying the following statements right out loud. Repeat them often, until they are a part of the fabric of your individual teaching style. Make up some of your own and circulate them around to other teachers. Even though they are meant to be fun, humor in the classroom is serious business:

A day without laughter,

Is not what I'm after.

Funny from this day I will be,

With a ha, ha, ha, and a tee, hee, hee.

From my students all the while,

I shall seek to gain a smile.

My teaching style is not effective,

Till humor is the first elective.

Today, tomorrow, and ever after,

I'll fill my days and theirs with laughter.

Anyone without a sense of humor is at the mercy of everyone else.

—William E. Rothschild

Six—

Humor In The Workplace

Any man who has had the job I've had, and didn't have a sense of humor, wouldn't still be here.

—Harry S Truman

"A company that has fun, where employees put cartoons on the wall and celebrate, is spirited, creative, and usually profitable." So says an expert in the field of humor and work.

One reputable life insurance company published a pamphlet for college graduates who were preparing for their first job interviews. A section of the pamphlet included information about the traits that most often lead to rejections of the applicants. One of the factors on the list cited that the applicant lacked a sense of humor.

Another survey by a national employment agency found more than ninety percent of executives from some of the largest corporations in the United States reported having a sense of humor is a key ingredient in career advancement. A sense of humor demonstrates your self-confidence in a non-threatening way. Humor also arms you with an added weapon because people are more comfortable around you, and you will likely be more persuasive as a result.

The chairman of Southwest Airlines is well known for his use of humor in the workplace. Anyone who questions humor's effectiveness in this environment need only look at the decades during which Southwest became the most profitable airline in the United States.

If there is one place in our lives where humor could be misused, misunderstood, and dangerous, it would be where we work. The turf wars, power struggles, mind games, and chain of command make this arena seem like a minefield.

A common theme in most corporations today is change. Management understands their employees tend to resist change. Many companies have become leaner in recent years requiring a need to do more with less. The constant pressure to increase productivity, perform faster, learn new information more quickly, and adopt new skills, while assimilating that information, all have added to increased stress on the job.

This conflict came into sharp focus recently at an aerospace company. If you fly commercially on an American carrier, chances are some of the components on your aircraft came from this company. So, keeping employees like that happy is important. The problem in question involved a total revamping of the corporation's benefits plan. As is so often the case, this meant the employees were about to get fewer benefits while at the same time paying extra into the plan. Unfortunately, the alternative would have required the company to take drastic action if their workforce refused to go along with the intended changes.

The communications department at corporate headquarters was charged with the task to "make it happen." A clever plan was devised. In the early stages, a survey went out to workers throughout the entire company that asked pointed questions about the proposed choices. From

The Sense of Humor

this survey came responses falling into similar categories. Some people were simply opposed to change. Others were afraid of losing benefits. Still others resisted additional costs. Opinions also tended to fall into categories depending on the age and seniority of the respondents.

After all the data had been tabulated and analyzed, the company decided that, along with the human resources presentations and printed materials, a humorous video program would be produced. What was different from a normal presentation is the fact this would be a puppet video in the spirit of the Muppets. The rationale for this decision came from understanding when you have to deal with a difficult subject, especially when the subject involves money, real people wouldn't be able to pull it off. A cartoon, which also would have worked, was too expensive. I was called in to work on the video production.

From survey results, characters were crafted to look and sound like the various groups who raised particular concerns. An older puppet represented those who had been with the company for a long time and were set in their ways. His character took on that kind of crusty voice, appearance, and personality.

There was a younger character, another with small children, and so on. As each character appeared in the program, they were able to voice the concerns of the group they represented in a humorous, non-threatening way. The information campaign was a success, resulting in a seventy-five percent sign up rate after only the first phase.

For those who can use this technique effectively, humor provides a valuable communications tool in many situations. Presentations become more interesting, employees are more attentive and working relationships are generally made stronger.

Another aerospace company was experiencing a higher than usual rejection rate on some of their smaller precision-machined parts. In this bottom line, just-in-time, lean manufacturing climate commonplace in

American corporate culture, the company had to do something about the problem … and fast. Again, video was called upon to get the message out. The method selected involved a short video that would follow these small, delicate parts all the way from machining, through polishing, inspection, and into storage where they were held until needed for final assembly. But there was a twist.

For purposes of demonstration, the delicate parts were replaced by dozens of raw eggs. Immediately, the viewer knew what would happen if an egg were to be mishandled, dropped to the floor, struck by another, larger object, or spilled out onto a hard surface. To make the point even stronger, these things were done to the eggs and the end results were obvious.

Again, as in the example of understanding on the part of employees and their changing benefits plan, here too people immediately understood, made the connection between fragile eggs, and the equally, if not more fragile parts they were handling. The humor campaign resulted in a dramatic reduction in failed parts, directly affecting productivity and the bottom line.

Neither jokes nor funny stories were used in these two examples, but humor was implemented as a tool and was effective.

In this context of mixing humor with work, note that humor in the workplace has emerged as one of the most serious issues today. A number of human resources consultants have issued warnings against humor as a form of sexual harassment. They cite everything from off-color remarks, to jokes with a double meaning, to gender-related humor.

The Harvard Business School published, "Uses and Abuses of Humor in the Office." Their extensive report reached the conclusion that humor in the office can be just the right thing when used in the right place. The publication went on to encourage would-be office comics to stick to the kind of humor that keeps the organization going, bolsters morale and allows co-workers to laugh together.

The Sense of Humor

This form of laughing together finds its way into another area of corporate America involving team spirit, team building, and functioning as a team.

Corporations are finding the use of humor increases creativity. Old solutions to problems have been replaced by new thinking— thinking outside the box. But this new approach to problem solving is an atmosphere that has to be embraced first, and then implemented by management. Improving your own sense of humor has been proven to boost scores on creativity tests. The appropriate use of humor and laughter at work are effective tools to sustain a mental state and work environment known to be most conducive to creative problem solving.

A key watchword found in industry is teamwork. For the last several years, this concept is being taught in US schools from college down to high school and even into some of the lower grades. Years ago, a typical science fair featured elaborate projects made by individual students— and probably their parents in many cases. This practice was changed to team projects. Now, several students began to collaborate on research, model building, written reports, and other visuals.

The idea of a teamwork model was brought to America from Japanese industry which operated at the time with a cradle to the grave commitment between industry and workers. Close ties were fostered so workers felt like they were actually a part of the company and its products. Group morning exercises were a common occurrence followed by teams working to solve complex problems, develop and market new products, or assemble intricate electronic devices.

Most corporations now promote the importance of team building, making the employees understand that they are an important part of something bigger. This has resulted in a sense of belonging as people work together to achieve common goals and objectives. While throwing a group of people together and calling them a team may be easy, building a team isn't quite that simple. Individuals may not feel like they are part of the team automatically. Shared positive humor helps to create an emotional bond between various employees working together. This bond strengthens the whole team.

The communications examples mentioned earlier are examples of improved communication where humor is used. One of the most common complaints in many organizations is the lack of good communication with management. This leads to mistrust between both groups and, an "us versus them" mentality develops. Management might begin to be referred to as the "suits," further dividing people who should all be working together for the common good of the company and of each individual. When trust is lost, there is no way for the team concept to flourish. Humor is often referred to as "social lubricant" making difficult forms of communication easier and more effective. Taking a lighter approach helps in dealing with awkward situations or more serious problems and conflicts.

Beyond the internal benefits corporations can achieve by including humor, humor can also be a powerful weapon in sales and advertising. How many times have you returned to work on Monday following the Super Bowl? Remember how all the discussion surrounded the television commercials, especially the funny ones? When we can laugh in connection with a new product, or even one that has been in the marketplace for a long time, we form a positive opinion toward that product. However, if you are already predisposed against a particular product, this may not hold true such as in the case of the advertising for beer products. Even if it's funny, and a lot of those TV spots are, they wouldn't likely sway you to become a new customer.

People are often afraid if they use humor and no one laughs, then something terrible will happen, though no one has yet figured out what that terrible thing might be. In a situation like this, a speaker could say something like, "Well, your boss thought it was funny." The floor isn't likely to open and swallow them up, yet the fear of failing with humor is so overwhelming, they choose to avoid trying altogether. While there is always a risk in using humor, we should take the risk so we can make the places where we work better. Many feel humor is something they should leave at home when they come to work. Since you already spend so much of your life at work, why not make the job as fun as possible? Humor helps you keep everything in perspective.

The most important thing to decide right now is you want to improve your sense of humor where you work. Knowing more about how humor reduces stress, advances good health, and enhances job performance should be all a good manager needs for motivation. When you add to this equation a better bottom line, you and your company will be on your way.

Next time you are back at work, look for others there who have a good sense of humor. Begin spending more time around them and less time with people who are negative. This is an easy one because you can already visualize the people who come to you consistently with complaints, negative attitudes, and a "what have they done for us lately" frame of mind. These people will not help you on your path to becoming a more humor-minded person. Remember, negativity breeds negativity, while humor only serves to build us up, to improve our outlook and our performance.

If you have your own personal workspace, begin dressing your space up with items that are either fun or make you think happy thoughts. At a recent company meeting, management handed out a small box to everyone who attended. Printed on the outside of each box in bold letters was the word *FUN*. The box contained a multicolored plastic Slinky, a large rubber ball, and a set of jacks. All of these items immediately caused the recipients to be transferred back to their childhoods as they remembered, probably quite happily, another time and place. The employees were encouraged to actually take the items from the box and play with them from time to time.

High pressure work environments, like law offices and advertising agencies, have developed entire rooms devoted to nothing but fun. The rooms can be simple with smaller objects, or they might be elaborate with pool tables, Ping-Pong, putting greens, pinball machines, and foosball tables. The idea is to have a room that feels safe, where fun is encouraged, and where stress can be relieved.

Over the years, I've worked on the editing of my video projects in various post-production facilities. Some were pretty bare bones, while a few included a fun room. You can imagine, whenever I had the choice, I took my work to a facility with a fun room. This room was a great place to relax, particularly when the inevitable technical problems caused my edit session to be delayed.

Actively look for humor at work every day. Tell your coworkers funny stories and ask them to share with you funny stories of their own. These will likely include humorous incidents they've experienced at home and other places away from work. But make sure this doesn't take away from the time you should spend working. The comments or incidents can take place just before a meeting is supposed to start, at lunch, or while you're on break.

While on your humor journey, spend more time thinking of things that are funny to you. Telling a joke or hearing one told are ways to focus on a lighter level, but humor can be found in many different forms.

Try poking fun at yourself. A sign that we are a healthy, well-rounded person, is when we can laugh at ourselves. Life is too short, so why take everything, including yourself, too seriously? This is one of the most difficult humor skills to learn and master, but when you do, self-deprecating humor becomes one of the most powerful stress reducers, especially when you are able to defuse a mistake you've made in an ordinarily stressful workday. If you have been working all along to improve your humor skills during times when you're in a good mood, then when the tough times come you will be able to draw on this well within yourself to help you cope with anything that might come your way.

The key here is to take your work seriously, but take yourself lightly. While maintaining your level of professionalism, you will learn, through humor, how to manage conflicts more effectively, become more persuasive, release creativity, and work better as a member of your team. Not only will your employer get a better performance from you, you will find more enjoyment in the work you do.

Logically, if a good sense of humor is high on the agenda of your human resources department when hiring people in the first place, these same people are most likely to be retained during any downsizing the company may initiate in the future. Remember, "He who laughs … lasts."

Many organizations are using humorists to teach people how the use of humor can enhance job performance. At one medical conference, Dr. Allen, mentioned in the medical chapter, stood before a live audience of doctors, nurses, and other health professionals. His message was intended to help them lighten up and relieve the obvious stress associated with their work. As he talked, he began teaching them how to juggle. But to make juggling easier, he used different colored handkerchiefs. They floated slowly in the air, making juggling more simple. Not only did he have them, but each member of the audience had a set as well.

As he began to engage the audience, and everyone followed his instructions from the stage, the room became ablaze with color, movement, and increasingly, laughter. By the time he was finished, these stiff, serious, tense medical staff members smiled and laughed like children. Each person was handed a prescription that read on one side, "NOT for EMERGENCY USE ONLY." The other side listed the steps for proper juggling technique. At the top he had printed, "Rx for Health through Creative Silliness," and at the bottom, "Juggle twice each day as needed to reduce stress."

Finding the benefits of humor as a valuable tool in management isn't so much about being funny, but about developing a sense of humor, appreciating the value of humor, and applying its positive qualities. Rather than concentrating on making people laugh, a corporate culture that welcomes laughter is most important. In the Southwest Airlines example, we see that their mission is to provide the best possible air service, but service is delivered in the context of having fun. Laughter is welcomed in this setting which fosters higher ambition, greater initiative, good morale, higher productivity, and lower employee turnover. After all, who would want to leave a job that is truly fun?

You may wonder if the benefits of including humor at work can be measured. Studies show that approximately eighty percent of all humor, fun, and laughter is unplanned. Knowing this may help employers to encourage an atmosphere of spontaneity. According to one survey of employers:

• 55% report that fun and humor reduce stress at work
• 34% find humor increases job satisfaction
• 28% notice humor stimulates creativity and innovation
• 24% cite that humor strengthens employee loyalty
• 22% see an improvement in customer service
• 16% say humor increases productivity.

Realizing the importance of laughter and fun at work, some companies have begun adding a humor consultant to their staff. Not only are they charged with the task of elevating the use of humor, they also must work to dispel the perception that humor at work might seem unprofessional. An interesting dynamic can be seen when corporate meetings are held away from the office. Most people in this environment become more relaxed, and even playful. In such a setting, humor can be more readily added to the meeting agenda for its maximum positive effect. The trick is in not leaving this new lighter spirit behind at the offsite meeting, but to bring levity back into the company for all the good humor will provide.

Humor at work will:

- Improve communication
- Reduce conflict and tension
- Promote teamwork
- Enhance employee relations
- Enliven your workplace
- Build trust with your customers
- Stimulate creativity
- Strengthen mental fitness
- Cause us to do our best
- Increase morale and motivation

And Prevent burnout.

Always laugh heartily at the jokes your boss tells, it may be a loyalty test.

—Source Unknown

Seven—

Humor and Relationships

Humor is the great thing, the saving thing. The minute it crops up, all our irritations and resentments slip away, and a sunny spirit takes their place.

—Mark Twain

If you are like most people, you breathe in and breathe out every hour of the day and night, but you probably never think about breathing. Your heart beats, pumping life giving oxygen from that breathing, throughout your body every second of your life. But, unless you suffer from heart trouble, chances are you never give your heartbeat a second thought. Yet, if either of these vital systems within your body were to stop, even just for a short time, the result would be fatal.

Your sense of humor, and laughter for that matter, are proving to be just as vital as your heartbeat or breathing. We have learned about the countless physical and psychological benefits derived from humor. There is another part of your life that could wither and die, without the exercise of humor—that vital component is relationship.

Relationship, as defined in the dictionary is, "The state of being related or interrelated, and the relation connecting or binding participants in a relationship: as kinship."

Before relationship can develop, there must first be friendship. The dictionary gives a thorough definition of this term, but omits a major component. Most enduring friendships are characterized by the laughter that fills the air when good friends get together. You'll hear laughter in back yards, at restaurants, or any place where friends gather. Without humor and laughter, friendship is incomplete.

When you mention relationship, there is a tendency to jump ahead to dating, engagement, and marriage. We'll get to those subjects, but friendships and relationships exist in many other forms and settings, without progressing this way.

Some friendships start out on the playground at school or in a Sunday school class. Children begin by simply playing together. In these settings, they discover other children who think like they do, have the same interests, and likely share a compatible sense of humor. Often such friendships continue through high school and college, even lasting an entire lifetime. When these friends get together, especially after being apart for months or years, the time of separation is quickly dissolved by laughter.

There are entire sections in any greeting card display devoted to friends. You've probably heard of the practice where two friends send a recurring gift each year. Some choose to alternate each Christmas, while others select birthdays. The gift can be the same silly item or might evolve every time it is sent, becoming more and more outlandish and bizarre each year.

Friendships may be casual, with no other connections, or they might develop when people attend the same church, work together, belong to the same club, etc. Though we likely have several friendships, not many will develop into relationships. A relationship takes much more time and effort, leaving little room for any but a select few.

Here are two humorous little stories about friendships. See if you think there is a deeper relationship in either one.

1. Two friends were standing in a line at the bank when a pair of robbers came in. Not only did the thieves clean out all the cash drawers, but they also walked around with bags and ordered everyone to drop in their valuables.

    Just as the robbers got to the pair of friends, one turned to the other and, as he passed him a bill said, "By the way, here's that twenty bucks I owe you."

2. A very cheap man was looking for a gift for his friend. Everything in the shop was very expensive except for a broken glass vase he could buy for almost nothing. He asked the store to mail the vase for him, hoping his friend would think it had been broken on the way.

A few days later, he received a thank you note from his friend. "Thanks for the beautiful vase. You were so thoughtful to wrap each piece separately."

What did you decide—friendships or relationships? Probably neither term applies because in each case the friendship is only superficial.

Relationships within the family were explored in chapter three as the benefits of using humor were discussed. There is an added dimension of relationships with extended family. A trip to any family reunion yields some interesting results as you observe the interaction of various members who attend. Small groups will invariably gather. A common characteristic of these groups is laughter.

Then there are the loners, the sulkers, and those wounded by something said or done so long ago by another family member that only *they* can remember anymore. Humor and laughter can be especially useful under these circumstances. You will also enjoy noticing the families at your reunion who seem to get along well as a unit. There is a lot of good give and take, self-deprecating humor, and a general sense of well-being. Other families not doing so well might likely display biting, cutting humor, often characterized by sarcasm or you'll detect no humor at all.

All around you in your daily life are opportunities to observe:

• How humor is well used in various situations.

• How humor is not used.

• How humor could make a certain situation better.

You'll be amazed how quickly you will become aware of these interpersonal relationships. When you see opportunities to alleviate difficult situations with humor, you will begin to do so. Armed with the information in these pages, you can also have the confidence that your interventions will likely have a positive end result, making your world, and that of others around you, a better place to live.

We know from our previous chapter that strong alliances are formed at work using humor. These alliances can become friendships, leading to long-term relationships in business. A sense of humor helps relationships within the company and in dealing with customers and suppliers. One company, for example, has the following phrase written in their mission statement:

We seek to consistently demonstrate a sense of warmth, humor, and mutual respect in our relationships with our customers, to be a company with which they most enjoy working.

How refreshing to read a statement like that in an otherwise cutthroat, bottom line, dog-eat-dog corporate environment. If more company managers truly understood the value found in using humor, they would begin to see tangible results in their business.

The Sense of Humor

The relationship information of interest to many people centers around dating and marriage. In most studies, a good sense of humor ranks at or near the top of the list of qualities men and women value in a potential mate. In both informal as well as academic research, humor has been cited as an important component of couples' interactions in successful relationships. These findings demonstrate an interesting picture for the role each partner's sense of humor plays in their romantic relationships.

Recently I contacted a national online e-dating service. I wanted to know about their experience with the importance of a sense of humor when applicants looked for a possible "match."

They say of themselves that their service is not one which simply matches individuals in the superficial areas. Rather, this service strives to match people in the deeper, more important dimensions that make a difference in a relationship.

When asked about how applicants valued humor, the president of this service told me, "We have fifty of the most popular 'must haves' on our site. A good sense of humor is always ranked in the top five for both men and women. I see humor as incredibly important to a great marriage."

We can all agree that the use of humor in this next example is designed to be fatal to the relationship.

A soldier is stationed overseas far from home when he gets a dreadful "Dear John" letter from his girlfriend back home breaking off their engagement. And, to make situation even worse, she asks him to return her picture. So he goes around collecting all the unwanted pictures of other girls from several of his friends and writes her a letter saying, "Regret I can't remember which one is you ... please keep your picture and return the rest."

Sense of humor is one of the foremost qualities people identify as attractive in others and equally important in their relationships. In this critical area of relationship building and maintenance, negative humor is to be most avoided. Sarcastic, hostile, destructive, cutting humor should not be permitted to enter any relationship. Positive use of humor will foster fairness, trust, honesty, open communication, long-term commitment, and loyalty.

There may be a selfish reason for trying humor in your marriage relationship. People who are married enjoy better health, they make more money, and they are happier. Yet we are watching a divorce rate of nearly sixty percent; a rate that has increased more than two hundred percent in the past thirty years. Experts tell us one of the main reasons is because falling in love is easy. People find staying in love much more difficult.

Anyone who has been married for a number of years knows how the relationship changes over time. Studies and writings abound on this subject. Since we know all the other positive effects derived from humor, we can conclude using humor in marriage will help ensure your chances for a long and successful life together. Additional studies show marriage lengthens our lives—some people say they only feel longer—promotes better physical and emotional health, and reduces depression.

Too many couples stop dating once they get married. In our next example, dating didn't last long at all:

"If you'll make the toast and pour the juice, sweetheart," said the newlywed bride, "breakfast will be ready."

"Good, what are we having for breakfast?" asked her new husband.

"Toast and juice."

A common phrase during the dating phase is, "Let's go do something fun." When the complaint, "The spark is gone," is heard a few months or years later, likely the fun has gone out of the relationship. Possibly, increasing your use of a positive sense of humor might be one of the components that would put your marriage back on the right track. As we have heard from so many different sectors on this subject, you may survey your own marriage or relationships and say, "Now that you mention ..." If this happens, take steps immediately to change course.

Interestingly, women consistently rate this quality a little higher than men. That may be because, studies indicate, men initiate humor, jokes, and funny stories while women tend to enjoy hearing them.

As you move forward into the various friendships and relationships in your life, take this short quiz to see if you have already reached the peak of your sense of humor potential, realizing its positive effects on others, or if there is room for improvement.

Is There Enough Laughology in *Your* Life?

Score 1 point if you agree.

Score 5 points if you disagree.

1. I believe I have a good sense of humor _____
2. When faced with a tense situation, I usually try to change it with humor _____
3. I like to laugh and it happens easily _____
4. I am able to laugh when I'm alone, at a movie, or a watching a sitcom _____
5. I make a point of passing along the funny stories, jokes, and cartoons I find _____
6. It's easy for me to make people laugh _____
7. I laugh a lot at work and so do my coworkers _____
8. I've always had people tell me I have a good sense of humor _____
9. I'm always on the lookout for other people who make me laugh

    _____

10. I like laughing at home around my family, and they enjoy it, too

    _____

Total _____

40—50 Are you still alive? Time to get started by watching a funny movie, buying a good joke book, anything to get your pulse going again.

30—40 You already recognize laughter is a good thing, now get out there and use it even more.

20—30 You aren't too far off the mark, but any improvement will only make things better.

10—20 You're the kind of person the rest of the world is looking for, now go out and help as may other people as you can.

Humor is often created when there is a change in traditional relationships. Citing "The Far Side" again, much of Gary Larson's humor comes from turning these relationships around. He will often give human characteristics to animals or completely bend reality. One of his cartoons shows three extremely small men reading a large book. They sit in an oversized chair and everything in the frame is exaggerated. And the name of the book they're reading? *Little Women.*

In another, two fish are swimming in a bowl high on a tall table. They think a third fish has escaped to safety wherever that is. But on the floor beneath them, we see the skeletal remains of a dead fish. When you understand how changing traditional relationships between objects, animals, and people become funny, you can come up with your own original humor.

Humor in any loving relationship should express affection. The form this takes will vary with each couple. The rule still applies that if it doesn't feel right, it probably isn't. Affectionate humor will never cut the other person down. Humor may be used to help get at some of the difficult areas of the relationship that, much like the puppets were used in the company benefits plan change in chapter six, can only be reached in a humorous way.

Remember that humor is not simply the telling of jokes. With a little research, you'll discover finding good jokes that don't make someone else look bad is difficult. Why do we rarely tell jokes that end with people looking smarter, braver, more capable, or more generous? This is one of the main reasons you need to develop a well-rounded sense of

The Sense of Humor

humor that can include some such jokes, but is not totally dependent on them in order for you to enjoy humor, and provide levity to the people who are special in your life.

The use of humor helps strengthen interpersonal relationships at all levels and wherever you find them. Working together toward a common goal becomes that much more enjoyable for everyone involved. Look for ways to better use this powerful tool in all areas of your personal and professional relationships.

You may think being funny is a gift, like salesmanship, music, or athletic ability. That may be so, and there are the true standouts in every field. But it doesn't mean you can't increase your humor ability with practice. You may not be able to star in a Hollywood comedy, or travel the stand-up comic circuits, but if you practice, practice, practice your own brand of *laughology*, your style will emerge. Your style will be unique to your personality and perfect for the relationships you choose to pursue.

"Laughter is the best way to make somebody's heart beat."

—Robert Holden

Eight—

Humor as a Tool of Ministry

Laughter is the shortest distance between two people.
—Victor Borge, pianist and comedian

Jesus used "… the weapon of wit and the saber of satire" in his running verbal battles with the religious power structure, according to Randall O'Brien of Baylor University, author of *I Feel Better All Over Than I Do Any Place Else.*

Interestingly, there are no jokes in the Bible. Moses and the profits never told a joke. John the Baptist was not noted for humorous anecdotes, and the Son of God never entertained people with a funny story. None of the Apostolic writings contain humor.

You will find no entertaining humor—none at all. Nothing in God's Word is calculated to promote empty laughter.

Given O. Blakely has noted, "Church history records few moments of humor. The total absence of humor from the Bible is one of the most singular things in all of literature.

"As early as the eleventh century, the influential leader John of Chrysostom insisted Jesus never laughed. Through the centuries, artists overwhelmingly have followed the saint's argument. How many paintings have you seen where the Son of God grins from ear to ear?

"Humor was often the howitzer he used to shell the veneer of piety surrounding 'Fortress Pharisee.' Who couldn't help but laugh when Jesus exposed the arrogance of blindness of the religious leaders, calling them 'blind guides' … straining out a gnat and swallowing a camel ... cleaning the outside of a cup but leaving the inside filthy ... and like tombs, whitewashed on the outside but rotting on the inside?"

According to Francis of Assisi, "Leave sadness to the devil. The devil has reason to be sad."

A clergyman selected Hebrews 9:27 as his Sunday morning text.

It is appointed unto men once to die, and after that the judgment.

His announced topic was, "As Sure as Death and Taxes." No more sobering statement exists in the Bible than that quote from Hebrews. Not so much as a hint of levity—no joking matter. Or, was it?

Stepping to the pulpit, the pastor began his sermon by asking, "Did you hear about the man who said he wished he knew where he was going to die because, if he knew, he wouldn't go within fifty miles of that place for as long as he lived?"

With tact and wit, he set up his audience for a sobering look at the shortness of life and the certainty of death and the inevitability of judgment.

Another pastor, who had a tendency of going overtime with his sermons, also stepped up to the pulpit. Opening his Bible, he took out a pink note, which he held up to the audience. Those seated in the front pews could make out the letters KISS. It was his wife's doing, of course, and her husband explained that the letters simply meant, "**K**eep **I**t **S**hort, **S**weetheart!"

The Sense of Humor

In so doing, he set up for himself and the congregation a "teaching moment," in which he informed his people that long windedness was something he was working on, but also suggesting some texts need more preaching time than others. With a touch of humor, he suggested on a future Sunday when, as the audience sat engrossed in the grip of a thought-provoking sermon, he would break from his message to add a whimsical, "Aren't you glad I haven't stopped preaching yet?"

Such a moment did come and, aware of how their pastor had disciplined himself to be a good steward of time, theirs was a full and overflowing blessedness.

Another pastor became a useful "lab-specimen" during the designing and now the writing of this chapter. For example, on a Sunday morning when he reminded parishioners to sign the register sheets on each aisle, he said, "Just your name, address, telephone number … and, if you insist, your checkbook balance."

This congregation is predominant with professionally-oriented people. Yet, they responded with laughter at the pastor's quip.

Why?

Because, though our worship services tend to be in a serious vein, a mood of fellowship okays an admittedly corny quip like the checkbook ad lib. Occasionally, during the sermon, he used the names of people from the audience. "What would you have done, Jim?" he may ask or, "How about you, Mary Ann, if it were up to you to make the decision?"

Every Christmas season, our church has a tradition by which families take their turns at the advent display which consists of five unlit candles, marking the weeks until Christmas. Parents and children from one family come up each Sunday, present an advent message, and light one of the candles. This past Yule season, the Taylor family took their turn at the candles, but the one they were supposed to light refused to cooperate. The mother had the excruciating experience. The delay became nearly exasperating. When Mrs. Taylor was about to give up, the candlewick at last responded. Just as the family returned to their pew, the pastor said, "She never met a candle she couldn't light!"

Another time, during the pastoral prayer, a baby began chattering the way little ones do just before they learn to say *mama* or *dada*. As the child's happy chatter intensified, the pastor paused and, looking out toward the child, said pleasantly, "Listen to that voice. That baby might just make a great preacher one day." Then he added, "Finish yours, sweetheart, and then we'll go back to mine." To the congregation he remarked, "Babies reach out to God, too, you know."

Church History tells us the use of humor during worship, or life in general, was labeled taboo by many Christians through the centuries. One Bishop, as a warning to the general public, is said to have pontificated, "The church will declare anathema if laughter is heard."

Yet, we read the following in Proverbs 15:13 *A happy heart makes the face cheerful,* Proverbs 15:15 says *but the cheerful heart has a continual feast,* or in Proverbs 17:22 *A cheerful heart is good medicin*e. And Psalms 2 tells us God laughs at those who rebelled against his Kingship.

One of the funniest accounts to me is found in 1 Samuel 5:1-5 where the Philistines captured the Ark of the Covenant and put the Ark right beside their dragon idol. The next day they found their idol flat on its face. So they set their god back up, only to find him in the same position the next morning. But this time, the head and hands were cut off.

In 1995, scholars gathered in Turin and insisted that the Scriptures were filled with humor and clever wordplay. They called the gathering, "Laughter and Comedy in Ancient Christianity." Studies began to focus on Jesus' sense of humor.

Let's take a random look at the Bible to see if there is any evidence of levity in its pages.

Remember Job's three so-called friends, Bildad, Eliphaz and Zophar?

The Sense of Humor

Crepehangers they were, actually adding to their friend's torment with accusations and predictions which gave Job nightmares. In the eighth chapter of the book, Bildad takes his turn. Sarcasm must have been heard in his voice as he lashed out with, *Your words are a blustering wind.*

Can't you imagine Zophar and Eliphaz having a good laugh out of that tirade? In fact, the entire chapter sounds like an effort at being cruel and comical at the same time. On and on Bildad goes, snarling, scoffing, playing holier-than-thou.

But now, have a look at verse twenty-one. Bildad sounds like he has become positive, as though he wants to be a genuine friend. *He will yet fill your mouth with laughter and your lips with shouts of joy.* What is Bildad saying? We can only wonder but he certainly seems to be speaking of humor.

After telling the aged Abraham and Sarah they will give birth to a son, God adds a little twist to the story. That little surprise package, about which Abraham and Sarah snickered in disbelief, will be named, "Isaac," which is in Hebrew, "laughter."

"There is a real theological aspect here," says Mark Biddle, a professor at Baptist Theological Seminary, in Richmond, Va. "Since we are created in the image of God and we have an innate sense of humor, could that mean God has a sense of humor too?"

Let us look even further into the Creator's method. From what we know today, the human brain was designed with two divisions. These divisions are known simply as the right hemisphere and the left hemisphere. The right hemisphere controls our aesthetic feelings toward such things as music, beauty, flowers, fragrance and taste. The left hemisphere is the "nuts and bolts" side of the brain. Mathematics, routine handwork, all kinds of manual skills are controlled by the left hemisphere.

Take a close note of a fascinating fact. Artists of the past, the greatest names of all time, together with contemporary artists, show a high majority painting with their left hands. Why? Because the right hemisphere of the brain imagines the beauty to be created and sends instructions to the opposite side of the brain informing the left hand how to move the paintbrush.

Humor perception involves the whole brain and serves to integrate and balance activity in both hemispheres. A professor at the college of William and Mary in Williamsburg has shown there is a unique pattern of brain wave activity during the perception of humor. EEG's were recorded on subjects while they were presented with humorous material. During the setup to the joke, the cortex's left hemisphere began its analytical function of processing words. Shortly afterward, most of the brain activity moved to the frontal lobe which is the center of emotionality. Moments later the right hemisphere's synthesis capabilities joined with the left's processing to find the pattern—to 'get the joke.' A few milliseconds later, before the subject had enough time to laugh, an increased brain wave activity spread to the sensory processing areas of the brain, the occipital lobe. The increased fluctuations in delta waves reached a crescendo of activity and crested as the brain 'got' the joke and the external expression of laughter began. His findings show that humor pulls the various parts of the brain together rather than activating a component in only one area.

Charles R Swindoll published a book titled, *Laugh Again,* with a subtitle, *Experience Outrageous Joy.* Chapter titles include: "Your Smile Increases Your Face Value," "Laughing Through Life's Dilemmas," "Freeing Yourself Up To Laugh Again," and "While Laughing, Keep Your Balance!" In his chapter titled, "Defusing Disharmony," and dealing with church members who cause problems, Swindoll writes. "These dragons are all too common. As one veteran pastor says, 'Anyone

The Sense of Humor

who's been in ministry more than an hour and a half knows the wrath of a dragon.'"

Nick Foster, humorist and pastor says, "Humor is disarming." He explains "It makes us deal with issues we wouldn't face otherwise. Humor is more than a joke at the end of a sermon. It does not even necessarily produce laughter and it might even produce tears. A lot of the Bible is narrative, and lots of the narrative is funny. It makes the characters human. And if Peter and Paul are not human, they don't have anything to teach us."

Once I heard my dad relate this story. "At a country church in Michigan, my wife and I discovered a humor-based Sunday school class. The teacher operates a large dairy farm in the community. Class members, young adults, tend to be more interested in grain futures and egg prices than they are in Old Testament genealogies and varieties of doctrine. Speaking of doctrine, he has been known to introduce a subject topic of Christ's return by telling of the man who was such a dogmatic premillennialist, he wouldn't eat Post-Toasties.

"He bases Sunday morning levity mostly on reports of the previous week's experience of personal happenings in the lives of class members. After a Scripture text and prayer, he will ask, 'Well, what's happened to you this past week?'"

One week, the following dialogue occurred: "I had the awfulest thing happen to me!" began one young farmer's wife. "I mean to tell you," her husband breaks in. "She just about ..." "Let me tell it, will ya?" his wife scolds. "Okay, tell it," her husband snaps back playfully. "I was riding our power mower in the back yard when a mosquito bit me right between the shoulders." She took a deep breath and blurted, "I didn't watch where I was going and drove right into our swimming pool!"

A cloud burst of laughter echoes through the church building. The leader waits a moment, then calls for attention. There are numerous quips during the class. The lesson is a continuation of Israel's wilderness wandering. Someone mentions the problem of obtaining water. A burly farmer, who would normally be asleep by this time, pops up with, "What? No swimming pools?"

The class leader, a warmly gregarious person, has a lot of confidence in the Bible, with a strong personal commitment to Jesus Christ. He is no goof-off. Mirth describes the mood of the class but though they may not make any claim to being scholars, class members share a strong interest in the Bible and its teachings.

"It's a great fellowship," he said. "I thank God for it. It gives us a sense of sharing which naturally translates into pleasant rapport with each other. I can't explain how it works, but this rapport gives the feeling of spiritual comradeship somehow."

Frequently, someone has a new joke to share. The leader likes this. "It's a lot better than having them sit staring off into space. The point is," he observes, "humor establishes a communication mode which really works. I find this kind of teaching method especially effective with the marginal student. That is, the person who is along because his wife attends and otherwise would be turned off by conventional methods of teaching."

This class provides an excellent example of how to use humor effectively. Others in the church, hearing frequent laughter have asked, "Why can't we have that much fun in our class?"

As we broadened our research, we were continually surprised and pleased to find the role of humor expanding among church-related communications. We found a clergyman in one of the southern states who had a small but thriving church. He was painfully aware much of the growth came from transfer letters with anyone joining the church on a statement of faith a rarity. Beside a fine sense of humor, he ran a good program. But he wasn't reaching people with the Gospel.

The Sense of Humor

One day he got an idea!

He found a neutral spot downtown where he could experiment with some meetings and announced *Comedy Thursday*. The idea spread to other communities. Before long, people began coming in throngs. The pastor gave them a thirty-minute program: twenty-five minutes of humor, two to five minutes of "preaching."

Scores of people became Christians and dozens joined the church. Critics began coming out of the woodwork. "Christian comedy," snarled one of them, "what's that supposed to be, an oxymoron?" Someone else wanted to know, "Why aren't you trying to reach the lost the way the Bible tells us to?" Some critics began calling them, "Fun-damn-mentalists."

But, fortunately, more people praised the idea than slandered it. "To me," said one such person, "this is really what it means to be in the world but not of the world!" According to one youth pastor, "The way to a youth's heart is through his funny bone, and our youth ministry uses humor, games, and wild events to reach those hearts for Jesus Christ."

Incidentally, Oswald Chambers, the famous author of *My Utmost for His Highest*, wrote, "Obey God with glad, reckless joy!"

You have likely noticed the trend toward casual funerals, especially in the case of deceased believers. First, there is a graveside internment, attended by family and closest of friends. As much as a week later, a memorial service convenes. Often humor is evident.

Another story my dad enjoyed telling is this one. "I cherish memories of Jim Irvin, one of the astronauts who walked on the moon's surface. Jim told my wife and me how, on August 8, 1971, he observed earth-rise on the lunar horizon. Closing his left eye, Jim brought his thumb toward his right eye until it completely blotted out planet earth!

When I consider the heavens, the work of thy fingers, the moon and the stars, which thou hast ordained, what is man that thou art mindful of him.

"Jim remembers reciting the words in Sunday school as a boy. He whispered them now on the moon. Subsequent to his resignation from the Air Force, Jim took an active interest in searching for Noah's Ark.

"So, during the funeral service, a NASA friend looked at the casket and said, 'We know what's happening, Jim. When you first got to heaven—after you met the Lord—you went looking for Noah. When you found him, you said, 'Okay, Noah! Where did you park that ark?'"

The first time I attended a funeral where humor predominated was for the father of a close friend of mine, a God-fearing man who had devoted his life to personal witness. One after another, friends told of comical experiences this man had had in the way he gave his witness to many people. I laughed so frequently and so fully at times, I felt just a bit bewildered as I stood outside the church waiting for the family to come with the remains. As they went by, I heard someone say, "Now that's what I call a Christian celebration!"

I have attended many such farewells since that initial experience.

Wedding receptions, birthdays, anniversaries, all offer opportunity for witness with humor. Remember, you can often stimulate high amusement by cracking a joke. A simple observation of the people involved will often provide all the humorous info you need.

Many have watched the life and ministry of Billy Graham with considerable interest. I especially noticed the intense seriousness of his crusades. Wise and consistently tactful, Billy realizes the importance of humor in programming, however.

For example, at one crusade I remember his calling George Beverly Shea to the podium to sing but, instead of stepping away, Billy remained to inform Mr. Shea he would sing with him.

Immediately audience interest was obvious.

But then, Billy also requested song leader Cliff Barrows to join them. The trio sang together *This Little Light of Mine* and when they came to the line, "Hide it under a bushel?" doing a solo, Billy bellowed, "No!"

The audience loved it.

Here's another story my father told me. "My work has taken me to over one hundred and thirty countries across the world. Usually, I was a guest of an international family, or in a missionary home.

"I got to be known as a joke teller, which disturbed me somewhat. I especially remember one morning in Taiwan. The mission, for whom I was doing a film, had its headquarters on the mission field. Its general director served on the front lines while an associate remained back in the US.

"One evening, after we had a social time together with several missionaries, the director turned to me and said, 'I understand you are an early riser, Ken.' With that he invited me to come to his office at five the next morning for a time of special fellowship.

"I thought I caught a hint of reproof in his voice.

"When I prayed before retiring, I told the Lord this might be a little tough to take.

"All I ask is that you help me to be a genuine Christian in my attitude and my willingness to learn.

"Five o'clock came.

"I arrived at the headquarters' office and was welcomed in. The general director had been spending several mornings with the fifteenth chapter of John and shared some highlights with me. It was also a chapter I had logged a good bit of time in myself, so he asked me to share as well.

"It seemed so definite he was setting me up for the 'kill.'

"Finally, moments until time for breakfast, he looked at me with an expression on his face which I couldn't immediately interpret. 'I want to especially thank you, Ken,' he began, 'because of the influence you are having with our staff. Many of them are young, new in the disciplines of missionary life, and it's my job to help them keep one foot in the contemporary world, the other foot in the realm of dedication and commitment.'

"He hesitated a moment, tears moistening his eyes, then he continued saying, 'It's tremendous, watching you guys put things together in the motion picture, the way you blend a light touch with the reality of missionary life and ministry. Most of all, I want to thank you for your humor. You're like a shot in the arm when you come. You have had a close enough look to realize this is pretty serious business.'

"I was smitten with gratitude!"

Here's another experience my father related concerning humor. "I especially remember later—when I was back home in the US—receiving a letter marked Urgent!

"It came from a missionary in Pakistan who had helped us on another film production. He told me he had been asked to bring the commencement address at a missionary high school. 'I've got to have some real good and fresh jokes,' he pleaded.

"I sent him several.

"This gave me a feeling of fulfillment. Rather than being asked my opinion on a deep theological issue, I was providing some beautiful people a supply of what proved to be hilarious amusement.

"I considered the opportunity a sacred mission!"

As you continue your own search into increasing your use of humor in ministry, you may be interested in starting what we like to call a Joy Club in your church, Sunday school class, retirement home or other setting where you regularly meet with other Christian people.

A quick Internet search under the subject Laughter Clubs will yield a number of choices. Some are of the opinion that you, or a member of your intended group, should become a certified laughter specialist. This is probably a good idea since there are a few health concerns relative to the use of laughter with certain age groups or physical conditions.

But be aware of this: most of what you will encounter includes a strong New Age component. Our suggestion is that you find out all you can about beginning a club. Go to the meetings. Get certified if you feel this is necessary. Then set out to craft your own criteria for what is important to your particular group in your setting.

A couple places to look for information include, but are not limited to, The World Laughter Tour, Laughter Clubs International, Laughter Clubs USA, and The Humor Project. If you live in a large city, there will already be laughter clubs you can visit for more information. Some meet in churches. Again, if you do a diligent Internet search, the information is out there.

Laughter is the sun that drives winter from the human face.

—Victor Hugo

Nine—

Humor International

In polite society one laughs at all the jokes, including the ones one has heard before.

—Frank Dane

It has been said that humor is the first of the gifts to perish when translated into a foreign tongue.

This brings to mind a joke where a man from Latvia has been in the United States for only a few months. During that time, he has begun taking a class in basic English. On this evening the instructor is giving the students an opportunity to try out what they have learned.

She approaches the student, points to her elbow, and asks him, "What is this?"

With great difficulty, and much thought, the young man says, "That's my elbow."

"Correct, very good." Next she points to her ear, "What is this?" she asks.

"Um," he begins thinking, "Um, oh, I know, that's my ear."

"Right again," she tells him. Then she points to her nose. "And this?"

Now he really has to think hard. Sweat begins to form on his upper lip. Finally he calls out, "My-my nose?"

"Excellent, now tell me, how are you able to remember your English so well?"

The man points to his temple and, with a broad smile, tells her, "It's easy, I keep it all up here in my kidneys."

There have been some real-life miscues involving international humor. In these cases, the humor was inadvertent. Years ago, General Motors made a car called the Nova. When the new model was introduced to Central and South America, GM proudly advertised the name, "Nova," far and wide. The only problem was that in Spanish, the phrase, "No va" means, "It doesn't go."

Gerber Foods is famous for that adorable little picture of a baby on the label of all their products. Unfortunately, in Africa, companies traditionally put a picture on the outside of their containers to tell consumers what's inside, because so much of the rural population is unable to read. Imagine the horror of thinking the jars contained, well, you get the picture.

Colgate in Spanish is the word that means, "Hang yourself."

An American air carrier launched an ad campaign in Mexico using the catchy slogan, "Fly In Leather," but translated, they were encouraging their passengers to "Fly Naked," (vuela en cuero).

Pepsi Cola marched proudly into the vast Chinese market by encouraging the Chinese to, "Come Alive With The Pepsi Generation," but what they were actually telling the people was, "Pepsi Brings Your Dead Ancestors Back From The Grave."

There are many more examples, but most of them are too graphic or crude to be listed here.

The Sense of Humor

We have discussed how jokes are regional and cultural, depending on where you live within the United States. Just imagine how the understanding of jokes changes when you travel to an entirely different country where, along with everything else, the language is completely different.

American businessmen have had to grapple with this issue while transacting international business. Some very clever television commercials have been produced to illustrate these differences, but things, as they say, often do get lost in the translation.

One high-powered American executive was making a presentation to his Japanese colleagues. He decided to tell a typical American joke after which his audience erupted into laughter. He thought he'd really hit a home run until he learned later that the translator had told the attendees, "This kind American has just told a joke that is very culturally bound. Would you all therefore please laugh now?"

In a similar incident, an American speaker told a joke lasting nearly two minutes. The translator repeated the joke in the local language, using just a few words. No matter. Everyone laughed. After the meeting he asked his host, "How were you able to translate my joke and make it so short?"

Much like the previous example, the translator replied, "I simply told them our guest has just told a joke. Everyone please laugh."

Lest we only make fun of some of our attempts at humor in other parts of the world, see what you think of these examples of jokes that have come to us from different countries. Some you will see translate into English quite well, and they're funny, but others don't make much sense at all. Keep in mind that these are translations of actual jokes from the countries listed. You'll be able to identify some of the vintage problems from the old Russia. The Czech jokes stemmed from a hatred and mistrust of both the government and the police.

RUSSIA

A guy cries over a grave:

"Why did you pass away so early?"

"Whom are you mourning over?"

"This is the first husband of my wife."

ASIA

A wife wakes her husband up in the middle of the night after hearing a noise.

"Go to sleep," he says. "Before a burglar could steal something from this house, he would have to bring something in."

ENGLAND

A young Winston Churchill was making a speech when he was hit by a cabbage. He responded, "I asked for the gentleman's ears, not his head."

RUSSIA

"Ivan, do you know Einstein is coming to Odessa?"

"Who is he? Is he a famous pharmacist?"

"No, he is a famous physicist. He is the author of the *Theory of the Relativity.*"

"What's that?"

"Well, how can I explain this? You see, you have two hairs on your head. Is that a lot or a little?"

"A little."

"And now let's imagine you found the same number of hairs in your soup."

"Can it be true? He is coming to Odessa with this stupid joke?"

RUSSIA

"What feet you have, Vasily Ivanovich. They're even dirtier than mine."

"That's because I'm much older then you, Petka."

RUSSIA

A sergeant instructs a sentry:

The Sense of Humor

"When the general comes, report to me immediately."

The general doesn't show.

The sergeant gets nervous and every hour reminds the sentry to report about the general's arrival.

Finally, the general comes.

"Where have you been?" asks the sentry. "The sergeant has already asked about you four times."

INDIA

"You admit that you stole jewels and furs in addition to the money?"

"Yes," said the thief. "I was taught that money alone does not bring happiness."

RUSSIA

Brezhnev complains to Gromyko that he can't get used to summer and wintertime time changes.

"It's simple," replies Gromyko. "Just move the hands on your clock one-hour ahead in spring and then move them one-hour back in autumn."

"Well," says Breznev, "that sounds really simple. Nevertheless, when I sent a telegram of my condolences to Egypt regarding Anwar Sadat's assassination last summer, it arrived one hour before his death."

RUSSIA

A teacher asks:

"Vovochka, who is your father?"

"Comrade Stalin."

"Well, who is your mother?"

"Our Soviet motherland."

"And what do you want to be?"

"An orphan."

RUSSIA

"What was the nationality of Adam and Eve?"

"Russian, of course. Why else would they think they're in Paradise

115

when they were homeless, naked, and just had one apple for both of them?"

CZECH

"What is the relation between salary and work in socialism?"

"Salary is punishment for discharged duty, or workers pretend to work and the state pretends to pay them."

CZECH

"Are there any countries where it is not possible to build socialism?"

"Yes, countries like Luxembourg are far too small for such a big mess."

CZECH

A Czech agricultural scientist performs an experiment to train cows not to eat:

The experiment continued successfully for several weeks, but just before reaching complete success, all cows accidentally died.

CZECH

The chief of police arranges a police action and tells his men: "The operation will begin precisely at 11.48. For those of you with digital watches, that's 'truncheon—truncheon—upside down chair—snowman.'"

RUSSIA

Two men in the Ukraine meet on a train. "Where are you going," asks the first.

"I'm going to Moscow to buy meat," says the second.

"Me, too," says the first. The train winds its way through the USSR and finally gets to Kiev, where the second man starts to get off.

"I thought you were going to Moscow to buy meat," says the first.

"I am. The line starts here."

CHINA

A man had two pairs of boots; one with thick soles and the other with thin soles. One morning, he made the mistake of putting one of each of the boots on. While walking, he felt very uncomfortable. "How strange! How it is that my legs are not the same length today?" he said in surprise.

A passerby told him, "Your boots are not a pair."

Hearing this, he hurried home to change boots. But when he got home and saw the other boots, he thought for a moment and said, "There is no need to change. These other two are not a pair either. One has a thick sole and the other has a thin sole."

CHINA

A grocer once had a daughter born to him. One day, a friend of his made a match for his baby girl and told him the future husband was only one year older than she was.

The grocer discussed this marriage in private with his wife. "Our daughter is just one, the boy's age is the double of hers; when she is twenty and gets married, her husband will be forty," he said. "How do we have the heart to marry off our daughter to such an old man?"

His wife smiled and said, "You are really dumb. Our daughter is now one year old; in one year won't she be the same age as the boy?"

CHINA

Two men, A and B, once came to blows. A bit off B's nose, so B, in much pain, took A to the county magistrate to the have the case judged.

"How dare you bite off B's nose!" the magistrate said.

"B bit off his own nose. It has nothing to do with me," A answered.

"Nonsense! Everyone knows the nose is higher than the mouth. How can the mouth reach the nose?" the magistrate said severely.

"By standing on a bench," A said cunningly.

"Oh, so that is how it is!" said the magistrate nodding his head slightly.

CHINA

A bookworm was once walking slowly in the heavy rain. A passerby asked, "Why are you walking so slowly in this heavy rain?"

"What's the use of hurrying?" the bookworm said leisurely. "Isn't it raining up ahead, too?"

CHINA

In a village lived a family whose members were all ignorant. One day, while eating grain from a pot, their cow got its head stuck in the pot and couldn't get it out. Not knowing what to do, they asked their uncle for help.

The uncle came and had a look. "That's an easy job," he said in a decisive manner. "Just cut off the cow's head!"

One of his nephews cut off the cow's head according to his uncle's idea, but the head was still stuck in the pot. They felt quite helpless and asked the uncle for help again.

"That's easy, just break up the pot!" the uncle said complacently.

The pot was broken up and the cow's head came out. Everyone praised the uncle for his incomparable cleverness. On the contrary, at this very moment the uncle burst out crying. They felt puzzled and asked him why he was so sad.

The uncle wiped his eyes. "I'm now too old and won't live long. I will die someday after all. When I'm gone, who will come to help you out if you have any trouble then!"

CHINA

The immortal Cripple Li once crossed a small bridge which was made by two planks, one thick and the other thin. So one side of the bridge was higher than the other side. In this way, Lame Li could walk steadily when crossing the bridge.

"This bridge is the best in the world," he said favorably. But while returning, he crossed the bridge again from the opposite direction. This time Lame Li's lame leg was on the lower side and he became more lame than usual. "This is the worst bridge in the world," he said in a fury.

The Sense of Humor

AUSTRALIA

"What do you call a boomerang that doesn't come back?"

"A stick."

EGYPT

In Egypt, light comments and smart responses play an important part in the Egyptian sense of humor. Egyptian people laugh at several things, often just the contradictions in life. As in America, humor can vary depending on what region of that country a person is from. Subjects range from intellectual to the ridiculous. One Egyptian joke, reported to be a true story, is translated like this:

The editor of a local newspaper needed to finish an obituary. He was tired, and in a hurry to be on his way home. So he wrote a note at the bottom of it that said, "Only if there is a space for it." The next morning the obituary ran in the paper. It read, "Mr. *XYZ* died recently. May God let him into paradise ... only if there is a space for him."

The more widely circulated Egyptian jokes are usually more common, and often deal with the village idiot. But, there are gems like this one.

One boy says to another, "Everybody stands up for my father at work."

"What does your father do?"

"He's a judge."

"So what? People bow their heads to my dad at work, including *your* dad."

"Wow, what does he do?"

"He's a barber."

INDONESIA

A report out of Indonesia demonstrates just how difficult translation can be. Here an American film was being translated.

The English line went like this, "I smell something fishy around

119

here." In Indonesia, something fishy actually means it smells like fish, while in the US something fishy can smell like fish or the phrase can mean something's suspicious. So the translators said that the main character in the film smelled like fish.

SWEDEN

In Sweden, where both American films as well as American television situation comedies are common, viewers seem to have a better handle on American humor.

"I don't think Sweden is much different from the US when it comes to humor and comedy," one Swede noted. "The comedies we see are mostly American shows, and the ones made in Sweden are mostly copies of American shows."

Another added, "The funny movies that are made in Sweden are more subtle and realistic. For a few years now, most of these movies have been about guys in their thirties trying to adjust to some kind of adult life."

Still another observed, "The most popular shows here are British series like *Monty Python's Flying Circus, Fawlty Towers*, programs like that."

America is famous for its standup comics. But in Japan, there is a major style of humor called Rakugo: Japanese Sit-Down Comedy. Rakugo is best described as comic story telling. The performer sits on a mattress. His only props include a fan and towel. The fan can be chopsticks, scissors, a pen, or some other similar object. The towel becomes a book, bills, or simply a towel. This performer is dressed in a Kimono and does the entire act by himself. Only conversations appear in the story, and the performer has to do all the characters.

Western humor entered Japan in the latter part of the 19th century, when Japan opened the door to the outside world. A joke book was published in Japan at that time titled "Kaiko-Showa," meaning, "is to allow one's mouth to open with laughter." The idea was to expose the Japanese people to American jokes and humor. Often the Japanese people would read the jokes and laugh, but they never really got the point of the humor. English jokes were also blended in. The people didn't get into the habit of verbally exchanging the jokes with one another, preferring only to read them.

Throughout history and within many different cultures, the sense of humor has been valued. Court jesters were employed at most royal gatherings. Native Americans used clowns in some of their ceremonies, evoking laughter and a lighthearted spirit among the people.

One thing is sure, no matter what country you visit, laughter is the same everywhere. If something is funny in China, they don't pull on their ears. People in Africa don't touch their knees or elbows in their reaction to humor. Everywhere in the world, when something is funny, people laugh. It doesn't matter how you get there, so long as you enjoy the journey. A smile is the same the world over, and laughter, like music, is a universal language.

The happiness or unhappiness of men depends as much on their humors as on fortune.

—Francois de la Rochefoucauld

Ten—

Humor That Is No Laughing Matter

Any discussion of the problems of being funny in America will not make sense unless we substitute the word wit for humor. Humor inspires sympathetic good-natured laughter and is favored by the healing-power gang. Wit goes for the jugular, not the jocular, and it's the opposite of football; instead of building character, it tears it down.

—Florence King

As with beauty, so we find humor is in the eye of the beholder. What is funny to you may not necessarily be funny to someone else. And at times, humor can not only be harmful, but can actually hurt others. What is the comedian really saying when he quips, "Take my wife, please?"

Or in a nursing home joke, where two men were playing checkers and one of the women residents decided to streak through the room to see if they would notice her.

One man looked at the other and asked, "Who was that?"

To which the other said, "I don't know, but that dress she was wearing sure could use some ironing."

The problem here is that the joke is funny at some level, but takes a shot at an entire segment of our population. It's actually the young not wanting to admit that one day they too will be old and may need care. Worst of all, it is insensitive, obvious, and may hurt the feelings of another person.

It's important to remember that humor can have a dark side. I had to learn this the hard way because, when I was younger, I enjoyed a sarcastic brand of humor. To me, the most fun came when I was able to make someone else the brunt of a cutting remark, and I was pretty quick to offer them. Looking back, I can see how this made me feel better about myself whenever I could make another person feel smaller. I honestly don't think this was a calculated and conscious effort on my part. The humor simply worked, so I continued to use this style. Others standing by found the quips funny. But, as a result, things that I thought were funny actually hurt other people.

I clearly remember one day when a friend confronted me and said, "You have no idea how much what you said hurt me."

I totally changed my personal use of humor from that moment to today. If another person is hurt, humor isn't funny. Humor can also be insensitive, malicious, exclusive, and biting. Humor can be used to ridicule, slander, or put people down. This includes racial and sexual subjects directed at others or their situations in life. Humor, used inappropriately, can be harmful. In all cases, we should ensure we don't use any humor that does harm.

So, as you can see, humor truly is in the eye of the beholder. But we firmly believe that used properly, humor helps us feel better about our lives and circumstances, helps people to learn better, helps us in our places of work and in our interpersonal relationships.

The Sense of Humor

Recognizing inappropriate or destructive humor is the easy part. The joke just doesn't feel quite right. Humor that hurts, is mean, or ostracizes others is cruel humor. Humor that is racist, sexist, or crude can now lead to sanctions, termination of employment, and even lawsuits. Humor can be insulting, especially when used with a person you don't know very well. In those situations, you're better off not using any at all.

Adults should be cautious in the kinds of humor they use around younger people. Young people are more impressionable. They may think mean spirited humor is the norm, and begin using it as well. Humor should never be used to cause suffering for another person.

Some have suggested that slapstick humor is destructive and therefore negative. They believe we are laughing at a person like Charlie Chaplin or Buster Keaton because we know something bad is about to happen to them. What makes the situation funny is also what makes it nasty, in their opinion. They cite the humiliation and the pretended harm.

Psychologists tell us of the lifelong damage that comes from negative self-talk in adults. All through their lives, these people have stored up negative images of themselves and their abilities. Looking back on your own childhood, you will probably remember such seemingly harmless things your parents said to you including, "If your head wasn't connected, you'd probably forget that too." "Close the door. Were you born in a barn?" "Act your age, not your IQ."

At the time, these were simply silly sayings, but they can begin, over time, a pattern of negative thoughts and feelings in children that last.

A common racial joke will employ a typical stereotype. Added to this is something degrading, disgusting, or humiliating. People who use this type of humor speak loudly about some of the beliefs and prejudices they may hold. Some may even be suppressed, but they're still in there, hidden so that the joke teller may be unaware on the surface.

125

Off-color, or sexual joke telling, which will be visited later, takes something beautiful that God made for man's enjoyment, and attempts to turn it into something filthy or ugly. Sure, some of these jokes are extremely funny. But have you ever asked yourself why? Jokes of this type may tell us a lot about the joke teller as well. Beyond that, the jokes can hurt other people.

Sarcasm usually has the effect of hurting the feelings of the other person. While sarcasm is most often used between friends, and is seen as friendly backstabbing, it finds its way into casual friendships, and even includes people with whom we are only slightly acquainted.

A typical sarcastic cut might go like this. Two men meet, and one says to the other, "Where did you find that jacket, in the dumpster?"

The friend laughs off the remark, but may be proud of his new jacket and may even have taken great pains to pick it out at the store. Now, does this mean the friend likes his choice or is he saying something else?

Or a woman may know that her friend was going to the hair dresser just prior to their lunch date.

When they meet, she might say, "I thought you were going to have your hair done this morning."

In each case, what is said might seem funny, but why use it in the first place? Why does the sarcastic person choose those words instead of complimenting their friends on the jacket or the hair color?

Parents are especially guilty of using sarcasm with their children. If this is allowed, trouble in their teen years could make the terrible two's seem like classical music.

Children may hear comments such as, "Your room looks like the city dump." Or, "You're about as graceful as a three-legged horse."

Parents use this form of humor to express their own disappointment in the behavior of their children. But children process and store our words. For this reason, parents would do much better not to use sarcasm.

The Sense of Humor

Choosing not to use any humor in some situations may prove to be one of the best uses of humor.

Sarcasm leads to feelings of poor self-worth, self-image, self-esteem, increasing feelings of anger and resentment. No one, no matter what their age, enjoys the feeling of being put down or embarrassed. This is especially true when it happens in a group. My experience when my friend corrected me for my use of sarcasm happened in high school. High school's a real pressure cooker for students who are trying their best to fit in, be included and feel popular. Like so many pressures that used to only hit young people in their high school years, many of these problems have now found their way into the realms of junior high, middle, and elementary school.

When we attack another person or group with our humor and we hear the laughter, we might interpret that response as good. The problem with all negative humor—to be funny, someone else has to be hurt. They may laugh as a defensive response covering up what is really going on inside.

Negative humor might also be used as a device to gain power or supremacy. If we are able to put another person down, that elevates us; it gives us power over the person or situation.

The cutting remark can be a signal of anger on the part of the teller. When called on it, the teller might respond, "What's the matter, can't you take a joke?"

This is a direct attack on the listener who may have been offended or hurt by the joke.

There was a famous comedian who could often be found on television or on the comedy circuit. His brand of humor cut down, ridiculed, and berated everyone and everything in his path. One wonders why and even if this was truly funny. Fortunately, the use of biting humor, and comedians who make jokes about being drunk, have somewhat faded from the humor landscape. But that's not to say the genre has disappeared entirely.

Humor should bring people together, while negative humor has the opposite effect. Negative humor divides by ethnic, social, religious, economic, and a multitude of other divisive labels.

Cutting remarks should never be made in a marriage relationship. Here, a person may not like the way his or her spouse does certain things. Instead of tackling the issue head on, a husband might say, "Is that the best you can cook, clean, look, dress?" or other personal observations.

Thinking that a touch of "humor" might correct the behavior or performance, the cut is made. This allows for the potential of hurt and resentment that can only grow with time.

Much has been written about marriages that seem to start out well, but quickly degenerate into abusive relationships. Young couples who are dating, with an eye toward possible marriage in the future, would do well to be especially observant of negative humor in their relationship. The observation should go both ways. If you are the one who initiates negative humor, ask yourself what is at the root. If you are the recipient of cuts and put downs, project into the future and see if this is the kind of person you want to spend your life with.

Go out of your way to find something good to say, be complimentary, and make sure the funny things you say aren't meant to hurt or to cover up what you are really thinking about the other person's actions or personality. You should talk out your differences about the use of humor in your marriage.

If humor has a dark as well as a lighter side, then we would do well to call dark humor what it is. Darkness is reserved for the Evil One. Logic says that dark humor, hurtful humor, the tearing down of another person, must come from his influence. How better to destroy relationships than with the subtleties of negative humor? Here, as in so many other areas of our lives, we are able to see how the Devil takes something created for our good, changes it only slightly sometimes, and then uses it to hurt us or others. We are instructed to resist the Devil. This image applies no less in our use of humor as in any other areas of our lives.

It has been said that only about one third of the population has a sense of humor, which they have unleashed on the other two thirds who didn't think it was funny.

If someone uses negative humor against you, there are several steps you can take. The most obvious would be to tell them you don't appreciate their form of humor, and ask them to stop.

Another effective response would be not to react at all, thus discouraging similar events in the future. Taking this a step further, you could frown or shake your head. Some people will go so far as to actually tell the other person the joke was offensive and why. Since many people who use negative humor might actually be unaware of its effect, we are helping them if their error is brought to light.

Humor with a double meaning should also be avoided. In communication, we attempt to make our messages clear and concise. When a joke with a double meaning is told, we open the door to misinterpretation. Did we tell the joke with the good meaning in mind, or the bad? Do we even know the joke has a double meaning? Or, was the joke told for the express purpose of the second meaning?

We've all heard jokes like, "I went fishing, just for the halibut." Sure, it's cute, but brings to mind a second meaning with a darker connotation.

An expert made a breakdown of the difference between the two forms of humor. Constructive humor creates positive environments where people support each other, promote self-esteem, and create mutually beneficial connections.

Destructive humor does the reverse. It goes for the throat, reminding us how important it is for humor to be a shared, nurturing, and constructive exchange between both parties.

The best practice is to realize if humor is God given, then it probably was intended for our good and that of others around us. If humor is negative, or hurts, then the source is likely coming from someplace else. With this as our guide, we cannot only begin to reform the ways we use and perceive humor, we will also be able to identify negative humor in others. You may find yourself in a position to actually take some of the new information you are learning, and alter negative humor use in someone else. Look for opportunities to do that in creative ways, and see what happens. A little song says, "Brighten the corner, where you are." Proper use of humor will do exactly that.

Imagination was given man to compensate for what he is not, and a sense of humor to console him for what he is.

—Francis Bacon

Eleven—

How to Make 'em Laugh

Good humor isn't a trait of character, it is an art which requires practice.

—David Seabury

Earlier I mentioned I'm not much of a joke teller. My style of humor tends to be more in the moment, within normal conversation. But I do enjoy hearing jokes when they're told well. I don't aspire to be good at telling jokes, plus I can't remember them well and easily forget the punch line. This can be deadly in joke telling. My dad, on the other hand, was a great story and joke teller. My barber is a very good joke teller too.

What follows falls more into the category of, "Do as I say, not as I do." Still, I do enjoy hearing a good joke.

In so many areas of our lives, we hear said, "Timing is everything." Never is this a more accurate statement than where humor is concerned. You've likely heard of the importance of comedic timing or the proper way to deliver a punch line.

Have you ever been flipping channels and stopped when you found a standup comic? If most of us are honest, we listen to the comedian and say to ourselves, "How can one person be so funny and I'm not?" We further ask ourselves, "I wonder if I could make people laugh like that?"

The truth is, probably not. That is, not without a lot of practice. Because by the time we see the typical comedian on a stage for the first time, that person has worked for years to develop their craft with just the right timing, material, and delivery. And let's face it, some people are simply funnier than others, naturally. Of the few performers you see, there are literally thousands of others who never succeed professionally. A good example is the TV show *Last Comic Standing*. Here, the good and the bad are quickly separated.

Some people may be uniquely created with an innate ability to make us laugh. There are a few comedians who could simply order from a menu and make us laugh. The rest of us have to work at the skill. And that is the focus of this chapter.

In real estate, the three most important words are location, location, location. The three most important elements in comedy are timing, timing, and timing. Beyond that, as you develop your own style, will come facial expression, tone of voice, gestures, and other nuances that will make your delivery unique. Thinking of the standup comics you know or enjoy, you'll notice how no two have the exact same style. They also use different material. So, you should search for your own unique humor ability too.

One of the most successful comics of our time is Jerry Seinfeld. You know an entertainer has reached the top when people know who they are simply by one name like … Seinfeld. Watching him perform, you might think his humor comes easily, but that isn't the case. There are many other comedians you can find on places like YouTube. There you can spend time studying what each comic does that makes you laugh.

In a documentary, *Comedian*, cameras present a behind the scenes look at the agony that goes into each performance. Comics are constantly editing, rewriting, and reworking their material. Each time they offer a new joke, there is risk involved. This is a good picture to have in your own mind when you begin telling jokes. In your situation you might ask yourself, "What do I have to lose?"

Most professional comics would admit to insecurities and self-doubt. If the skill is so difficult for the professionals, what makes you think you should be able to discover an easier path? Comedy takes hard work, practice, and effort for the standup comic to come up with routines that connect with their audiences. Making it look easy is the key. The degree to which you would like to be successful in your circle of influence, using humor, will determine the amount of work you are willing to put in, but the rewards will be well worth the journey.

A joke is a short story with a funny ending, some say.

The better you know a joke, the more you will be able to work on delivery. Comedians call this "selling" the joke. So learn your material well. You might start keeping a joke file or notebook. Your computer can be useful here since you can easily move material around. Put your jokes in subject order for easy retrieval.

You want to be careful that you don't become some kind of joke spewing robot, but at the same time, memorizing the joke is important. This allows you the flexibility to work on telling it effectively. If you can picture in your mind the circumstances and characters in your joke, the story will become more real, making the telling more fluid.

When telling jokes and funny stories, you need to be yourself. The style you use, your timing, voice, and gestures need to be your own. The more comfortable you are in your delivery, the better job you'll do at being funny. Don't try to imitate anyone else. Your own style, when it fits your personality, will be evident. When you are able to keep the process fun along the way, then everyone will benefit from the laughter.

Be prepared to adapt your joke for the audience or individual you are telling it to. Then fix the image of the characters in your mind so they become like real people. This makes it almost seem as if you're telling a true story about real people.

Good fiction writers know that before they begin to write, their story must have a beginning, a middle, and an end. So with a joke. Fix in your mind the start, the track you will take through the middle of the story, and then on to the end. Nothing is worse than coming to the end of a joke and finding you forgot the punch line or muffed the delivery.

Never try telling a joke that you don't get. This fits into the practice area again. Make sure you understand the material you plan to deliver.

Selecting your jokes depending on their appropriateness for your audience is critical. You'll often hear professional comedians complain that they "died" on stage, or the audience was dead. Sometimes this simply indicates that the material didn't fit the audience.

Take your time in setting up the joke. Establishing the characters and the situation will lead to a better pay-off at the end. Once the setup is complete, the importance of timing comes into play. Don't rush through the material. Allow your audience to enjoy the story along with you as you spin the yarn. Here is where practice becomes critical as well. If you have a friend or spouse who is willing, rehearse your material in front of them. See how they react. Ask for suggestions. If this approach is uncomfortable, then practice in front of a mirror.

Remember, the very act of practicing will make or break your delivery in front of a live audience. Once you feel you have the material down, set up a video camera, your smart phone, or some other electronic device, and record yourself telling jokes. This will do one of two things. You may like everything and decide you're ready for prime time. Or, if

The Sense of Humor

you're honest, you'll see numerous areas that could use improvement. Being able to objectively stand back and watch yourself might be painful, but will help you move toward better timing and delivery.

Some joke experts suggest an exercise you might like to try. The next time you see one of those stand up shows, actually count the number of lines in each joke. You will find that less is best. The more you remove unnecessary words, the better the joke. Think about the times you've endured jokes by family or friends where the story seemed to go on endlessly. By the time the teller hit the punch line, who cared?

Since humor is the most effective tool you can use to capture an audience's attention, work to be the best you can be with the humor you plan to use. With all we have learned about the benefits of humor and laughter, you'll appreciate knowing how much enjoyment you've brought to audiences, family, friends, colleagues, and others by helping them learn to laugh.

On your journey to better joke telling, practice on your friends and family every day. And don't be discouraged if you don't hit a home run every time. Even the pros face this. Humor, good humor, is a process. Read the writings of funny people like Dave Barry or others you enjoy. Listen to performers who tell funny stories well. Study their delivery, their timing. Seek out the situation comedy television programs that are most like your own style of humor.

When you encounter something that strikes you as extremely funny, ask yourself, "What made me laugh at that? Why did I laugh?" Equally important, when humor didn't strike your funny bone, ask the same questions, "Why or why not?"

Now, go out there and make 'em laugh!

Laughter is a highly addictive positive contagious: if somebody starts, it's very difficult to stop.

—Robert Holden

135

Twelve–

Jokes and Other Humor

Humor is a whisper from the soul, imploring mind and body to relax, let go and be at peace again.

—Source Unknown

Now that you have a better understanding of humor and its benefits when used properly, we have assembled hundreds of jokes and funny stories for your enjoyment. This material has been arranged according to several of the major subject headings. Each section will relate to the corresponding chapter subjects.

At the end you will find a miscellaneous section with material that didn't especially fit into a particular subject or category.

While you read these jokes and stories, I hope you will find examples that fit perfectly into your needs for funny material. As you begin to memorize and tell some of your favorites, I believe your life, and the lives of those closest to you, will be better as a direct result.

Have fun!

HEALTH HUMOR

A distraught patient called her doctor's office asking if it was true the pills the doctor had prescribed were to be taken for the rest of her life.

The doctor assured her it was true.

After a moment of silence, the woman said, "Then I'm really worried about my condition because the label says, 'No refills!'"

A man woke up in a hospital bed after his operation and found the curtains were drawn around him. "Why are my curtains closed?" he asked. "Is there something wrong?"

The nurse told him, "No, it's just that there's a big fire across the street, and we didn't want you to wake up and think the operation wasn't successful."

A woman came to the hospital to visit a friend. She hadn't been in a hospital for several years, so she felt uneasy not knowing about all the new technology. A technician followed her onto the elevator, pushing a large machine with intimidating looking tubes, wires, and dials.

"Boy, I'd hate to be hooked up to that thing," she said.

"So would I," said the technician. "This is a carpet cleaner."

The man told his doctor he wasn't able to do all the things around the house he used to do. When the examination was over, he said, "Now, Doc, I can take it. Tell me in plain English exactly what's wrong with me."

"Well, in plain English," the doctor said, "you're just lazy."

"Okay," the man said. "Now give me the medical term so I can tell my wife."

My therapist told me the way to achieve true inner peace is to finish what I start.

So far today, I have finished two bags of chips and a chocolate cake. I feel better already.

A man was having some physical problems so his doctor told him to drink warm water one hour before breakfast. At the end of a week, he came back and the doctor asked if he was feeling any better. The man said he actually felt worse.

"Did you drink warm water an hour before breakfast each day?"

"No," the man said, "I could only do it for about fifteen minutes!"

Doctors at a hospital have gone on strike. Hospital officials say they will find out what the doctors' demands are as soon as they can get a pharmacist to come over and read their picket signs!

An artist asked the gallery owner if there had been any interest in his paintings on display at that time.

"I have good news and bad news," the owner told him. "The good news is a man asked about your work and wondered if it would appreciate in value after your death. When I told him it would, he bought all your paintings."

"That's wonderful," the artist said. "What's the bad news?"

"The guy said he was your cardiologist."

The Sense of Humor

Two little boys were examining digital bathroom scales at a department store.

"Have you ever seen one of these before?" one asked.

"Yeah, my mom and dad have one," the other said.

"What's it for?"

"I don't know for sure," the second boy answered. "I think you stand on it and it makes you mad."

A concerned husband went to the doctor to talk about his wife.

"Doctor, I think my wife is deaf because she never hears me the first time, and I always have to repeat myself."

"Well," the doctor told him, "Go home, and tonight, stand about fifteen feet away from her and say something. If she doesn't answer, move about five feet closer and say it again. Keep doing this so we can get an idea how deaf she is."

So the husband goes home and does exactly as instructed. He starts off about fifteen feet from his wife in the kitchen as she is chopping some vegetables and says, "Honey, what's for dinner?" He hears nothing. So he moves about five feet closer and asks again. Still no answer. He moves five feet closer. Nothing. Finally he gets fed up, moves right behind her, and asks again, "Honey, what's for dinner?"

She turns around and says, "That's the fourth time you asked me. It's meatloaf!"

Three old pilots are walking on the ramp.

First one says, "Windy, isn't it?"

Second one says, "No, it's Thursday."

Third one says, "So am I. Let's go get something to drink."

A patient complained to his doctor, "This hospital is no good ... you treat us like dogs."

"Oh, Mr. Jones, you know that's not true," his doctor responded with a bit of disgust in his voice, "Now, roll over!"

At a nursing home, a group of seniors were sitting around talking about all their ailments. "My arms have gotten so weak I can hardly lift this cup of coffee," said one.

"Yes, I know," said another. "My cataracts are so bad I can barely see my coffee."

"I couldn't even mark an "X" when I voted, my hands are so crippled," volunteered a third.

"What? Speak up! What? I can't hear you! I can't turn my head because of the arthritis in my neck," said a fourth.

"My blood pressure pills make me so dizzy!" exclaimed another.

"I forget where I am, and where I'm going," said another.

"I guess that's the price we pay for getting old," winced an old man as he slowly shook his head. The others nodded in agreement.

"Well, count your blessings," said one woman cheerfully, "Thank goodness we can all still drive."

An elderly woman called 911 on her cell phone to report her car had been broken into. She is hysterical as she tries to explain her situation to the dispatcher. "They've stolen the stereo, the steering wheel, the brake pedal, and even the accelerator!"

The dispatcher said, "Stay calm. An officer is on the way." A few minutes later, the officer radios in. "Disregard," he says. "She got in the back-seat by mistake."

The Sense of Humor

A man was telling his neighbor, "I just bought a new hearing aid. It cost me four thousand dollars, but it's state of the art. It's perfect."

"Really?" answered the neighbor. "What kind is it?"

"Twelve thirty."

An exhausted looking man drags himself into the doctor's office. "Doctor, you gotta help me, there are dogs all over my neighborhood. They bark day and night, and I can't get any sleep."

"I have good news for you," the doctor answered, rummaging through a drawer full of sample medications. "Here are some new sleeping pills that work like a dream. A few of these and your troubles will be over."

"Great," the man answered, "I'll try them."

A few weeks later, the man comes back, looking worse. "Doctor, your plan didn't work, I'm more tired than before!"

"I don't understand," said the doctor, shaking his head. "They're the strongest sleeping pills on the market!"

"That may be true," answered the man wearily, "but I'm still up all night chasing those dogs and when I finally catch one, it's impossible to get him to swallow one of those pills!"

A man was jogging in the park, and decided to sit down and rest for a while. He spotted the nearest bench and sat next to a man with a dog at his feet. "Does your dog bite?" he asked. =

"No," the man said. A few minutes later the jogger reached over to pet the dog and it took a big chunk out of his hand.

"I thought you said your dog doesn't bite, what's the deal?"

Without looking up the man answered, "That's not my dog."

Three sisters, ninety-two, ninety-four, and ninety-six, live in a house together. One night, the ninety-six-year-old runs a bath. She puts her foot in and pauses. She yells to the other sisters, "Was I getting in or out of the bath?"

The ninety-four-year-old yells back, "I don't know. I'll come up and see." She starts up the stairs and pauses, "Was I going up the stairs or down?"

The ninety-two-year-old is sitting at the kitchen table having tea, listening to her sisters. She shakes her head and says, "I sure hope I never get that forgetful, knock on wood." She then yells, "I'll come up and help both of you as soon as I see who's at the door."

You don't stop laughing because you grow old; you grow old because you stop laughing.

Late one night at a mental hospital, one inmate shouted,
"I am Napoleon!"
Another one said, "How do you know?"
The first inmate said, "Because God told me!"
Just then, a voice from another room shouted, "I did not!"

A lady noticed her husband standing on the bathroom scale, sucking in his stomach. Thinking he was trying to weigh less she commented, "I don't think that will help."
"Sure it does," he told her. "It's the only way I can see the numbers."

A woman went to her psychiatrist and said, "Doctor, doctor, I want to talk to you about a problem my husband has. He thinks he's a refrigerator."
"That's not so bad," said the doctor. "It's rather harmless."

The Sense of Humor

"Well, that could be," she said. "But now, every time he sleeps with his mouth open, the light keeps me awake."

A new nurse listened while the doctor barked out, "Typhoid! Tetanus! Measles!"

She asked another nurse, "Why does he do that?"

The other nurse told her, "Oh, he just likes to call the shots around here."

While making rounds, a doctor points out an X-ray to a group of medical students.

"As you can see," she said, "because his left fibula and tibia are radically arched, the patient limps. Sterling, what would you do in a case like this?"

"Well, I'd probably limp too."

A scientist has just developed a "magic" pill that dissolves excess body fat and will cure obesity. It's also reported that he is the front-runner to receive this year's Nobelly prize.

An accountant is having trouble sleeping and goes for a checkup.

"Doctor, I just can't get to sleep at night."

"Have you tried counting sheep?"

"That's the problem. I make a mistake and then spend hours trying to find it."

Mr. Jones is driving past the state mental hospital when his left rear tire goes flat. While he's changing the tire, another car goes by, runs over the hub cap where he was keeping the lug nuts, and knocks them all down a nearby drain.

He's at a loss for what to do next and is about to start walking when he hears a voice from behind the hospital fence, where a patient has been watching the whole thing.

"Hey, pal! Why don't you just take one lug nut off each of the other three wheels and use them to replace the missing ones? That'll hold your tires on until you can get to a garage."

Mr. Jones is startled by the patient's rationality, realizes the plan will work and puts the spare tire on without any problem. Before he leaves, he calls back to the patient. "Hey, you know, that was a pretty smart idea. What are you doing in a mental hospital?"

The patient smiled and said, "I'm in here because I'm crazy, not because I'm stupid."

Five doctors went duck hunting one day. Included in the group were a GP, a pediatrician, a psychiatrist, a surgeon, and a pathologist. After a while, a bird came flying right over their heads. The first to react was the GP, who raised his shotgun, but then hesitated.

"I'm not quite sure if it's a duck," he said, "I think I'll have to get a second opinion." And, of course, by that time, the bird was gone.

Another bird flew by, and this time, the pediatrician drew a bead on it. But he wasn't sure if it was a duck either and, besides, it might have babies

Next to see a bird was the psychiatrist. "Now, I know that's a duck, but does he know he's a duck?" The lucky bird disappeared while the doctor wrestled with his dilemma.

Finally, a fourth bird flew past and this time the surgeon lifted his shotgun and, boom! He lowered the smoking gun, turned to the pathologist behind him and said,

"Go see if that was a duck, will you?"

The Sense of Humor

The doctor in a small clinic asked a weather-beaten mountaineer how he was feeling.

"Well ... it's like this," drawled the man. "I'm still a-kickin', but I ain't raisin' no dust."

One day at a trial, an eminent psychologist was called to testify. A severe, no-nonsense professional, she sat down in the witness chair, unaware that its rear legs were set precariously on the back of the raised platform.

"Will you state your name?" asked the district attorney. Tilting back in her chair she opened her mouth to answer, but instead catapulted head-over-heels backward and landed in a stack of exhibits and recording equipment.

Everyone watched in stunned silence as she extricated herself, rearranged her disheveled dress and hair and was reseated on the witness stand. The glare she directed at onlookers dared anyone to so much as smirk.

"Well, doctor," continued the district attorney without changing his expression, "we *could* start with an easier question."

A customer in a bakery was carefully examining all the rich-looking pastries displayed in the glass cases.

The clerk approached him and asked, "What would you like?" and he said, "I'd *like* that chocolate-covered, cream-filled doughnut, that jelly-filled doughnut, and that cheese Danish." Then with a sigh he added, "But I'll just take an oat-bran muffin."

I don't usually pass on news like this, but sometimes we have to pause and truly remember what life is all about. So I pass on this sad, sad news. There was a great loss today in the entertainment world. The man who wrote the song "Hokey Pokey" died. What was really terrible is they had trouble keeping the body in the casket.

They'd put his left leg in, and ... well, you know the rest.

A cardiologist came up with a new operating procedure that would cut down the time heart surgery takes, causing less trauma to the patient. He was praised by his peers when he presented it at a medical convention. He was also paid $100,000 to present his findings. He did a couple more of these presentations and realized it would be more lucrative to do lectures about his procedure than to work as a surgeon. So he decided to give the lectures full-time. He purchased a limousine and hired a driver.

One day, after he'd been doing the lecture circuit for about a year, his driver said to him, "You know ... this is totally unfair."

"What do you mean?" asked the surgeon.

"Well, you get paid $100,000 every time you give this lecture and that's more money than I get paid in a whole year."

The surgeon explained to him it's a very complicated procedure and he is the only person that can give the lecture.

"That's not true. I can do your lecture blindfolded. I've heard it so many times now, I know it by heart," the driver said.

"Well, if that's true, I'll tell you what. You give the next lecture and you can keep the $100,000 if you do it right." So the driver agrees.

They arrive at the lecture hall, where the surgeon and the driver change coats. The surgeon puts on the driver's hat and sits in the back of the room.

The driver nails the presentation. Not only that, but he also answers all the questions without any problems. Just when the driver thinks he's finished, an audience member wearing a lab coat stands up and asks a very complex question that the driver is not able to answer.

"You know," the driver said, "I have given this lecture 287 times and I have never been asked such a dumb question. In fact, it's *so* stupid; I'm going to let my driver answer it."

The Sense of Humor

A group of parachute trainees were being taken up for their very first jump. The instructor gave out last minute instructions. "After you jump, count to eight and pull the rip cord. If the chute doesn't open, pull the chord for the backup parachute. After you reach the ground, a green truck will be there to bring you back to the airport." When it came time for Joe to jump, he did as he had been instructed. After counting to eight, he pulled the rip cord, but his parachute didn't open. So he pulled the backup chute, but that didn't open either. He was very disappointed and thought to himself, *With my luck, I'll bet that green truck won't be there either.*

Being an Astrologer is not easy. It takes hard work, great sensitivity, a clear analytical mind, and the ability to keep a straight face.

Every lunch hour, a man picked up a can of dog food at the grocery store, went across the street to a park bench and ate it. A doctor, who happened to pass through the park regularly, couldn't help noticing his behavior and one day decided to offer some advice. "I'm an internist," he explained, "and I think you should know that stuff isn't very healthy for people. In fact, eating it could kill you."

"Thanks for the advice, Doc, but I've been eating dog food for years and I feel just fine."

The doctor shrugged his shoulders and walked off. A few weeks later he noticed the man was missing from his bench, and asked another park regular what had happened.

"He's dead."

The doctor shook his head. "I told him dog food would kill him."

"Oh it wasn't the dog food. He got run over chasing a car."

An American pilot was living in Australia. One day, while flying in the outback, he lost control of his plane and crashed. He was discovered by a rancher, who drove him to a hospital, where it was determined that he had no life threatening injuries, but he was unconscious. When he woke up the next day, he saw that he was in a hospital, and realized he could barely move his heavily bandaged limbs. He asked the nurse standing near his bed, "Did they bring me here to die?"

"No," she said cheerfully. "They brought you here yester*die*."

At a play, when the usher noticed a man stretched out across three seats during the intermission, he walked over and whispered, "I'm sorry, sir, but you are only allowed one seat." The man mumbled but didn't move.

"Sir, if you don't move, I'll have to call the manager." The man moaned again but stayed where he was. The usher left and returned with the manager, who called the police. The officer looked at the man and said. "All right buddy, what's your name?"

"Henry," he mumbled.

"And where are you from, Henry?"

"I'm from … from … the … balcony."

A man goes to the dentist because something's wrong in his mouth. The dentist examines him and says, "That new upper plate I put in for you six months ago is eroding. What have you been eating?"

"All I can think of is about four months ago, my wife made asparagus and put some stuff on it that was delicious. She said it was Hollandaise sauce and I loved it so much, now I put it on everything—meatloaf, toast, fish, vegetables—everything."

"Well," the dentist said, "that's probably the problem. Hollandaise sauce is made with lots of lemon juice, which is very corrosive. It's eaten away your upper plate. I'll make you a new one, and this time we'll use chrome."

"Why chrome?" he asked.

"It's simple. Everyone knows ... there's no plate like chrome for the Hollandaise!"

A man and his wife loved to hunt for mushrooms. One day they collected a basket full, and decided to throw a mushroom party. Everybody loved them, including the cat. But later they saw her writhing on the kitchen floor. They called the doctor and asked, "We think we've eaten poisoned mushrooms, what should we do?"

The doctor told them to bring their guests to the emergency room right away. They all had to have their stomachs pumped. By the time they got back home, the cat was lying contentedly in the corner ... with six newborn kittens.

Patient: "Doctor, I don't know what's wrong with me but I hurt all over. If I touch my shoulder here, it hurts and if I touch my leg here, it hurts and if I touch my head here, it hurts, and if I touch my foot here, it hurts."

Doctor: "I think you have a broken finger."

"Doctor, am I going to die?"

"That is the *last* thing you're going to do."

Monday I had a near death experience and it's changed my life forever. I went horseback riding. Everything was going fine until the horse started bouncing out of control. I tried with all my might to hang on, but he finally threw me off. Just when things couldn't possibly get worse, my foot got caught in the stirrup. I fell head first to the ground.

My head kept bouncing harder and harder because the horse wouldn't stop. He didn't even slow down. Lucky for me the store manager ran up and unplugged the beast just in time.

Feeling edgy, a man took a hot bath to relax. Just as he got comfortable, the doorbell rang. He climbed out of the tub, put on his robe and slippers and went to the door.

A man wanted to know if he needed anything fixed around the house. He slammed the door and went back to his bath. The doorbell rang again. On went the robe and slippers. The man started for the door again. He took one step, slipped on a wet spot, fell backward and hit the back of his head hard against the bathtub. The man struggled into his clothes and though he was in great pain, drove to the doctor.

After examining him, the doctor said, "You know, it could have been much worse. Nothing is broken. But you need to relax. Why don't you go home and take a nice hot bath?"

Three men are on the golf course, and they start talking.

"When you're in your casket, and friends and family are crying, what would you like to hear them say about you?" one of them asked.

The first guy said, "I'd like to hear them say I was a great doctor, and a good family man."

The second guy says, "I'd like to hear that I was a wonderful husband and teacher who made a big difference in my students' lives."

Then the last guy said, "I think I'd like to hear them say ... 'Hey look ... he's moving!'"

Old Fred was in the hospital, near death. The family called their pastor to be with them. As the pastor stood next to the bed, Fred's condition deteriorated very fast, and he motioned frantically for something to write on. The pastor handed him a pen and a piece of paper, and Fred used his last bit of energy to scribble a note, then he died.

The pastor thought it best not to look at the note at that time, so he put it in his pocket. At the funeral, he finished his message and realized he was wearing the same jacket he wore when ol' Fred passed away.

He said, "You know, Fred handed me a note just before he died. I haven't looked at it yet, but knowing Fred, I'm sure there's a word of inspiration here for all of us."

He opened the note and read, "Hey! You're standing on my oxygen tube!"

An old man had never been to Florida. Now, on his birthday, his kids gave him a trip to the beach. He had a wonderful time spending day after day by the ocean in the sunlight, and he got a great tan.

Unfortunately, the day before heading back, he suffered a massive heart attack and died.

Back home, in the funeral home, two old lifelong friends came up and looked at their friend. One of them sniffed, wiped his eyes and said to the other,

"Don't he look just wonderful! So nice and peaceful?"

The other friend, standing beside him sniffed and said,

"Really peaceful—and that tan. It looks like the trip did him a lot of good."

Within a few hours of the death of a congressman, an eager prospective candidate telephoned the Speaker of the House.

"I was very sorry to hear of the congressman's death, is there any chance that I could take his place?"

The Speaker said, "It's fine with me, unless the funeral director has an objection."

A woman told the vet something was wrong with her dog. He examined the animal and told her the dog was dead.

"I don't believe you," she said, "I'd like a second opinion."

So the vet went into another room and got a cat. He put the cat up on the table with the dog. The cat sniffed the dog and jumped down.

Then the vet went out and got a black lab, put him on the table, the lab sniffed the dog and jumped down.

Again the vet said, "I'm sorry, but your dog is definitely dead. That will be $5,500 for the exam."

"$5,500! You can't be serious! What are the charges for?"

"$100 is for me and it's only $5,400 for the CAT scan and lab work."

A geneticist, a lawyer, and a family counselor meet over lunch to decide once and for all when life really begins.

The geneticist spoke first, "I've done many, many tests, and have come to the conclusion that life begins at conception."

The lawyer spoke next. "I am a person who interprets the written law, and, therefore, I believe life begins at different times depending on what state one lives in."

"Well, I'm afraid that I must disagree with both of you," responds the family counselor. "Over the years, I've met with thousands of parents and attended dozens of workshops. I have come to the conclusion that life really begins once your youngest child goes off to college and your dog dies."

A man stubbed his toe. It hurt so bad, he decided to go to the doctor and have it checked out. A nurse came in and informed him he had to remove his clothes and put on a gown.

"That's ridiculous," he objected, "I only hurt my toe. The rest of my

The Sense of Humor

body is fine."

"Those are the rules," she retorted.

He was about halfway undressed when a voice from the other side of the curtain sheepishly whimpered, "You think you've got it bad? They made me do the same thing, and I'm just here to fix their copier."

"It's been six weeks, doctor, and I still feel terrible," a patient complained.

"Did you follow my instructions on your medicine exactly?" he asked.

"Yes," the woman said proudly, "The label on the bottle said, 'keep closed tightly', so I did."

A man goes to the doctor for a routine exam. The doctor is interested in what the man has been eating.

"Well, for breakfast, I drink a gallon of grapefruit juice, a quart of prune juice, and eat a box of cooked oatmeal. Then I follow that with a package of English muffins, a dozen scrambled eggs, and coffee.

"For lunch, I have a side of ham, a gallon of soup, two pounds of fries, a dozen doughnuts, and coffee.

"Then for supper I eat shrimp, lobster, three kinds of steak, a dozen biscuits, half a pie topped with ice cream, and coffee.

"Now before you say anything doc, I know what you're gonna tell me."

"What would that be?" asked the doctor.

You're gonna tell me I'm drinking way too much coffee."

Two men were traveling on a train when one asked the other, "W-w-w-where do y-y-y-you g-g-get off?"

"D-d-d-denver," said the second man.

"W-w-w-what's in D-d-d-denver?"

"M-m-m-my d-d-d-doctor s-s-s-sent m-m-m-me to a sp-sp-sp-specialist to s-s-s-see if h-h-h-he could h-h-h-help m-m-m-my s-s-s-stuttering.."

"W-w-w-who is it?"

"D-d-d-d-doctor Mac-mac-mac Whorter."

Th-th-th-that's w-w-w-wonderful, h-h-h-he's the s-s-s-same d-d-d-doctor w-w-w-who c-c-c-cured m-m-m-me of m-m-m-my s-s-s-s-s-stuttering."

"I'm afraid I have some bad news. You're dying and you don't have much time," the doctor said.

"Oh no, that's terrible. How long have I got?" the man asked.

"Ten ..." the doctor answered.

"Ten? Ten what? Months? Weeks? What!" he asked desperately.

The doctor looked at his watch, held up one finger, and began counting, "10...9...8...7..."

Doctor: "I've got bad news. You have high blood pressure and Alzheimer's"

Patient: "Whew! At least I don't have high blood pressure."

He is not dead, he is electroencephalographically challenged.

"Are you an organ donor?"

"No, but I once gave an old piano to the Salvation Army."

What's the difference between a general practitioner and a specialist? One treats what you have, the other thinks you have what he treats.

What's one thing a patient doesn't want to hear in the operating room?

The Sense of Humor

"Oops!"

What is a patient's famous last word in surgery?
"Ouch!"

What nuts give you a cold?
Cachoo (cashew) nuts.

When they take out an appendix, it's an appendectomy; when they remove your tonsils, it's a tonsillectomy. What is it when they remove a growth from your head?
A haircut.

Why are doctors stingy?
First they *say* they'll treat you, and then they make you *pay* for it.

It is well documented that for every minute you exercise, you add a minute to your life. This enables you, at eighty-five years of age, to spend an additional five months in a nursing home at thousands of dollars per month!

I joined a health club last year and spent about five hundred bucks. Haven't lost a pound, though. I guess you have to actually show up.

I have to exercise early in the morning before my brain figures out what I'm doing and puts a stop to it.

The advantage of exercising every day is that you die healthier.

I don't exercise because, every time I try, it makes the ice jump right out of my glass!

"I operated on Mr. Jones the other day," said the surgeon.
"What for?" asked his colleague.
"About $12,000."
"What did he have?"
"Oh ... about $12,000."

A doctor called one of his patients,
"I hate to bother you with this, but the check you gave me just came back."
"Humm, that's funny," the patient said. "So did my warts."

The hypochondriac manic-depressive seems to feel bad when he feels good in the fear he's going to feel even worse, when he gets better.

A little old lady told her friend, "I know a man who is so full of antibiotics, any time he sneezes, everyone in the room gets better."

A boy said to his friend, "My uncle can't watch football on TV anymore."
"Why?" asked his friend.
"My mother said he's neurotic."
"What does that mean?"
"I don't know, but every time the teams get in a huddle, he thinks they're whispering about him."

A patient was waiting nervously in the examination room of a famous specialist.
"So, who did you see before coming to me?" asked the doctor.

The Sense of Humor

"My local general practitioner."

"Your GP?" scoffed the doctor. "What a waste of time. Tell me, what sort of useless advice did he give you?"

"He told me to come and see you."

The patient shook his doctor's hand in gratitude and said, "Since we're the best of friends, I wouldn't want to insult you by offering payment. But I *would* like for you to know that I've mentioned you in my will."

"That is very kind of you," said the doctor emotionally, and then added, "May I see that prescription I just gave you? I'd like to make a little change ..."

Mr. Lee was terribly overweight, so his doctor put him on a diet.

"I want you to eat regularly for two days, then skip a day, and repeat this procedure for two weeks. The next time I see you, you'll have lost at least five pounds."

When Mr. Lee returned, he shocked the doctor by losing nearly twenty pounds.

"Why, that's amazing! the doctor said, "Did you follow my instructions?"

Mr. Lee nodded. "I'll tell you, though. I thought I was going to drop dead that third day."

"From hunger?" the doctor asked.

"No. From all that skipping."

There was a case in one hospital's intensive care unit where patients always died in the same bed, on Sunday morning, at about eleven a.m., regardless of their medical condition. This puzzled the doctors and some even thought it had something to do with the supernatural. No one

159

could solve the mystery as to why the deaths occurred around eleven a.m. on Sundays. So, a worldwide team of experts was assembled to investigate the cause of the incidents. The next Sunday morning, a few minutes before eleven a.m., all the doctors and nurses nervously waited outside the room to see for themselves what the terrible phenomenon was all about. Some were holding wooden crosses, prayer books, and other objects to ward off the evil spirits.

Just when the clock struck eleven ... Lloyd, the part-time Sunday maintenance man, entered the room and unplugged the life support system so he could use the vacuum cleaner.

FAMILY HUMOR

"Did you have a nice Christmas?" a friend asked a woman as they shopped in the grocery store.

"Well, I had a nice visit. A bearded man came to my door with a big bag over his shoulder."

"Of course. It was Santa."

"No, it was my son bringing his laundry home from college."

A mother opened her back door to check on her four-year-old son, who was playing in the yard with some older children. She was horrified to see them feeding him an earthworm.

She screamed at them, "Don't feed him worms! They'll make him sick!"

They looked puzzled and asked, "Was he sick yesterday?"

A little boy asked his father, "How are people born?"

His father answered, "Adam and Eve had babies, then their babies became adults and had babies, and it's been like that right up to today."

The boy then went to his mother, asked the same question and she said, "We were monkeys then we evolved to become people like we are now."

The boy ran back to his father and said, "You lied to me. Mom said we all came from monkeys!"

His father looked down to him and smiled. "No, your mom was talking about *her* side of the family."

A teenager, who had just received her learner's permit, offered to drive her parents to church. After a wild ride, they finally reached their destination. The driver's mother stumbled out of the car and in a most grateful voice, said, "Thank you."

"Anytime," her daughter said.

Her mother replied, "Honey, I wasn't talking to you. I was talking to God."

An organic gardener came home from a nearby farm with two buckets of cow manure.

"What's that for?" asked her five-year-old daughter.

"The strawberries," Mom answered.

After staring at the buckets for a moment, the girl said, "Mom, if it's okay with you, can I have mine with whipped cream instead?"

Deep in a forest, a little turtle began to climb a tree. After hours of struggle and effort, he reached the top, jumped into the air waving his front legs and crashed all the way to the ground. After recovering, he slowly climbed the tree again, jumped and fell to the ground. The turtle tried over and over again while a couple of birds, sitting on a nearby branch, watched his sad efforts.

Finally, the female bird turned to her mate. "Dear," she chirped, "I think it's time to tell him he's adopted."

Daryl and his two brothers, Darryl and Darrryl were on a road trip.

The Sense of Humor

Daryl, the driver, noticed the car was low on gas, so he stopped at a gas station and got out to fill up, while his brother Darryl went in to get something to drink. While pumping gas, he realized he had locked the keys in the car. When he went inside to pay, he asked the attendant for a coat hanger so he could try to open the door himself.

Ten minutes later, the attendant came out to see how he was doing.

Outside the car, Daryl, with his brother Darryl helping, was moving the hanger around and around while the third Darrryl, who was inside the car, kept saying, "A little more to the left ... a little more to the ..."

A man is listening to the radio and hears that a car is headed the wrong direction on the freeway, forcing people off the road. He realizes his wife is on that same highway and quickly calls her cell phone.

"Honey," he says, "be careful. There's a car going the wrong way and running everyone off the road!"

She screams back, "It's not just one car! There's *hundreds* of them!"

Samantha was never fun to have around as a child, so her mother shipped her off to spend the summers with relatives. One summer, Samantha was visiting an uncle in the country where, to try to keep her entertained, he had an idea.

"Why don't you grab a rifle, take my dogs and go shootin?"

Samantha, being a tomboy, thought that was a great idea. So, off she went toward the woods, with the gun on her shoulder and the dogs trailing close behind. After a couple of hours, Samantha returned with a big smile.

Her uncle looked up and said: "Did you have a good time?"

"Oh, yes, it was great", she said. "You got any more dogs?"

After trying a new shampoo for the first time, a guy wrote an enthusiastic letter of approval to the manufacturer. Several weeks later he came home from work to find a large carton in the middle of the living room floor. Inside were free samples of the many products the company made: soaps, detergents, tooth paste, and paper items.

"Well, what do you think" his wife asked smiling.

"I think next time I'm gonna write to Lexus!"

When David was younger, he hated going to weddings. It seemed that all of his aunts and the grandmother types used to come up to him, poke him in the ribs, cackle, and say, "You're next, you're next."

They stopped saying that later on after he started doing the same thing to them at funerals, "You're next, you're next."

A little boy has been the center of attention until his new baby sister comes along. It's hard for him to share their attention, and he's a little jealous.

On his sister's first birthday, his mother and father take him aside to tell him that since the baby is getting bigger, their house is too small and they'll have to move.

"That won't work," he said. "She's crawling pretty good now, so she'll probably just follow us."

A reclusive rancher is looking for a way to celebrate his fiftieth wedding anniversary. He's eating breakfast in a northern Arizona café with a longtime friend when their conversation turns to "the good old days."

"But about your fiftieth anniversary, Roy," his friend asked, "are you gonna do anything special?"

"Yup, we sure are," Roy said. "For our twenty-fifth anniversary, I took my wife to Tucson. For our fiftieth, I think I'll drive down there and bring her back."

The Sense of Humor

Who is bigger, Mr. Bigger, or Mr. Bigger's baby?
Answer- The Baby is a *little* Bigger.

A six-year-old and his four-year-old brother had a difference of opinion that finally led to a fight.

"Children! Children!" their mother called out. "Haven't you heard of the Golden Rule?"

"Yes," sputtered the six-year-old, "but he did unto me first!"

A man couldn't think of the right gift so he bought his mother-in-law a large cemetery plot. On her next birthday, he didn't give her anything.

She was quick to tell him how thoughtlessness he was. So he said, "What'd you expect? You haven't even used the gift I gave you *last* year."

While driving in Pennsylvania, a family drove up behind an Amish buggy.

The owner of the buggy obviously had a sense of humor, because on the back was a hand printed sign ...

Energy efficient vehicle.

Runs on oats and grass.

Caution: Do not step in the exhaust.

One day, a married couple had twin sons. They didn't have enough money to raise them, so they put the boys up for adoption. One of the boys went to a Spanish family and they named him Juan. The other boy went to an Egyptian family and they named him Amal.

Years later, Juan was curious about his real parents. After some research, he finally located them, and sent a nice letter with a picture of himself.

The original mother said "I'm so glad he's happy and what a wonderful picture. I wish we had a picture of Amal too. I wonder what he looks like."

Her husband turned to her and said, "You know what they say. When you've seen Juan, you've seen Amal."

One summer there was a violent thunderstorm as a mother tucked her little boy into bed. She was about to turn off the light when he asked her, with a tremble in his voice, "Mommy, could you sleep with me tonight?"

His mother smiled and gave him a big hug. "I can't honey," she said. "I have to sleep in Daddy's room."

After a long silence with a shaky little voice he said, "The big sissy."

A frustrated father shook his head and said, "When I was a kid, my parents punished me by sending me to my room without any supper. But my son's room has a flat screen TV, video games, a smart phone, computer and a DVD."

"So how do you discipline him?" asked his friend.

"That's easy. Now we send him to *our* room."

Over breakfast one morning, a woman said to her husband, "I bet you don't know what day this is."

"Of course, I do," he said as he left for the office.

At ten a.m., the doorbell rang. When his wife opened the door, she was handed a box containing a dozen long-stemmed, red roses.

At one p.m., a foil-wrapped, two-pound box of her favorite chocolates was delivered.

Later, a boutique sent over a designer dress.

The Sense of Humor

The woman couldn't wait for her husband to come home. "First the flowers, next the chocolates and then the dress!" she said. "This was the best Groundhog Day ever!"

A man and his wife were sitting down to their usual morning cup of coffee, listening to the weather report on the radio.

"There will be three to five inches of snow today and a snow emergency has been declared. You must park your cars on the odd-numbered side of the street."

He gets up from his coffee and says, "Okay."

Two days later, again they're both sitting down to coffee and the weather forecaster announces, "There will be two to four inches of snow today and a snow emergency has been declared. You must park your cars on the even-numbered side of the street."

Again he gets up and says, "Okay."

Three days later, they're again sitting with their cups of coffee and the weather forecaster says, "There will be six to eight inches of snow today and a snow emergency has been declared. You must park your cars on the ..." Right then the power went out and they didn't get the rest of the instructions.

The man says to his wife, "Now what am I going to do?"

She told him, "Why don't you just leave it in the garage this time?"

A girl wanted her boyfriend to meet her parents. "My mother has a great sense of humor," she told him. "You'll get along great."

They met her parents at a restaurant, and right away her mom launched into one joke after another. Her boyfriend fired right back and soon they were all laughing hysterically.

After a few minutes, the girl noticed that no one was sitting anywhere near their table. "Maybe we're being too loud," she said.

"No," her boyfriend said, "the hostess is probably asking customers if they'd like to sit in 'Joking' or 'Non-joking'!!"

Years ago, a couple toured Russia. Their guide argued with them about everything. As they were leaving Moscow, the husband said, "Look, it's snowing."

The guide disagreed, "No, sir, it is raining."

"I still think it's snowing," said Mr. Smith.

"Raining"

"Snowing"

"Raining"

Finally, his wife said, "He must be right because … Rudolph the *Red* knows rain, dear."

A very dirty little boy came in from playing outside and asked his mother, "Who am I?"

"I don't know! Who are you?" she asked.

"Wow!" the boy said. "Mrs. Johnson *was* right! She told me I was so dirty, even my own mother wouldn't recognize me!"

"My uncle tried to make a new kind of car. He took the engine from a Ford, the transmission from a Chevy, the tires off a Honda and the exhaust system from a Chrysler."

"Really? What did he get?"

"About twenty years."

A little boy has a new baby sister and she's screaming like mad.

He asked his mother, "Where'd we get her anyway?"

His mother told him, "Your sister came from heaven."

He said, "Wow! Now I see why they threw her out!"

The Sense of Humor

A son called his mother in Florida and asked, "How are you doing?"
She said, "Not too good. I've been very weak."
Her son asked why she was so weak.
"Because I've hardly eaten anything in thirty-eight days."
He asked her, "Why haven't you eaten in thirty-eight days?"
"Because I didn't want my mouth to be full of food when you called."

Two elderly men were playing cards on Saturday night as they've done for the past thirty-five years. Larry, the older, had been having problems remembering which cards were which and usually needed help from his wife.

At the end of the card game, Ed said to Larry, "You did very well tonight. You didn't need any help at all. Why is that?"

"Well, ever since my wife sent me to that memory school, I haven't had any problems at all."

"Memory school? What memory school?"

Larry thought for a minute, "Oh, what's that flower that's red and has thorns? You know, a really pretty flower ...?"

"A rose?"

"Rose, yeah ... that's it!" Larry turned to his wife and hollered, "Hey, Rose! What's the name of that memory school you sent me to?"

During a recent little league game, the coach said to one of his young players, "Do you understand what cooperation is? What it means to be a team?"

The little boy nodded yes.

"Do you understand that what matters is how we play together as a team?"

The little boy nodded.

"So," the coach continued, "when a strike is called, or you're out at first, you don't argue or curse or attack the umpire. Do you understand that?"

Again the boy nodded.

"Good," said the coach. "Then would please you go over and explain that to your parents."

A father and son went fishing one day. After a couple hours out in the boat, the boy asked his father, "How does this boat float?"

The father thought for a moment, then replied, "I don't really know, sn."

Then the boy turned back to his father and asked, "How do fish breathe underwatr?"

"I don't really know, so."

A little later the boy asked his father, "Why is the sky ble?"

Again, the father said. "I don't really know, sn."

Worried he was starting to annoy his father, he said, "Dad. Do you mind my asking you so many questions?"

"Of course not, son. How you gonna learn anything if you don't ask questions!
"

"Thanks for the harmonica you gave me for Christmas," a little boy said to his uncle. "It's the best present I ever got."

"That's great," said his uncle. "Do you know how to play it yet?"

"Oh, I don't play it," the boy said.

"Why not?"

"My mom gives me a dollar a day not to play the thing during the daytime, and my dad gives me five bucks a week not to play it at night."

The Sense of Humor

Unable to attend the funeral after his father died, a son who lived far away called his brother and told him, "Do something nice for Dad and send me the bill."

Later, he got a bill for $300.00, which he paid. The next month, he got another bill for $300.00, which he also paid, figuring it was some incidental expense.

Bills for $300.00 kept arriving every month and, finally, the man called his brother again to find out what was going on.

His brother told him, "You said to do something nice for Dad. So I rented him a tuxedo."

A man in a grocery store pushed a shopping cart that contained, among other things, a screaming baby. As he moved along the aisles, he kept repeating softly, "Keep calm, George. Don't get excited, George. Don't yell, George."

A lady came up to him and said, "I'm amazed at your patience in trying to quiet little George."

"*Little* George? *I'm* George!"

The mother of a large family explained why she dressed all her children alike, right down to the youngest baby.

"When we had just four children, I dressed them alike so we wouldn't lose any of them. Now, I dress them alike so we won't pick up any that don't belong to us."

A wife said to her husband one morning, "We've got such a clever dog. He brings in the newspaper every morning."

Her husband said, "Lots of dogs can do that."

"Well, yes ... but we don't subscribe to any papers!"

When a mother returned from the grocery store, her little boy pulled out the box of animal crackers he had begged for. He spread the animal-shaped crackers all over the kitchen counter.

"What are you doing?" his mom asked.

"The box says you shouldn't eat them if the seal is broken, so I'm looking for the seal."

A boy from New York was being led through the swamps of Louisiana by his cousin.

"Is it true that an alligator won't attack you if you carry a flashlight?"

With a big Louisiana smile his cousin said, "That depends on how fast ya *carry* the flashlight."

A three-year-old boy went with his dad to see a new litter of kittens.

He couldn't wait to get home and tell his mother. "There were two boy kittens and two girl kittens."

"How did you know that?" his mother asked.

"Daddy picked them up and looked underneath. I think it's printed on the bottom someplace."

A man frantically dialed 911, "My wife is pregnant and her contractions are only two minutes apart!"

"Is this her first child?" the operator asked.

"No!" the man shouted, "This is her husband!"

An efficiency expert finished his lecture with a note of caution.

"You don't want to try these techniques at home."

"Why not?" asked someone from the back of the audience.

"Well, I watched my wife's routine at breakfast for years. She made lots of trips to the refrigerator, stove, table and cabinets, often carrying just a single item at a time. 'Honey,' I asked her, 'why don't you try carrying several things at once?'"

The same person asked, "Did it save time?"

"Actually, yes. It used to take her twenty minutes to get breakfast ready. Now I do it in seven."

A little boy practiced his violin in the living room while his father was trying to read in the den. The family dog was lying in the den, and as the screeching sounds of the violin reached his ears, he began to howl.

The boy's father listened to the dog and the violin for about as long as he could. Then he jumped up, threw his paper to the floor and yelled,

"Could you please play something the dog *doesn't* know?"

A man, his wife, and their son from the country go to a big hotel in the city. When they get into the lobby, they're directed to the front desk to check in. While the wife is taking care of the paper work, her husband looks at all the amazing things they have. One that catches his eye is a recessed wall with a crack in it. Just then, an elderly woman walks up, pushes a button next to the recess, and the wall opens up to a small room! She walks in, the wall closes, and lights above the secret doors flash along the top. Then they start flashing in the opposite direction and a minute later, the wall opens again. But this time, a beautiful young lady steps out.

The man looks back at the doors in the wall, and says to his son, "Boy, you go git 'cher mama!"

An elderly gentleman had a serious hearing problem for years. He went to the doctor and was fitted with a set of hearing aids that allowed him to hear perfectly.

A month later he went back for a checkup and the doctor said, "Your hearing is perfect. Your family must be happy you can hear again."

"Oh, I haven't said anything to my family yet," he told the doctor, "I just sit around and listen to their conversations ... changed my will three times already!"

A couple's happy married life was being tested because of old Aunt Emma.

For seventeen long years she lived with them, always crotchety, and always demanding.

Finally, Emma died.

On the way back from the cemetery, the husband confessed to his wife, "Honey, if I didn't love you so much, I don't think I would have put up with your Aunt Emma in the house all these years."

His wife looked at him in shock. "*My* Aunt Emma! - I thought she was *your* Aunt Emma!"

A prisoner got a letter from his wife.

"I've decided to plant a garden in the back yard. When is the best time to plant the seeds?"

Since he knew the guards read all the mail, he wrote back to her.

"Whatever you do, do not touch the back yard! That's where I hid all the loot."

A week later, he got another letter from his wife.

"You wouldn't believe what happened. Some men came to the house with picks and shovels and dug up the whole garden."

The prisoner wrote another letter to his wife. "Now is the best time to plant the seeds!"

A pregnant woman gets in an accident and falls into a deep coma. Asleep for nearly six months, when she wakes up she notices that she's no longer pregnant and frantically asks the doctor what happened.

"Ma'am you had twins! A boy and a girl. Your brother came in and named them."

She thinks to herself, *Oh no, not my brother... he's an idiot!*

She asks the doctor, "What's the girl's name?"

"Denise."

"That's not such a bad name. I like it! What's the boy's name?"

"De-nephew."

A police officer in a small town stopped a young driver who was speeding down Main Street.

"But officer," the man said, "I can explain."

"Just be quiet," snapped the officer. "I'm going to let you cool off in jail till the chief gets back."

"But, officer, I just wanted to say ..."

"I told you to be quiet! You're going to jail!"

A few hours later, the officer looked in on his prisoner and said, "Lucky for you the chief's at his daughter's wedding. He'll be in a real good mood when he gets back."

"Don't count on it," the man in the cell told him. "I'm the groom."

A man left the icy streets of Chicago for a vacation in Florida. His wife was on a business trip and was planning to meet him there the next day. When he reached his motel in Florida, he decided to send her a quick email. He couldn't find the note where he had written her email address, so he did his best to type it from memory. Unfortunately, he missed one letter and his note was sent instead to an elderly preacher's wife whose husband had just died a day earlier. When the widow checked her email, she took one look at the monitor, screamed and fainted. Her family rushed into the room and read the message:

Dearest wife,

Just checked in.

Everything is prepared for your arrival.

P.S. Sure is hot down here!

A man is staying overnight with a farm family. When they sit down to dinner, there's a pig at the table. The pig has three medals hanging around his neck and one wooden leg. The man says, "Hmm, I see there's a pig having dinner with us."

"Yep," the farmer said. "That's because he's a very special pig. You see those medals around his neck? The first one is from when our baby son fell in the pond and was about to drown. That pig dove in, swam out, and saved his life.

The second medal, that's from when our daughter was trapped in the burning barn, and the pig raced inside, carried her out, and saved *her* life.

And the third medal is from when our oldest boy was cornered by an angry bull, and that there pig ran under the fence, bit the bull's tail and saved the boy's life."

"I can see why you let a pig like that sit at the table and have dinner with you. And I can see why he got all those medals. But how did he get the wooden leg?"

"Well," said the farmer, "you don't eat a pig like that all at once."

There was a family named Father, Mother, and Baby Tomato. One of their favorite activities was to go window-shopping in town. The only problem was Baby Tomato could never keep up. He would get all interested in something and fall way behind his parents. So here it was Saturday night and the family was window-shopping. But before long, Father Tomato noticed that Baby Tomato wasn't anywhere near them.

He looked back and there, almost two blocks back, he saw Baby Tomato looking in a window.

So Father Tomato walked all the way back and told him, "You're going to have to keep up with Mother Tomato and me."

"Ohhhh kaaaay, I'll try."

A little later, the same thing happened, and again, Father Tomato had to go back and get him.

"Ohhhh Kaaaay, I'll try," he said again, but before too long, he was a full three blocks back. That was it! Father Tomato had had all he could stand. He stormed back to where Baby Tomato was standing, and kicked him to smithereens.

Then he looked down at what was left of Baby Tomato and said, "Now…catch up!"

A little boy found a cat and brought it home to see if his parents would let him keep it.

"Is it a boy or a girl," his dad asked?

"I don't know, must be a boy."

The next morning, he got up early to check on his new friend, but when he looked in the box, there were six baby kittens. He ran back upstairs to his parent's bedroom and screamed, "Dad, Mom, come quick! That cat I brought home last night just fell apart."

A little boy walked up to the librarian to check out a book entitled, "Comprehensive Guide for Mothers."

When the librarian asked him if it was for his mother, he told her no.

"Then why are you checking it out?"

"Because," the boy said, beaming from ear to ear, "I just started collecting moths last week!"

Cindy's mother sent her to the store to buy more diapers.

"That's eight dollars for the diapers," said the clerk, "and twenty six cents for the tax."

"We don't need any tacks," Cindy protested. "Whenever my mom puts a clean diaper on *our* baby, she just uses the tapes."

Jimmy went away on a trip and his sister, Sarah, promised to take good care of his cat. A few days later he called home to see how the cat was getting along.

"Oh," his sister told him, "your cat's dead."

"Dead?" he protested. "You could have broken it to me more gently."

"Well, what did you expect me to say?" she asked.

"You could have told me something like the cat got stuck on the roof, Mom had to call, and the fire department came to get her. Then the next time I called, you could say the cat fell from the ladder. Maybe the next time you could have told me the vet did everything he could, but my cat didn't pull through."

"Well, I didn't think first. I'm sorry," she said.

"That's okay, I guess," Jimmy said, "so tell me, how's mom?"

"Um…she's on the roof, but, the firemen are up there right now trying to get her down," she began.

A boy accidentally broke the neighbor's window with his baseball.

His father scolded him saying, "What did he say when you broke his window?"

"Do you want it with, or without all the bad words?"

"Without, of course," his father growled.

The boy thought for a moment and then said, "The man didn't say anything to me at all."

The Sense of Humor

A man was pulled over by a motorcycle patrolman. "Did you know your tail light was out?" he asked.

The man jumped out of the car and as he ran to the back he cried, "Oh this is terrible!"

"Now take it easy," comforted the policeman. "It's not a serious problem."

"Just wait till my wife and kids find out about this."

"Your wife and kids, where are they?"

"They're in the trailer that used to be hooked on back here!"

A little baby boy was born, and he didn't make a sound.

At first, this was great because his parents were able to sleep through the night as soon as they brought him home.

As the boy grew, the parents became concerned because he hadn't spoken a word yet.

All of a sudden, when he was ten years old and sitting at the dinner table, he said, "Pass the bread."

The parents were shocked, and his father asked, "Son, why have you never spoken before?"

"Well," the boy said, "up until now, everything was okay."

A man in the city had three cousins visiting and they didn't speak a word of English. He asked his friend to drive them home. Thirty minutes later the friend returned with all three cousins.

"What happened?" asked the man.

"Your cousins can't speak English," his friend said.

"I know. That's why I told you the one on the left lived on 23rd street, the one on the right lives on 45th street and the one in the middle went to Broadway."

"I know, I know," his friend said, "but when I hit a big bump, they all flew into the air, and came down in different seats. So I had to bring them back and have you sort them out for me all over again."

A woman reported the disappearance of her husband to the police. An officer in charge looked at the photograph she handed him, questioned her and then asked if she wished to give her husband any message if they found him.

"Yes," she said. "Tell him my mother didn't come visit us after all."

A small boy was attending his first wedding. After the service, his cousin asked him, "How many women can a man marry?"

"Sixteen," the boy responded.

His cousin was amazed that he had an answer so quickly. "How do you know that?"

"Easy," the little boy said. "All you have to do is add it up, like the preacher said: four better, four worse, four richer, four poorer."

Attending her first wedding, a little girl whispered to her mother, "Why is the bride dressed in white?"

"Because white is the color of happiness and today is the happiest day of her life," her mother explained, keeping it simple.

The child thought about this for a moment, then said, "So, how come the groom's wearing black?"

A small boy is sent to bed by his father. Not five minutes later ... "Da-ad ..."

"What?"

"I'm thirsty. Can you bring me a drink of water?"

"No. You had your chance. Lights out."

Five minutes later, "Da-aaaad ..."

The Sense of Humor

"What?"

"I'm thirsty. Can I have a drink of water?"

"I told you no! If you ask again, I'll have to spank you!"

Five minutes later ... "Daaaa-aaaad!"

"What!"

"When you come in to spank me, can you bring a glass of water?"

My grandmother started walking five miles a day when she was sixty. Now she's ninety-seven and we don't know *where* she is!

A young boy had just gotten his driving permit. He asked his father if they could discuss his use of the family car.

His father took him into his study and said, "I'll make a deal with you. You study hard, bring your grades up, get your hair cut, and then we'll talk about it."

After about a month, the boy came back and asked his father if they could discuss his use of the car.

They again went into the study where the father said, "Son, I'm very proud of you. You've brought your grades up, you've studied hard, but you didn't get your hair cut."

The young man waited a moment and then replied, "I've been thinking about that. You know, Samson had long hair. Moses had long hair. Noah had long hair. Even Jesus had long hair."

His father said, "Yes, and everywhere they went, *they* had to walk."

Jimmy was a little five-year-old boy his mom loved very much. Being a worrier, she was concerned about him walking to school when he started Kindergarten. She walked with him to school the first couple of days but when he came home one day, he told his mother that he didn't want her walking him to school every day. He wanted to be like

181

the "big boys." He protested loudly, so she had an idea of how to handle it.

She asked a neighbor, Mrs. Goodnest, if she would follow her son to school, at a distance, so he wouldn't likely notice, but close enough to keep an eye on him.

Mrs. Goodnest said that since she was up early with her toddler anyway, it would be a good way for them to get some exercise, so she agreed.

The next school day, Mrs. Goodnest and her little girl, Marcy, set out following behind Jimmy as he walked to school with another neighbor boy he knew. She did this for the whole week.

As the boys walked and talked, kicking stones and twigs, Jimmy's little friend noticed this same lady was following them as she seemed to do every day.

Finally, he asked Jimmy, "Have you noticed that lady following us all week? Do you know her?"

Jimmy nonchalantly replied, "Yea, I know who she is."

The little friend said, "Well who is she?"

"Oh, that's just Shirley Goodnest."

"Shirley Goodnest? Who's she, and why is she following us?"

"Well," Jimmy explained, "every night my Mom makes me say the 23rd Psalm with my prayers 'cuz she worries about me so much. And in it, the prayer says, 'Shirley Goodnest and Marcy shall follow me all the days of my life.' So I guess I'll just have to get used to it."

A little boy ran frantically up and down the aisles of the grocery store yelling, "Louise! Louise!"

His mother ran up behind him," Please, you know I hate that name. If you ever get lost, just call mother."

"I was going to do that, but I figured this place was probably full of mothers."

The Sense of Humor

A very successful businessman had a meeting with his new son-in-law. "I love my daughter, and now I welcome you into the family," said the man. "To show you how much we care for you, I'm making you a fifty-fifty partner in my business. All you have to do is go to the factory every day and learn the operations."

The son-in-law interrupted, "I hate factories. I can't stand the noise."

"I see," replied the father-in-law. "Well, then you'll work in the office and take charge of some of the departments."

"I hate office work," said the son-on-law. "I can't stand being stuck behind a desk all day."

"Wait a minute," said the father-in-law. "I just made you half-owner of a money-making organization, but you don't like factories and won't work in an office. What am I going to do with you?"

"Easy," said the young man. "Why don't you just buy me out?"

Two men are playing golf when one of them hits a terrible slice.

"I call that my son in law shot," he said.

"Your son in law shot?" his friend asked. "What's that supposed to mean."

After a long sigh the man responded, " Not...*exactly* what I had in mind."

EDUCATION HUMOR

The academic dean came to the football coach to complain about one of his players.

Dean: "Harris over there has four Fs and a D. What do you think about that?"

Coach: "Looks to me like he's concentrating too much on one subject."

Timmy's English teacher was a perfectionist and demanded the very best from his pupils. So it was only to be expected that he would get furious when little Timmy handed in a poor paper.

"This is the worst essay it has ever been my misfortune to read," ranted the teacher. "It has too many mistakes. I can't understand how one person could have made so many errors."

"One person didn't," replied Timmy defensively. "My mother, my father, and my sister all helped me."

A high-school student came home from school one afternoon, looking very depressed. "What's the matter," asked his mother.

The boy said, "Aw, it's my grades. They're all wet."

"What do you mean `all wet?"
"I mean they're all below C-level."

A mother mouse and a baby mouse are walking down the path, when all of a sudden they're attacked by a big cat. The mother mouse starts barking like a pit bull, scaring the cat away. "See?" the mother said, "that's why I always say it's important to learn a foreign language?"

A young weightlifter began to develop his arm and shoulder muscles by standing outside behind the house, with a five-pound potato sack in each hand, extending his arms straight out from his sides and holding them there as long as he could. Later he tried ten-pound sacks, then fifty-pound sacks and finally he got to where he could lift a one hundred-pound sack in each hand and hold his arms straight out for more than a full minute!
"Next time I'll start putting potatoes in the sacks," he said.

Robert and Peter both applied for jobs at a large company and had to take an intelligence test. They each thought the test was easy, except for the final question: "Name a fourteen-letter word for someone in charge of a plant."
"How did you answer that last one?" asked Robert.
"I thought it was tough at first ... then I said Superintendent."
"I think I got it right, too," Pete said, "but I put down Horticulturist."

Teacher: "If you had one dollar and you asked your father for another, how many dollars would you have?"
Bobby: "One dollar."
Teacher (sadly): "You don't know your arithmetic."
Bobby: (sadly): "No, you don't know my father."

The Sense of Humor

A college student, looking for a creative way to ask his father for some extra spending money wrote:

Dear Dad,

$chool i$ really great. I am making lot$ of friend$ and $tudying very hard. With all my $tuff, I $imply can't think of anything I need, $o if you would like, you can ju$t $end me a card, $ince I would love to hear from you.

Love,

Your $on

Not to be outdone, the father wrote back:

Dear Son,

I kNOw that astroNOmy, ecoNOmics, and oceaNOgraphy are eNOugh to keep even an hoNOr student busy. Do NOt forget that the pursuit of kNOwledge is a NOble task, and you can never study eNOugh.

Love,

Dad

Two college students are driving through Louisiana. They come to the town of Natchitoches and start arguing about how to pronounce the name. They argue back and forth until they stop for lunch.

As they're standing at the counter, one of them asks the manager, "Before we order, would you please settle an argument for us? Could you tell us where we are? We're having trouble pronouncing the name."

The manager leans over the counter and says very slowly, "Burrrrrrrr-grrrrrrr Kiiiiing."

"How much are the candy bars?" asked a customer.

"Two for a dollar," said the girl behind the counter.

"All right," said the man. "I'll take just one."

"That'll be sixty cents," replied the clerk.

The customer paid for the candy and left. A man who overheard the transaction came up to the counter. "Here's forty cents," he said. "I'll take the other one."

A fourth grade class was beginning their study of US Presidents and the teacher was giving them a trivia quiz. When asked which President had a stuffed animal named after him, the class immediately screamed, "Garfield!"

A tourist was visiting New Mexico. While admiring some dinosaur bones that were everywhere, he met an old Indian who acted as an unofficial guide.

"How old are these bones?" asked the tourist.

"Exactly one hundred million and three years old," the Indian said.

"How can you be so definite?" inquired the tourist.

"An evolutionist told me they were one hundred million years old and that was exactly three years ago today."

A zookeeper wanted to get some extra animals for the zoo, so he decided to write a letter. The only problem was he didn't know the plural of *Mongoose.* So he started the letter: "To whom it may concern, I need two Mongeese."

No, that won't work, he thought, so he tried again: "To whom it may concern, I need two Mongooses. *Is that right?* he wondered.

Finally, he got an idea: "To whom it may concern, I need a Mongoose and, while you're at it, why don't you send me two of them?"

A window salesman called one of his customers.

"I'm calling because our company replaced all the windows in your house with our top-of- the line, triple-glazed, weather-tight windows over a year ago and you still haven't sent us a payment."

The customer answered, "But you told me they'd pay for *themselves* in 12 months."

There were four people named Everybody, Somebody, Anybody, and Nobody.

An important job had to be done and Everybody was sure that Somebody would do it.

Anybody could have done it, but Nobody did.

Somebody got angry, because it was Everybody's job.

Everybody thought Anybody could do it, but Nobody realized that Everybody wouldn't do it.

Finally, Everybody blamed Somebody when Nobody did what Anybody could have done!

A strong young man was working at the construction site. He bragged that he could beat anyone when it came to strength. He especially made fun of one of the older men. A few minutes later, the older worker had had enough.

"Put your money where your mouth is," he said. "I'll bet I can carry something in a wheelbarrow over to that outbuilding and you won't be strong enough to wheel it back."

"You're on, old man," the braggart said. "Show me what you got."

The old man grabbed the wheelbarrow by the handles, looked at the younger man, and said, "Get in."

A marine biologist was telling friends about some of the unusual findings he had made. "For instance," he said, "some whales can communicate at a distance of three hundred miles."

"What on earth would one whale say to another three hundred miles away?" asked a sarcastic member of the group.

"I'm not absolutely sure," the expert said, "but it sounded something like: 'Heeeeeeey!, Stanley, can you hear me nowwww? Good."

George decided to redecorate his bedroom, but he wasn't sure how many rolls of wallpaper to buy. His friend, Daryl, who lived next door, had recently done that job and the two rooms were exactly the same size.

"Daryl," he asked, "how many rolls of wallpaper did you buy for your room?"

"Ten," he said.

So George bought ten rolls of paper, and did the job. But he still had two rolls left over.

"Daryl," he said, "I bought ten rolls of wallpaper just like you said, but now I've got two rolls left over."

Daryl looked at him with surprise and said, "So did I."

A teacher was taking her first golf lesson.

"Is the word spelled P-U-T or P-U-T-T?" she asked the instructor.

"P-U-T-T is correct," he replied. "P-U-T means to place a thing where you want it. And P-U-T-T means a vain attempt to do the same thing."

Jimmy's kindergarten class was on a field trip to the local police station. They saw pictures tacked to a big bulletin board. The sign said, "The 10 Most Wanted."

One of the children pointed to a picture and asked if it was the actual picture of a wanted person.

"Yes," said the policeman. "The detectives want him really bad."

The Sense of Humor

Jimmy tugged on the officer's belt and asked, "If you want them so bad, then why didn't you just keep them when you took their pictures?"

One day a little girl came home from school, and told her mother, "Mommy. Today I was punished at school for something I didn't do."

Her mother was outraged, "That is terrible! I'm going to call your teacher! What was it you didn't do?"

The little girl said, "My homework."

The children had just been photographed and their teacher was trying to persuade each student to buy a copy of the group picture. "Just think how nice it will be to look at it when you are all grown up and say, 'There's Jennifer; she's a lawyer,' or 'That's Michael, he's a doctor.'"

And from the back of the room a little voice said, "Yea, and look, there's the teacher ... she's dead."

Sandy began her job as an elementary school counselor and was eager to help. One day during recess, she noticed a little girl standing all by herself on one side of a playing field while the rest of the kids were having a great time playing soccer at the other end.

Sandy walked up and asked if she was all right. The girl said she was.

A little later, Sandy noticed the girl was still in the same spot, by herself.

She asked, "Would you like me to stay with you and be your friend?"

The little girl said, "No, thank you."

So finally Sandy asked her, "Why are you standing here all alone?"

"Because," the little girl said, "I'm the goalie!"

The dean of admissions at a school of agriculture was interviewing a prospective student. "Why have you chosen this field?"

"My dream is make a million dollars in farming, just like my father," the student said.

"Your father made a million dollars in farming?" the dean asked.

"No," the student said, "But he's always dreamed about it."

A robber walks into a bank, pulls a gun, points to the teller and says, "Give me the money or you'll be geography."

The teller looked up and asked, "Don't you mean history?"

The robber demanded, "Don't try to change the subject."

A little boy had been looking over a display of greeting cards for a long time when a clerk finally asked, "What is it you're looking for? A birthday greeting, message to a sick friend, anniversary, or a congratulation for your mom and dad?"

The boy shook his head and said, "You got anything that looks like a blank report card?"

The principal of a small rural school had a problem with some of the older girls who were wearing lipstick. When they applied it in the bathroom, they would press their lips against the mirror and leave lip prints.

Before things got out of hand, he thought of a plan to stop it. He told all the girls who wore lipstick to meet in the ladies' room at two p.m. There they found the principal and the school custodian waiting for them.

The principal explained it was becoming a problem for the custodian to clean the mirror every night. He said he felt the girls didn't fully appreciate just how big a job it was so he wanted them to see just how difficult a mess it was to clean.

The custodian took a long-handled brush out of a box, dipped it in the nearest toilet, walked over to the mirror and began to remove the lipstick.

That was the last day any girls pressed their lips on the mirror.

A rich man's son was asked to write a composition in school on the topic of "poor people." The child wrote, "Once there was a poor family. The father was poor. The mother was poor. The children were poor. The butler was poor. The maid was poor. The chauffeur was poor ..."

It had been snowing for hours when an announcement came over the intercom: "Will the students who are parked on University Drive please move your cars so we can begin plowing."

Twenty minutes later there was another announcement: "Will the twelve hundred students who went to move twenty-six cars please return to class."

The old pastor made it a practice to visit the parish school one day a week. He walked into the fourth grade class, where the children were studying the states, and asked them how many they could name. They came up with about forty names. He told them when he was in school; students knew the names of all the states.

"Oh sure," a little boy said, "but way back then, there were only thirteen of them."

A third-grade girl came home from school and seemed very happy. Her mother asked, "Why are you so happy?"

The girl said, "We learned how to make babies in school today!"

Thinking the worst, her mother asked, "And exactly how did you learn that?"

"Simple—you just drop the y, and add i ... e ... s."

The teacher of an earth science class was lecturing on map reading. After explaining latitude, longitude, degrees, and minutes, the teacher asked, "Suppose I invited you to meet me for lunch at twenty-three degrees, four minutes north latitude and forty-five degrees, fifteen minutes east longitude ...?"

After a confused silence, one student said, "I think you'd be eating by yourself."

On the first day in college, a student took a front row seat in his literature class.

The professor told the class they would be responsible for reading five books, and she would provide them with a list of authors from which they could choose.

Then the professor walked over to her desk, took out some notes and began ... "Anderson, Baker, Brightman, Brock, Carter, Cook ..."

The student started writing as fast as he could, trying to get all the names down, when he felt a tap on his shoulder from the student behind him who whispered, "She's just taking attendance."

Heinz, from Switzerland, looking for directions, pulls up at a bus stop where two Americans are waiting.

"Entschuldigung, koennen Sie Deutsch sprechen?" he asks.

The two Americans just stare at him.

"Excusez-moi, parlez vous Francais?" he tries.

The two continue to stare.

"Parlare Italiano?"

The Sense of Humor

No response.

"Hablan ustedes Espanol?"

Still nothing.

The Swiss guy drives off, extremely disgusted. The first American turns to the second and says, "Ya know, maybe we should learn a foreign language."

"Why?" says the other. "That guy knew *four* languages and it didn't do him a bit of good."

It's high school graduation day and everybody's going to get their diploma except Leonard. At the assembly, the senior class stands up and chants, "Let Leonard graduate, let Leonard graduate!"

The principal agrees to give Leonard one last chance. "If I have five apples in my right hand and five in my left hand, how many apples do I have?" he asked.

Leonard thought long and hard and then said: "Ten?"

The entire graduating class jumped to their feet and shouted, "Give Leonard another chance. Give Leonard another chance!"

A teacher asked a girl in the hall, "Do you mind telling me whose class you're cutting this hour?"

"Like," the girl said, "uh, see, okay, like it's like I really don't like think like that's really important, ya know, like because I'm ya know, like I don't get anything out of it."

The teacher said, "It's English class, *isn't* it?"

A little boy was caught swearing by his teacher.

"You shouldn't use such language. Where did you hear it?"

"From my dad."

"Well, that's no excuse; you don't even know what it means."

"I—do—too!" he said, "It means his car won't start."

Two molecules meet each other on the street, and one says to the other, "Are you all right?"

"No, I lost an electron!"

"Are you sure?"

"I'm *positive!*"

After seeing his test results, a student went to the teacher and said, "Professor, I did the best I could on this test. I really don't think I deserve a zero."

"Neither do I," the teacher said, "but that's the lowest grade I can give you."

A chemist, a shopkeeper and a teacher were sentenced to death by firing squad. The chemist was taken from his cell and as the soldiers took aim he shouted, "Avalanche!" The soldiers panicked and in the confusion the chemist escaped.

The shopkeeper was led out next. As the soldiers took aim he shouted, "Flood!" and he escaped.

The teacher was then led out. The squad took aim and the teacher, remembering how the other two had escaped, shouted "Fire!"

A panda walked into a restaurant, ordered his meal and ate it quietly. When he'd finished, he pulled out a gun and shot out the windows. As he was walking out, the manager ran up and asked, "What do you think you're doing?"

The bear told him to look up the word panda in a dictionary, and ran off.

When he looked in the dictionary, he read, "The panda is a tree-dwelling black and white animal that eats, shoots, and leaves."

What is the difference between ignorance, apathy and ambivalence? I don't know, and I don't care one way or the other ...

Donald MacDonald from Scotland went to study at an English university and lived in the residence hall with all the other students. After he had been there a month, his mother came to visit.

"And how do you find the English students, Donald?" she asked.

"Mother, they're such terrible, noisy people. The one on the right side keeps banging his head on the wall and won't stop. The one on the left side screams all night."

"Oh Donald! How do you manage to put up with these noisy English neighbors?"

"Mother, I do nothing. I just sit here quietly, playing my bagpipes."

A country boy went on a shopping trip to the big city, and bought a two hundred-piece puzzle. He worked on it faithfully for over two weeks, and finally finished it.

"Look what I've done," he told a friend.

"That's really something, how long did it take you?" the friend asked.

"I did it in only two weeks."

"Two weeks? I've never tried to put one together. Is that fast?"

"You bet it is. Look on the side of the box it says 'From one to five years.'"

The teacher announced that she was giving a true or false test today.

Danny was ready for her. He'd put a quarter in his pocket earlier this morning just in case. After the test had been distributed, he pulled the coin out and began flipping it; heads for true, tails for false.

197

But he was still in his seat flipping the coin long after the other students had left.

"Are you having any trouble?" asked his teacher.

"No, no," Danny said proudly. "I finished a half hour ago, but right now, I'm just checking my answers."

An absent-minded professor stood before his class and said, "Students, today we will be dissecting a frog in order to learn more about how his systems work."

He took a paper bag out of the refrigerator and emptied its contents onto the desk. Out came a sandwich, and a cookie.

"That's odd," he said, "I distinctly remember, I already ate my lunch."

Two friends were talking, and one said, "I don't believe you ever went to school."

"Yes, I did. I went to the Immoral School."

"Never heard of it. What kind of school was that?"

"Oh, you know, Immoral school. It had no principal and no class."

The teacher asked, "I have five apples and seven students. How would you divide the apples so each student could have an equal amount?"

"Simple," said a little boy from the back of the room. "I'd make applesauce."

"Honestly, Jimmy, your handwriting is atrocious," said the teacher. "You're going to have to learn to do better."

"If I did that," Jimmy complained, "*then* you'd probably start correcting my spelling."

The Sense of Humor

"Class, we've been studying about Russia, so who can tell me what their former ruler was called?" asked the teacher.

"Tsar," a boy answered.

"That's right, and who can tell me what his wife was called?"

"Tsarina," a girl answered.

"Right again. And what were the Tsar's children called?"

From the back of the class a voice answered, "Tsardines?"

"I had a terrible semester," a boy in high school told his girlfriend.

"It couldn't have been that bad," she said.

"Oh yes, it was. I failed everything except chemistry."

"How is that possible?" she asked.

"Simple," he told her. "I didn't take chemistry this semester."

A nursery school teacher was delivering a station wagon full of kids home one day when a fire truck rumbled past. Sitting in the front seat of the fire truck was a Dalmatian dog. The children started to discuss the dog's duties.

"They use him to keep crowds back," said one child.

"No," said another, "he's just for good luck."

Then a third child ended the argument. "They use the dog," she said, "to find the fire hydrant."

While waiting for her first appointment in the reception room of a new dentist, a woman noticed his certificate, which bore his full name.

Suddenly, she remembered that a tall, handsome boy with the same name had been in her high school class some forty years ago. Upon seeing him, however, she quickly discarded any such thought. This balding, gray-haired man with the deeply lined face was too old to have ever been her classmate.

After he examined her teeth, she asked him if he had attended the local high school.

"Yes," he said.

"When did you graduate?" she asked.

"Forty years ago."

"Why, you were in my class!" she exclaimed.

He looked at her closely and then asked, "What subject did you teach?

A college science class was preparing for their exam. They had been cramming for days. As the students came into their classroom on the day of the test, they noticed a dozen birds standing on perches. But, each bird had been covered with a cloth bag so only their feet were showing. The teacher explained they were to identify all twelve birds simply by looking at their feet.

One student, who had studied especially hard, simply blew up. In exasperation, he stormed to the front of the room, tossed his paper on the desk and turned to leave. He muttered, "That is the dumbest idea any teacher has ever had. Who could possibly identify even one of those stupid birds, just by looking at its feet?"

"Just one moment," the teacher protested, "What is your name?"

"My name?" the student asked in a huff. Then he pulled up his pant legs, looked down at his feet and demanded, "You tell me!"

Three children were making too much noise in the school library. The librarian scolded, "Shhh, please be quiet. The children next to you aren't able to read."

"That is so sad," one of the noisy students said, "I've been able to read since pre-school."

WORK

The man walked into a fast food restaurant and pointed a gun at the woman behind the counter. "Give me all the cash," he demanded.

"Is that for here or to go?" she asked.

A raw recruit began his work in the German coast guard. His superior officer sat him in front of all the radio equipment and a microphone. He gave only brief instructions, then left the young man alone. Within minutes there was a distress call on the radio.

"This is the captain of a cargo ship. We are sinking ... I repeat, we're sinking!"

The radio operator quickly looked around the room to see if anyone could help, but he was all alone. He swallowed hard, leaned into the microphone and tried to smile. Then he said, "Um ... what are you ... *sinking* ... about?"

A film crew is shooting on location deep in the desert. One day, an old Indian came up to the director and said, "Tomorrow rain." The next day it rained.

A week later, the Indian came up to the director again and said, "Tomorrow storm." The next day there was a terrible hailstorm.

"This Indian is incredible," said the director. He told his secretary to hire the Indian to predict the weather. But, after several successful predictions, the old Indian didn't show up for two weeks.

Finally the director sent for him. "I have to shoot my biggest scene tomorrow, and I'm depending on you. What will the weather be like?"

The Indian shrugged his shoulders. "Don't know—radio's broken."

A Texan lands in Sydney and is picked up by a taxi. After requesting a tour of the city, he starts into a tirade about the small town airport and how in Texas he has a bigger runway on his ranch. They're soon crossing the Sydney Harbor Bridge and the Texan says, "I have a duck pond bigger than that harbor and a walking bridge over it that makes this one look like a toy."

The taxi driver is pretty fed up just as a kangaroo jumps out in front of them. He swerved out of the way, slammed on the brakes, turned to the man in the back seat and said, "Lousy rabbits!"

An angry motorist in a beat up old car went back to the garage where he'd bought an expensive battery just six months earlier. "Listen," he grumbled to the owner, "when I bought this battery you said it would be the *last* battery my car would ever need. It died after only six months!"

"I'm sorry," the garage owner said, "but when I saw your car, I didn't think *it* would last that long."

A young man was taking his verbal test to join the police force. He was asked, "If you were driving your police car alone on a lonely road at night and were being chased by a gang of criminals with guns driving seventy miles an hour, what would you do?"

Without skipping a beat, he said, "I'd do eighty!"

The Sense of Humor

May I take your order?" the waiter asked.

"Yes, how do you prepare your chickens?"

"Oh, nothing special, sir. We just tell them straight out they're going to die."

A traveler was waiting at the airport for his flight to Pittsburgh. He sees a machine with a sign that reads: "Your Height, Your Weight, Your Fortune—One Dollar."

He stepped on the scale and pushed a dollar bill in the slot. Out came a card that said: "You are five-feet-ten-inches tall. You weigh one hundred sixty pounds and you are waiting for the flight to Pittsburgh."

The man thought, *How could a machine know all that?* Then he got an idea, *I'll fool it.* He ran to the men's room, rolled up his coat collar, put on a baseball cap and a fake beard. He slipped back out, sneaked along the wall, ran around the corner, jumped back on the scale and quickly fed another dollar into the slot.

Out popped a another card that read: "You are five-feet-ten-inches tall. You weigh one hundred sixty pounds and while you were messing around in the men's room, you missed your flight to Pittsburgh."

A foreman sent out two crews to put up power poles along a new stretch of highway. He asked them to report back at the end of the day. Both crews were gone the entire day and returned just as it was getting dark. He asked the leader of the first crew how many poles they had installed.

"Eleven."

The foreman patted the guy on the back and said, "That's not too bad." Then he went to the leader of the second crew and asked the same question.

"We put two in."

The foreman was furious. "Two! You only finished two? The other crew installed eleven!"

"Yeah," the leader said, "but you should have seen how much those guys left sticking out of the ground!"

It was Christmas, and the judge was in a merry mood as he asked the prisoner, "What are you charged with?"

"Doing my Christmas shopping early," said the defendant.

"That's no big offence," said the judge. "How early were you doing this shopping?" "Before the store was open."

A man got a job as a night watchman at a factory. There had been a lot of thefts by the workers at night. So every morning, when the night shift workers passed through the gate, it was his job to check their bags and pockets to make sure nothing was being stolen. Things were going along very well his first night on the job until a man pushing a wheelbarrow filled with aluminum cans came through the gate.

Aha, he thought, *that man thinks he can cover up what he's stealing with those cans.* The guard picked through the cans, only to find nothing. Still he felt that the man was acting strangely, so he questioned him about the empty cans.

"I get a little extra money when I recycle, so I go into the lunchroom and pick up all the ones people have thrown away."

The guard let him pass but decided to keep a close eye on him. The next night it was the same and the night after that. Week in, week out, this went on. The same guy would push the wheelbarrow full of cans past the guard's checkpoint. The guard would always check and find nothing.

Then one night about a year later, the guard reported for work and found a message left for him to report to his supervisor. He walked into the office but before he could say a word, his boss said, "You're fired!"

"Fired?" he asked in total surprise. "Why? What'd I do?"

"It was your job to make sure that no one stole anything from this plant and you've failed. So you're fired."

"Wait a minute, what do you mean failed? Nobody ever stole anything from this place while I was on guard."

"Oh, really," said the supervisor. "Then how come almost three hundred wheelbarrows are missing?"

The CEO called one of his employees into the office. "Rob," he said, "you've been with the company for a year. You started off in the mailroom, a month later you were promoted to a sales position and one month after that, you were promoted to district manager of the sales department. Just four months later, you were promoted to vice-chairman. Now it's time for me to retire and I want you to take over the company. What do you say to that?"

"Thanks," the employee said.

"Thanks?" the boss replied. "Is that all you can say? Thanks!"

"Okay, okay," the employee said. "Thanks ... Dad."

Martin was a slow worker and found it difficult to hold down a job. After a visit to the job center, he was offered work at the local zoo. When he arrived for his first day, the keeper, aware of his reputation, told him to take care of the tortoise section. Later, the keeper dropped by to see how Martin was getting along and found him standing by an empty cage. "Where are the tortoises?" he asked.

"I can't believe it," Martin said. "I just opened the door and then ... whooooosh!"

When the census taker knocked on Miss Whitman's door, she

answered all his questions except one. She refused to tell him how old she was.

"But everyone tells their age to the census taker," he said.

"Did Miss Maisy Hill and Miss Daisy Hill tell you their ages?"

"Certainly."

"Well, I'm the same age as they are," she snapped and shut the door. He wrote on her form, "As old as the Hills."

A man moves to Staten Island. He loves living there, but hates having to take the ferry home every day. If he misses one late at night, he has to wait another hour or so for the next ferry. One Friday night, after a long, hard day at work, he gets to the dock and there's the ferry. It's only twenty feet out. So he decides, *I'm not going to wait this time.* He runs, takes a flying leap, and skids across the deck on his hands and knees. He has a few cuts and bruises, and his pants are torn, but he's safe on the deck.

He gets up, dusts himself off and says to one of the passengers, "Whew, I just made it!"

"You sure did," the passenger said, "but if you'd waited another minute or two, this ferry is about to dock."

A woman is heading to Florida for her winter vacation. When she gets to the airline counter, she hands her ID to the agent and puts her luggage on the scale to be checked through.

She tells the agent, loud enough for everyone around her to hear, "I'd like you to send my green suitcase to Hawaii, my red suitcase to London, and my dog to Albuquerque."

The agent doesn't quite understand and says, "I'm sorry, but we can't do that."

"Oh really? I am so relieved to hear you say that, because that's exactly what you did when I went to Florida last year."

A man stops at a rural gas station to fill his tank. As he's pumping his gas, he sees these two men working along the roadside.

One man digs a hole two or three feet deep and then moves on.

Then another man comes along and fills each hole back up with dirt.

The man who's been watching asks them, "What on earth are you doing?"

"Well, we work for the county planting trees," one of the workmen says.

"But one of you is digging holes and the other fills them back up. You're not accomplishing a thing. Aren't you wasting the taxpayers money?"

"You don't understand, Mister," the other workman says, leaning on his shovel and wiping sweat from his forehead. "Usually there are three of us: me, Ralph, and Jerry. I dig the hole, Ralph sticks in the tree and Jerry fills in the dirt. Now, just because Ralph is sick today, that's no reason me and Jerry can't still do our work."

This guy moves from the city to the country, and decides he's going to be a farmer. He heads to the local farm supply and tells the man, "Give me a hundred baby chickens."

So the man fills his order.

A week later, the man comes back and says, "Give me two hundred baby chickens." The man fills this order just like before.

Another week goes by and the man is back again. "This time I'd better have five hundred baby chickens."

"Wow," says the clerk. "You must be doing really well."

"Naw," says the man with a sigh, "I must be plantin' the little critters either too deep or too far apart."

An American executive goes to Japan on a business trip for the first time. He hates Japanese food, so he asks the desk clerk at his hotel if there is anyplace he can get something different.

The clerk tells him there's a pizza place that delivers. Back in his room, the businessman orders a pizza. About thirty minutes later, the delivery man shows up at the door.

The businessman takes the pizza, but before he can even pay for it, he starts sneezing uncontrollably.

"What in the world did you put on my pizza?" he asks.

The delivery man bows deeply. "Just what you order, sir ... 'pepper *only.*'"

A department store manager hears one of his clerks saying to a customer, "No, ma'am, we haven't had any for some time now, and it doesn't look like we'll be getting more any time soon."

Shocked by what he hears, the manager rushes over to the customer, who is about to walk out the door. "That isn't true, ma'am," he says. "Of course, we'll have some soon. In fact, we placed an order for it just a few days ago."

Then the shopper smiled, turned, and left.

The manager takes the clerk aside and says, "Never, *never*, under any circumstances, tell a customer we don't have something. If we don't have it, you tell them we've ordered it, and it'll soon be delivered. Now, what was it she wanted?"

"Rain," the clerk told him.

A salesman gets tired of his job and gives it up to become a policeman. One day, at the coffee shop, he meets an old friend who asks him how he likes his new work.

The Sense of Humor

"Well," says the salesman-turned-cop, "the pay is good and the hours aren't too bad. But my favorite part is the customer's always wrong."

As the woman was instructing her new maid on the great care required in handling certain valuable household objects, she pointed to the dining room and said with pride, "That table goes back to Louis the Fourteenth!

"Oh, that's nothing," the maid said. "My whole living- room set goes back to Sears on the fifteenth."

The manager of a large office noticed a new man one day and told him to come into his office. "What's your name?" he asked the new guy.

"John," the new guy said.

The manager growled, "Look ... I don't know what kind of a namby-pamby place you used to work, but around here, I don't call *anyone* by their first name. It breeds familiarity and that leads to a breakdown in authority. I refer to *all* my employees by their last name *only*, no exceptions ... Smith, Jones, Baker ... and that's it. You, on the other hand, will call me Mr. Robertson. Now that we got that straight, what's *your* last name?"

"Darling. My name is John Darling."

"Right, so *John*, the next thing I wanted to tell you is …"

A veterinarian was feeling sick and went to see his doctor. The doctor asked all the usual questions, about his symptoms, what he had been eating and how long had he not felt well.

The veterinarian interrupted him and said, "Hey, I might be a vet—but at least I don't have to ask my patients all these questions. I can tell what's wrong just by looking. Can't you?"

So the doctor nodded, looked him over, wrote a prescription, handed it to him and said, "Here you are. Of course, if that doesn't work, we'll have to have you put to sleep."

Fred, Jim and Scott attended a convention and shared a large suite at the top of a seventy-five-story hotel. After a long day of meetings, they came back to find the elevators in their hotel were broken and they'd have to climb up seventy-five flights of stairs to get to their room.

About a fourth of the way up, Bill said to Jim and Scott, "I have an idea. Let's break the monotony and concentrate on something more pleasant. I'll tell jokes for twenty-five flights, Jim can sing songs for the next twenty-five flights and, Scott, you can tell sad stories the rest of the way."

At the twenty-sixth floor, Bill stopped telling his jokes and Jim started to sing. He had a terrible voice and they all laughed.

At the fifty-first floor, Jim stopped singing, and it was time for Scott to start telling sad stories.

"I'll tell my saddest story first," he said, "I left the key to our room down in the rental car!

A long train with two engines was crossing the country. After they had gone some distance, one of the engines broke down.

No problem, the engineer thought and he continued on at half power. A little farther the second engine conked out and the train came to a stop.

The engineer decided to tell the passengers why the train had stopped, so he made an announcement, "Ladies and gentlemen, I have some good news and some bad news. The bad news is that both engines have failed, and we may be stuck here for a while. The good news is you're not in an airplane."

During training exercises, a lieutenant was driving down a muddy back road when he saw another jeep stuck in the mud with an angry colonel behind the wheel.

The lieutenant pulled alongside and asked with a smile, "Is your jeep stuck, sir?"

The colonel walked over, handed him the keys and said, "Nope. Yours is."

A man went into a busy flower shop with a large sign that read, "Say It With Flowers."

"Wrap up one rose," he said.

"Only one?" the florist asked.

"Just one," he answered. "I'm a man of few words."

A salesman was demonstrating unbreakable combs at the mall by putting the comb through all kinds of rough treatment.

Finally, to make a lasting impression, he bent the comb completely in half, and it snapped with a loud crack. Without missing a beat, he held up both halves of the 'unbreakable' comb for everyone to see and said, "And this, ladies and gentlemen, is what an unbreakable comb looks like on the inside ..."

There was an engineer who had a gift for fixing mechanical problems. After serving his company well for over thirty years, he retired.

A few months later, the company called him about an impossible problem they were having with one of their multi-million dollar machines. They'd tried everything, and everyone, to fix it but nothing had helped. In desperation, they called on the retired engineer who had solved so many problems for them in the past.

The engineer reluctantly took the job. He spent an entire day studying the huge machine. At the end of the day, he marked a small "x" in chalk on a particular component of the machine and said proudly, "The problem is right here."

The defective part was replaced and the machine worked perfectly again. When the company got a bill for $50,000 from the engineer for his services, they demanded an itemized accounting of the charges.

The engineer wrote on the invoice:

Chalk mark $1

Knowing where to put the chalk mark ... $49,999

A New York family bought a ranch out West where they intended to raise cattle. Friends came to visit and asked if the ranch had a name.

"Well," said the would-be-cattleman, "I wanted to call it the Bar-J. My wife favored the Suzy-Q. One son liked the Flying-W, and the daughter wanted the Lazy-Y. So, we're calling it the Bar-J-Suzy-Q-Flying-W-Lazy-Y Ranch."

"But you don't have any cattle?"

"No, sir. So far none of them survived the branding."

A young man decided to join the police force. As a recruit, he was asked on an the exam, "What would you do if you had to arrest your own mother?"

He wrote, "I'd call for backup."

The optimist: The glass is half full.

The pessimist: The glass is half empty.

The engineer: This container is twice as large as it needs to be.

A rookie police officer was assigned to ride in a cruiser with a seasoned partner. They got a call on the radio telling them to disperse some people loitering on a street corner.

The Sense of Humor

The officers drove to the area and noticed a small crowd standing on a corner.

The rookie rolled down his window and said, "Okay, people. Let's get off the corner."

At first no one moved, so he barked out again, "I said *move* it!" The people didn't know quite what to do but they began to leave anyway. The rookie turned to his partner and asked, "So, how did I do?"

"Pretty good," the veteran said, "considering that's a bus stop."

"Flight 4112," the air traffic controller said, "turn right forty-five degrees for noise abatement."

"Roger," the pilot responded, "but…we're at thirty-five thousand feet. How much noise can we make up here?"

The controller asked him, "Captain, have you ever heard the racket a smaller jet makes when it hits a 747?"

A champion jockey is about to enter a big race on a new horse.

The horse's trainer meets him before the race and says, "This is the fastest horse in the race, but you have to remember one thing. Every time you approach a jump, you need to yell, "Allleee ooop!" in the horse's ear. If you do that, you'll win easily."

The jockey thinks the trainer is nuts but he promises to do what he says.

The race starts and they approach the first hurdle. The jockey ignores the trainer's advice and the horse crashes right through the center of the jump. As they approach the second hurdle, the jockey is embarrassed so he only whispers "Allleee ooop" in the horse's ear. The same thing happens … the horse crashes straight through the center of the jump. At the third hurdle, the jockey decides, he'd better do what the trainer told him and yells, "Allleee ooop!" in the horse's ear.

Sure enough, the horse glides right over the jump. This continues for the rest of the race, but because of the first two crashes, the horse only finishes third. The trainer is furious and asks the jockey what went wrong.

"There's nothing wrong with me, it's this crummy horse. What is he—deaf or something?"

The trainer says, "Deaf? *Deaf?* The horse is not deaf. He's blind!"

Officer: "Soldier, do you have change for a dollar?"

Soldier: "Just a minute, buddy. Let me look."

Officer: "That's no way to speak to an officer! Now let's try it again. Do you have change for a dollar?"

Soldier: "No, sir!"

Government engineers were surveying and found that in a certain area, the New Hampshire and Maine border had to be changed. They stopped to tell a farmer that he was no longer in Maine but now lived in New Hampshire.

After a long pause, the farmer grunted and said, "That's a relief. I couldn't take another one of those awful Maine winters."

An elderly fisherman wrote to a mail order house: "Please send me one of those gasoline engines for my boat you show on page 720, and if it's any good, I'll send you a check."

A short time later the company wrote: "Please send us a check and if it's any good, we'll send you the motor."

Someone broke into the police station and stole all the toilets.

A spokesperson was quoted as saying, "It's embarrassing, but we have absolutely nothing to go on."

The Sense of Humor

Some Boeing employees decided to steal a life raft for a 747. They were successful in getting the raft out of the plant and home. Later they took it out for a float down the river and were surprised when a Coast Guard helicopter hovered right above them. It was homing in on the emergency locator that is activated any time a life raft is inflated.

They don't work there anymore.

"Do you believe in life after death?" the boss asked one of his employees.

"Yes, sir, I do."

"Well, then, that clears up everything, because after you left here early yesterday to go to your grandmother's funeral, she dropped by to see you."

The owner of a large factory decided to make a surprise inspection and check up on his employees. He noticed one man leaning lazily against a post.

"Just how much are you being paid a week?" the owner grumbled.

"Three hundred and fifty bucks," the man told him.

The owner grabbed his wallet, counted out three-hundred-fifty dollars, slapped the money into the man's hand, and said, "Here's a week's pay. Now get out of here and don't you ever come back!"

The man turned to leave, and the owner asked another worker, "How long has that lazy bum been working for me anyway?"

"Oh, he doesn't work here. That's just the pizza delivery guy!"

This sportsman goes ice fishing, takes out an auger and starts drilling a hole in the ice.

LOUD VOICE FROM ABOVE: "There's no fish there."

The guy goes to another spot and drills again.

LOUD VOICE FROM ABOVE: "There's no fish there, either."

He tries a third spot.

LOUD VOICE FROM ABOVE: "None there either."

Getting a little nervous he looks up and asks: "Are you God?"

LOUD VOICE FROM ABOVE: "Nope. Just the arena manager."

Two gas company servicemen, a senior training supervisor, and a young trainee were out checking meters in a suburban neighborhood. They parked their truck at one end of an alley and worked their way to the other end. At the last house, a woman was looking out her kitchen window and watched the two men as they checked her gas meter.

After they finished the meter check, the senior supervisor challenged his younger coworker, "Last one to the truck is a rotten egg."

As they came running up to the truck, they saw the lady from that last house was huffing and puffing right behind them. They stopped and asked her what was wrong.

All out of breath she said, "When I see two men from the gas company running away from my house as fast as you were, I figured I'd better run, too!"

A fire started on some grassland near a farm. The county fire department was called, but the fire was more than they could handle. Someone suggested they call in a nearby volunteer crew, but it was doubtful they could be of much help.

The volunteers arrived in a dilapidated old fire truck, rumbled straight towards the fire, and stopped in the middle of the flames.

They jumped off the truck and frantically started spraying water in all directions. Soon they had broken the blaze into two easily controllable parts.

The Sense of Humor

Watching all this, the farmer was so impressed with the volunteers' work and so grateful his farm had been spared, that when it was all over, he gave them a check for a thousand dollars right on the spot.

A local news reporter asked the volunteer fire captain what he planned to do with the money. "That oughta be obvious," he said, wiping ashes off his coat. "The first thing we're gonna do is get the brakes fixed on that old truck!"

There is a dangerous computer virus going around and it is transmitted through email. If you get an email message with the subject: "Virus Alert!" do not open it. If you do, the virus scrambles the second half of every text file on your system.

Very important: If you do get this virus, the first thing dlkfjaid dfdjas nairb gfdq40wt yaj asdfsdg dluog av da agj asdfajpg as dflasidffnm asd difvu asdfa vgoiae vdsofj we dasdf 9efm sd dag0 g adf as dg 0vbwe ads gwefawe ads vewerwe dsf!

One night, a lady stumbled into the police station with a black eye. She said she heard a noise in her back yard and went to investigate. The next thing she knew, she was hit in the eye and knocked out cold.

An officer was dispatched to her house to check it out, and he came back an hour and a half later with a black eye.

"Did you get hit by the same person?" his captain asked.

"No. But I did step on the same rake."

A Texan was visiting a Maine farmer ("fahmah"). The Texas rancher was boasting about the size of his ranch: "I can get into my pickup, drive all day and still not reach the boundary of my ranch," he bragged.

The Mainer shook his head, "Aayuhh. I used to have a truck just like that."

An FBI agent was talking to a bank teller after the bank had been robbed for the third time by the same bandit. "Did you notice anything special about the man?" he asked.

"Yes. He seems to be wearing nicer clothes each time."

When he checked in to buy a ticket, a passenger didn't know that Indianapolis was on Eastern Standard Time and Chicago was on Central Standard Time.

"The next flight leaves at one p.m.," the ticket agent said, "and arrives in Chicago at one-oh-one p.m."

"Could you repeat that, please?" the passenger asked.

The agent said, "It leaves at one p.m., and gets into Chicago at one-oh-one p.m. "Would you like a reservation?"

The passenger thought for a minute and said, "No ... but I think I'll stick around and just watch that thing take off."

A farmer was suing a trucking company for injuries sustained in an accident. In court, the company's high priced lawyer questioned him.

"Didn't you say, at the scene of the accident, 'I'm fine'?" asked the lawyer.

The farmer said, "Well, I'll tell you what happened. I had just loaded my favorite mule, Jenny, into the ..."

"I didn't ask for any details," the lawyer interrupted. "Just answer the question. Did you or did you not say, at the scene of the accident, 'I'm fine'?"

The farmer continued, "As I was saying, I had just loaded Jenny into the trailer and I was driving down the road ..."

The lawyer interrupted again. "Judge, I am trying to establish the fact that, at the scene of the accident, this man told the Highway

The Sense of Humor

Patrolman he was just fine. *Now*, several months *after* the accident, he's suing my client. I believe he is a fraud. Please tell him to simply answer the question."

But the judge was interested in Farmer's side of the story and told the lawyer, "I'd like to hear what he has to say about his mule."

The farmer thanked the judge and proceeded. "Well, as I was saying, I had just loaded Jenny, my favorite mule, into the trailer and was driving her down the highway when this huge semi-truck and trailer ran the stop sign and smacked right into the side of my truck. I was thrown into one ditch and Jenny was thrown into the other. I was hurtin' real bad and didn't want to move, but I could hear ole Jenny moaning and groaning. I knew she was in terrible shape just by her sounds. Shortly after the accident, a highway patrolman came to the scene. He could hear Jenny moaning and groaning so he went over to her. After he looked at her, he took out his gun and shot her right between the eyes to put her out of her misery. Then the patrolman came across the road. With the gun still in his hand, he looked at me and said, 'Your mule was in pretty bad shape. I'm sorry, but I had to shoot her. So tell me. How are you feeling?'"

Scientists at NASA had developed a gun built specifically to launch dead chickens at the windshields of airliners, military jets, and space shuttles all traveling at maximum velocity. The idea was to simulate the frequent incidents of collisions with airborne birds to test the strength of the windshields.

British engineers heard about the gun and were eager to test it on the windshields of their new high-speed trains. Arrangements were made to borrow the gun. But when it was fired, the engineers were shocked as the chicken hurtled out of the barrel, crashed into the shatterproof windshield, smashed it to smithereens, crashed through the control console, snapped the engineer's backrest in two and embedded itself in the back wall of the cabin. The horrified Britons sent NASA the disastrous results of their experiment, along with the specifications of the windshield, and asked the U.S. scientists for suggestions.

NASA's response was simple:

"Next time, thaw ... out ... the ... chicken."

A young, foolish pilot wanted to sound cool on the aviation frequencies. So, as he made his first approach to the small field at night, instead of using any official language to the tower, he just said: "Guess who?"

The controller switched off the lights on the field and answered: "Guess where!"

In the employee's washroom at a restaurant, the manager had placed a sign directly above the sink that said, "Think!"

The next day, when he went to the washroom, to check on the sign, there, right above the soap dispenser, someone had carefully lettered another sign that said—"Thoap!"

There was a veterinarian who put himself through veterinary school working nights as a taxidermist. When he graduated, he decided he could combine his two vocations to better serve the needs of his patients and their owners, double his practice and his income. He opened his new offices with a sign on the door that said, "Hillcrest Veterinary Clinic and Taxidermy—Either way, you get your pet back!"

The police had a stroke of luck with a robbery suspect who just couldn't keep his mouth shut during a lineup. When detectives asked each man in the lineup to repeat the words, "Give me all your money or I'll shoot," the man shouted, "That's *not* what I said!"

The Sense of Humor

At the end of a job interview, the human resources director asked a young engineer fresh out of MIT, "And what starting salary were you looking for?"

The Engineer said, "Something in the neighborhood of one hundred fifty thousand dollars, depending on the benefits package."

So the interviewer said, "Well, what would you say to a package of five-weeks' vacation, fourteen paid holidays, full medical and dental, a company matching retirement fund to fifty percent of your salary and a company car leased every 2 years? Shall we say a red Lexus?"

The engineer sat straight up and said, "Wow! Are you kidding?"

"Yes I am, but you started it."

Marine Corporal Jones was assigned to the induction center to advise new recruits about their government benefits—especially their GI insurance.

It wasn't long before Captain Smith noticed that Jones had almost a hundred percent record for insurance sales, which had never happened before. Rather than ask how he did it, the captain stood in the back of the room and listened to the sales pitch.

Jones explained basics of the GI Insurance to the new recruits, then he said. "If you have GI Insurance, go into battle and are killed, the government has to pay your beneficiaries two hundred fifty thousand dollars. But if you don't have GI insurance, and you go into battle and get killed, the government only has to pay a maximum of six thousand dollars. Now, think about it. Who do you think they're going to send into battle first?"

It was snowing heavily and blowing to the point that visibility was almost zero when the new secretary got off work. She made her way to

221

her car and wondered how she was going to make it home. She sat in her car while it warmed up and thought about her situation. Finally, she remembered her daddy's advice that if she ever got caught in a blizzard, she should wait until a snowplow came by and follow it. That way she wouldn't get stuck in a drift.

Soon a plow did come by and she started to follow it, and this made her feel much better.

She followed the snowplow and was feeling pretty proud of herself. As they continued on, she was not having any problem with the blizzard conditions.

After quite some time, she was surprised when the snowplow stopped. The driver got out, came back to her car, and motioned for her to roll down the window.

The snowplow operator wanted to know if she was all right since she'd been following him for such a long time. She said she was fine and told him about her father's advice to always follow a snowplow if she was ever caught in a storm.

The driver said it was okay with him and she could continue if she wanted to, but he was finished with the Wal-Mart parking lot and was going over to do Target next.

A man wearing rumpled clothes walked into a bank in New York City and asked for the loan officer. He said he's going to Europe on business for two weeks and needs to borrow five thousand dollars.

The bank officer tells him the bank will need some kind of collateral for the loan. So the man hands over the keys to his new Rolls Royce parked on the street in front of the bank. The bank agrees to accept the car as security for the loan. A bank employee drives the Rolls into the bank's underground garage and parks it there.

Two weeks later, the man returns, pays back the five thousand dollars and the interest, which comes to just a few dollars.

The loan officer says, "We are very happy to have had your business, and this transaction has worked out quite nicely, but there is one question. While you were away, we checked and found out that you are a multi-millionaire. What I don't understand is why you would even bother to borrow five thousand dollars?"

The man said, "Oh that's simple. Where else could I park my car in New York City for two weeks for only a few bucks?"

Pulling his big rig into the parking lot of a small roadside diner, the trucker went in, sat on a stool at the counter and ordered a turkey club sandwich. Just after his food had been served, a group of ten bikers came in. The leader walked up to where the trucker was sitting, grabbed the sandwich from his plate, ate the rest of it and laughed. The truck driver didn't say a word. He got up, paid the bill, and walked out of the diner.

"He wasn't much of a man," the biker said.

"No," the owner said from behind the counter. "He's not much of a truck driver either. Look, he just backed his rig up and smashed ten motorcycles!"

A photographer for a big magazine was assigned to take pictures of a great forest fire. He was advised that a small plane would be waiting to fly him over the inferno.

The photographer arrived at the airstrip just an hour before sundown. Sure enough, a small Cessna was waiting. He jumped in with his equipment and shouted, "Let's go!" The tense man sitting in the pilot's seat swung the plane into the wind and soon they were in the air, but he was flying erratically.

"Fly over the north side of the fire," the photographer said. "And make several low-level passes."

"Why?" asked the nervous pilot.

"Because I'm going to take pictures!" yelled the photographer. "I'm a photographer, and photographers take pictures."

The pilot cried out, "I … I thought you were the *flight* instructor?"

A rancher bought two horses, but he could never tell them apart. A neighbor suggested he cut the tail of one horse and that worked great until the other horse got his tail caught in a gate. It tore just right and looked exactly like the other horse's tail.

Then the neighbor suggested he notch the ear of one horse. That worked fine until the other horse caught his ear on a barbed wire fence. Once again our friend couldn't tell them apart.

The neighbor suggested he measure the horses for height. When he did, he was very happy to find that the white horse was two inches taller than the black horse.

A big city lawyer was called in on a case between a farmer and a large railroad company. The farmer noticed his prize cow was missing from the field that the train ran through. He filed suit against the railroad for the value of the cow. The case was to be tried before the justice of the peace. The attorney immediately cornered the farmer and tried to get him to settle out of court. The lawyer did his best selling job, and the farmer reluctantly agreed to take half, of what he was claiming, to settle the case.

After the farmer signed the release and took the check, the young lawyer couldn't help but gloat a little over his success.

He told the farmer, "You know, I hate to tell you this but I put one over on you in there. I couldn't have won this case. The engineer was asleep when the train went through your property that night. I didn't have one witness to put on the stand."

The Sense of Humor

The old farmer said, "Well, I'll tell you, young feller, I was a little worried about winning the case myself because that dumb cow came back home this morning!"

The coast guard recently stopped a boat off the California coast that was loaded with marijuana. There was so much of the stuff that they couldn't decide how to get rid of it. Finally they located a company nearby that had a huge kiln with a tall chimney. They made a deal with the owners to burn the drugs.

For a time all went well, but then a flock of birds flew right through the smoke pouring out of the top of the stack. As it turned out, these birds were terns. They were native to the area and were endangered, so the environmentalists followed them to see if they were okay.

And, of course, they discovered that no tern was left unstoned.

A young executive was leaving the office one evening when he found the CEO standing in front of a shredder with a piece of paper in his hand.

"Listen," the CEO said. "This is a very important original document and my secretary is gone for the day. Can you make this thing work?"

"Certainly," said the young executive. He turned on the machine, inserted the paper, and pressed the start button.

"Excellent, excellent!" the CEO said, as his paper disappeared into the shredder.

"All I need is one copy."

An unemployed actor is getting pretty desperate for work. He finds this guy from the zoo who is looking for actors. The guy explains that they have spent so much money getting the habitat just right, they ran out of money to buy the ape they wanted. So they hired the actor to wear an ape costume and sit in the cage.

During the first few days, the actor just sat there thinking he doesn't look real and no one is stupid enough to fall for this stunt. Finally he gets bored and decides to walk around and examine his little cage. He notices that people are watching his every movement. He decides to give them a show. After a couple of weeks, he's swinging on the poles and dancing around making a lot of gorilla noises and is drawing quite a crowd.

One day he's showing off for a group of kids. He's swinging around and around a pole when all of a sudden, his hand slips and he goes flying up over the top of his cage, right into the lion's cage. Immediately, the lion gets up and walks toward him.

The actor backs up as far as he can, and screams at the top of his lungs, "Help me! Please! Somebody help me!"

"Shut up, you idiot!" the lion whispered, "or you're gonna get us both fired."

These two bumpkins decided to take a few days off from work and see the sights. So one morning, they stopped to pick up a few supplies at a local store. One of the men told the clerk, "We need some maters, taters, and onions.

The clerk said, "You're from the hills aren't you?"

And the bumpkins said, "Yea. How'd you know?"

The clerk said, "It's because of the way you talk."

So as they left, one looked at the other and said, "That was pretty neat. Can I try it the next time?"

The other one said, "Sure."

So the next morning, they went into a different store, and the second country boy said to the storekeeper, "We need some maters, taters, and onions."

The Sense of Humor

And the storekeeper said, "You're from the hills aren't you?"

Grinning the man said, "Yup, yup, and I bet you knew that because of the way I talk."

The storekeeper said, "No. It's because this is a *hardware* store!"

Some crusty old cowboys were sitting around the campfire bragging about some of the long cattle drives they'd been on during their lives. Each tale got bigger and better than the last.

Then one old timer bragged, "I was on a cattle drive that took four hundred head straight from Texas to London, England!"

After a brief silence someone asked, "How did you get across the Atlantic?"

He thought for a moment, then said, "Didn't go that way!"

Three lawyers and three engineers are traveling by train to the same conference. At the station, the three lawyers each buy tickets and watch as the three engineers buy only one ticket.

"How are three people going to travel on only one ticket?" a lawyer asked.

"Watch and you'll see," said one of the engineers.

They all board the train, and the lawyers take their seats, but all three engineers cram into a restroom and close the door. Shortly after the train leaves the station, the conductor comes around collecting tickets. He knocks on the restroom door and says, "Ticket, please."

The door opens just a crack and out comes a ticket. The conductor takes it and moves on.

The lawyers saw this and agreed it was a brilliant idea. So, after the conference, they decide to copy the engineers on the return trip and save some money. When they get to the station, they buy a single ticket. But this time, the engineers don't buy any tickets.

"How are you going to travel without a ticket," a lawyer asked.

"Watch and you'll see," the engineers told him.

When they board the train, the three lawyers cram into one restroom, and the three engineers cram into another one nearby.

After the train pulls out, one of the engineers leaves his restroom and walks over to the restroom where the lawyers are hiding.

He knocks on the door and says,

"Ticket, please."

After being bogged down in a muddy road, the driver paid a farmer fifty dollars to pull him out with a tractor.

After he was back on dry ground he said to the farmer, "At these prices, I'd think you'd be pulling people out of the mud day and night."

"Can't," the farmer told him. "At night, I have to haul more water for the hole."

On a foggy night at sea, the ship's captain saw what appeared to be the lights of another ship heading straight toward them. He told his signalman to contact the other ship by signal light. He sent the message, "Change your course ten degrees to the north."

The reply came, "Change your course ten degrees to the south."

The captain responded, "I am a captain. Change your course ten degrees to the north."

The response? "I am a seaman first class, but you change your course ten degrees to the south." The captain was furious. He had his signalman send,

"I am a battleship. You change your course ten degrees to the north."

The reply flashed back, "I am a lighthouse. Now you change your course ten degrees to the south."

The Sense of Humor

"Pilot to tower... we're four hundred miles from land, only eight hundred feet over the ocean and running out of fuel ... please instruct."

"Tower to pilot, tower to pilot ... repeat after me ... 'Our Father, who art in heaven ...'"

A guy walks into work and both of his ears are all bandaged up. The boss asks, "What happened to your ears?"

He says, "Yesterday I was ironing a shirt when the phone rang and I accidentally answered the iron."

The boss says, "Well, that explains one ear, but what happened to your other ear?"

"Well, I had to call the doctor, didn't I?"

A man was opening his new store and received a bouquet of flowers with a card that said, "Deepest Sympathy." While he was trying to figure it out, the phone rang. It was the florist apologizing for having sent the wrong card. "Oh, it's all right," said the storekeeper. "I'm a businessman and I understand how these things can happen."

"But," the florist said, "I accidentally sent your card to a funeral."

"Well, what did it say?" asked the storekeeper.

"'Congratulations on your new location'."

A man walks into a hardware store and asks for a chain saw that can cut six trees in an hour. The salesman recommends the top of the line model, and the man buys it.

The next day he brings it back and says, "This chainsaw is defective. I could only cut down one tree and it took me the whole day!"

The salesman takes the chain saw, starts it up to see what's wrng, and the man says, "Hey, what's that sound?"

229

A young businessman had just started his own firm. He'd rented a beautiful office and furnished it with antiques. He noticed a man coming into the outer office, so he picked up the phone and started to pretend he was closing a big deal. Finally, he hung up and asked the visitor, "Can I help you?"

The man said, "Sure buddy. I'm here to hook up your phones!"

A magician used to put on magic shows on a transatlantic liner, but he had a parrot that kept spoiling the tricks by saying "He's got it up his sleeve" or "That box has a false bottom." One day, the ship hit an iceberg and sank. The magician saved himself on a raft. Three days later, the parrot floated up on a crate and asked him, "Okay, I give up. Now tell me, where did you hide the boat?"

Three men were going to the guillotine. The first was a lawyer, who was led to the platform, blindfolded and his head was put on the block. The executioner pulled the lanyard but nothing happened. So, out of mercy, the authorities allowed him to go free.

The next man to the guillotine was a physician, and he laid his head on the block, they pulled the lanyard ... still nothing. The blade didn't come down. So, to be fair, they let him go, too.

The third man to the guillotine was an engineer. They led him to the guillotine and laid his head on the block. He looked up and said, "Hey, wait a minute. I think I see your problem."

"Hello? Is this the fire department?"

"Yes."

"Listen, my house is on fire, you've got to come right away, it's a big one."

"Okay, how do we get to your house?"

The Sense of Humor

"Don't you have those big, red trucks anymore?"

A state trooper was driving down the Interstate when he saw a truck driver pull over, walk to the side of his truck with a tire iron, bang on the side of truck several times, then get back in and drive away. Two miles down the road he did it again. Another two miles … same thing. The trooper pulled the trucker over and asked him to explain.

The driver told him, "The load limit is ten tons and I'm carrying fifteen tons of parakeets so I've got to keep some of them flying around all the time."

A dairy farmer is milking his cow and as he's milking, a fly comes along and goes right into the cow's ear. A little bit later, when the farmer notices the fly in the milk he says, "Hmmm. In one ear, out the udder."

A woman walked into a veterinarian's waiting room dragging a soaking wet rabbit on a leash. The rabbit does *not* want to be there.

"Sit, Fluffy, sit," she told the rabbit.

Fluffy just glared at her. Then he jumped up on another customer's lap and got water all over him.

"I said *sit*," the woman told the rabbit. She's embarrassed and tells the rabbit, "Come on, Fluffy. Will you please be good?"

Just then Fluffy picks a fight with a Doberman and chases it out of the office.

As she leaves to go after Fluffy, she turns to the rest of the people in the waiting room and says,

"I'm sorry, but I've just washed my hare, and can't do a thing with it!"

There was a Japanese man who went to America for sightseeing.

231

On the last day, he hailed a cab and told the driver to take him to the airport. During the journey, a Honda drove past the taxi. The Japanese man leaned out of the window excitedly and yelled, "Honda, very fast! Made in Japan!"

A little later, a Toyota sped past the taxi. Again, the Japanese man leaned out of the window and yelled, "Toyota, very fast! Made in Japan!"

Then a Mitsubishi sped past the taxi. For the third time, the man leaned out of the window and yelled, "Mitsubishi, very fast! Made in Japan!"

The cab driver was a little angry, but he kept quiet. And this went on until the taxi came to the airport. The fare was three hundred dollars. The Japanese man exclaimed, "Ahhh ... so expensive!" and the driver yelled back, "Meter, made in Japan. Very fast!"

A man was driving along a rural road one day when he saw a three-legged chicken running. So he drove alongside it for a while and, as he drove, he noticed the chicken was running at about thirty mph. *Pretty fast chicken,* he thought to himself. *I wonder how fast it can go?* So he sped up and the chicken did, too! They were both moving along at forty-five mph! The man in the car sped up again and, to his surprise, the chicken passed him at sixty mph!!! Suddenly the chicken turned off the road and ran down a long lane leading to a farmhouse. The man followed the chicken to the house and saw a man in the yard with dozens of three legged chickens.

The man in the car called out to the farmer "How did you get all these three legged chickens?"

The farmer told him, "I breed 'em that way. Ya see, it's me, my wife, and my son living here and we all like to eat the chicken leg. Since a chicken only has two legs, I started breeding this three-legged variety so we could all eat our favorite piece."

The Sense of Humor

"That's amazing! How do they taste?"

"Don't rightly know. We can't seem to catch 'em."

A police officer pulls over a car with three old ladies in it, and says, "Ma'am, this is a sixty-five mph highway. Why are you going so slow?"

She said, "Sir, I saw a lot of signs that said twenty-two, not sixty-five."

"That's not the speed limit. That's the name of the highway you're on!" he told her.

"Oh, how silly of me! Thank you for letting me know. I'll be more careful."

Then the officer looked in the backseat where two other women are shaking and trembling. "Excuse me," he asked, "but what's wrong with your friends back here? They're shaking something awful."

"Well, we just came off of highway one-twenty-six."

Sign in veterinarian's waiting room: "The doctor is in. Sit, Stay."

A woman went up to the manager of a department store and asked, "Are you hiring?"

"No we aren't. We already have all the help we can use."

"Then would it be asking too much for you to get someone to wait on me?"

A man was sent to prison. During his stay, he became a model prisoner who got along well with the guards and other inmates. The warden noticed this, and made arrangements for the prisoner to learn a skill in the carpenter shop. After a couple years, he was recognized as one of the best cabinetmakers around. The warden decided to do some remodeling by himself in his kitchen, but he had trouble getting the cabinets straight and especially in getting the counter to fit. So he asked the prisoner to come to his house and finish the job.

The prisoner objected and told the warden, "I'd really like to help you out, but it was "counter-fitting" that got me sent to prison in the first place."

A man went to a flight school, insisting he wanted to learn to fly that day. Since all the planes were currently in use, the busy owner agreed to instruct him on how to pilot the helicopter solely by radio.

He took him out, showed him how to start it, gave him the basics and then sent him on his way.

After the new pilot climbed a thousand feet, he radioed in. "I'm doing great! I love it up here! The view is so beautiful, and I'm starting to get the hang of this."

After two thousand feet, he radioed again, saying how easy it was to fly. The instructor watched him climb over three thousand feet, and was beginning to worry that he hadn't radioed in.

A few minutes later, the instructor watched in horror as the chopper crashed about half a mile away. He ran over and pulled the pilot from the wreckage.

When he asked what happened, the pilot said, "I don't know! Everything was going fine, but as I got higher, I started to get cold, but I can't remember anything after I turned off that big fan."

A jeweler watched as a huge truck pulled up in front of his store. The back came down and an elephant walked out. It broke one of the store's windows with its tusk and then, using its trunk like a vacuum cleaner, sucked up all of the jewelry. The elephant got back in the truck and it drove off.

When the jeweler finally regained his senses he called the police.

The Sense of Humor

Detectives came out and he told them his story.

"Could you describe the elephant?" a cop asked.

"An elephant is an elephant," he said. "You've seen one you've seen them all. What do you mean 'describe' him?"

"Well," said the policeman, "there are two kinds of elephants: African and Indian. The Indian elephant has smaller ears and is not as large as the African elephant."

"I can't help you out," said the frustrated jeweler. "This elephant had a stocking pulled over his head."

A man rushed in to his barber and yelled, "My hair is falling out. You gotta give me something to keep it in!"

"Of course," said the barber. Then he handed him a small paper sack and asked, "Will this be big enough?"

Harold got a new job painting yellow stripes out on the highway. On the first day, he put his brush into the paint and laid down a strip half a mile long. On the second day he only went half as far. By the third day he only went one block.

His boss noticed this and asked, "Why is it each time you go out, you paint a shorter and shorter line?"

"Well," said Harold, "each day I've had to start farther away from my bucket.

A salesman came back to the office, all excited. "I got my first two orders today!" he said.

"That's great, what were they?" asked the sales manager.

He opened his order book and read, "Get out, and stay out!"

Due to the current economic conditions, it was difficult to get a loan.

The vice president of a bank was listening to a junior executive talking on the phone. The junior executive said, "No … no … no … no … yes … no," and then he hung up the phone.

The vice president asked what he had agreed to when he told the customer, "yes."

"It's nothing to worry about," said the junior executive. "He just asked if I was still listening."

A man went on vacation and decided to call his partner to see how he was doing.

"How's everything at the office?" he asked.

"Things are okay, but I have some bad news."

"What is it?" he asked.

"We were robbed today."

"Robbed?" he asked.

"Yes, I'm afraid so."

"Don't be silly," the man told his partner. "Just put it back."

The president of a company came home one night, discouraged, and slumped into his favorite chair.

"What's wrong?" asked his wife.

"We're giving aptitude tests at the office this week. Today I took one and found out it's a good thing I own the company."

Two twin, stuttering blacksmiths, Buford and Bart, had just heated a piece of iron, and set it on the anvil.

Buford said, "H-h-h-h-hit it n-n-n-now."

"W-w-w-w-where?" asked Bart.

"Aw sh-sh-sh-shoot," Bufford grumbled, "n-n-now we'll h-h-h-have t-t-t-to h-h-h-heat it again.

The Sense of Humor

It was Bob's, the new mechanic for the neighborhood police department, first day on the job. The sarge told him to fix the flashers because they weren't working. Try as he might, he couldn't get the flashers to work properly so he brought the patrol car to a local garage to have it repaired.

Later in the day, the sarge returns to pick up his cruiser and asks Bob "Everything working okay with the car now?"

"Yep! I had to bring it into town though and was worried that the mechanic there might try to rip me off."

"Well?" asked the sarge.

"I was so relieved when he told me all I needed was twelve dollars' worth of blinker fluid."

Two cops, Harv and Marv, pull up to a Burger King on a lunch break. They go inside and Marv holds a table while Harv places their order at the counter. Marv looks out the window, notices someone taking off with their police car and runs outside. Harv, hearing all the commotion, runs outside and asks Marv what happened. "Someone just drove off with our squad car!"

"Did you try to stop him?" Harv asked.

"I did better than that! I got the license number!"

"You're a high-priced lawyer! If I give you a thousand dollars, will you answer two questions for me?"

"Absolutely! What's the second question?"

Some men in a pickup truck drove to a lumberyard. One of them walked into the office and said, "We need some four-by-twos."

The clerk asked, "You mean two-by-fours, don't you?"

The man said, "I'll go check," and went back to the truck. He returned shortly and said, "Yeah, I meant two-by-four."

"All right. How long do you need them?"

The customer paused for a moment and said, "I'd better go check."

After a while, he returned to the office and said, "A long time. We're gonna build a house with 'em."

A man was lying in his hospital bed when a new patient, bruised, and covered in bandages, was brought in and placed on the bed next to his.

"What happened to you?" he asked.

"I was working on the tenth floor of a building, clearing some bricks and mortar. I couldn't throw them to the ground, so I decided to send them down in a bucket. I pulled the bucket up with a rope. Then I put the end of the rope over a pulley and ran it down to the ground where I tied it to a tree. I went back up to the tenth floor and filled the bucket with bricks. Then I went back downstairs and prepared to lower the bricks."

"Sounds like a good plan to me," the other man said.

"I thought so, too, only now the bucket was heavier than I was so when I untied the rope, the bucket came down like …"

"A ton of bricks?"

"Very funny. Anyway, I held on to the rope and shot straight up like a rocket, but half way up, the bucket hit my shoulder and broke my collarbone."

"Ouch!"

"Well, I went clean up to the pulley, and the bucket hit the ground so hard all the bricks flew out. Now, I was heavier than the bucket, so before I knew it, as the bucket came back up, I went racing down."

"Like another ton of bricks?"

"Cut it out, it hurts too much to laugh. The bucket slammed into my leg and I broke my ankle. Then, when I hit the ground, I landed right on top the pile of broken bricks. After that I passed out. They tell me that's when I let go of the rope."

"That's good."

"Not really because that's when the bucket came back down and …"

Some county workers were out digging a trench along the county road. One of them, who was about as dumb as the dirt he was digging, asked, "How come we gotta be out here working in the hot sun, and the foreman gets to sit up there by that tree in the shade drinking lemonade?"

"Why don't you go over and ask him?" one of the workers said.

So he crawled out of the trench, walked over to the foreman and asked, "How come we have to work so hard and you don't do nothin'?"

"I got brains," the foreman said.

"What do ya mean, brains?" the worker asked.

"Here, let me demonstrate." He proceeded to place his hand on the big oak shade tree and told the worker, "Go ahead, smack my hand as hard as you can with your shovel."

The worker took his shovel, pulled it back, and swung it like a baseball bat. Just as it came to the tree, the foreman pulled his had out of the way. The shovel hit the tree so hard it bounced out of the worker's hands.

"Now do you understand?" the foreman asked.

"I think so." The worker went back and climbed down into the trench.

"Well," his friend wanted to know, "what did you find out?"

"Oh, nothin'. He just said it was because of his brains."

"His brains? What does that mean?"

"Here, I'll show you." The worker put his hand over his face and said, "Go ahead, smack my hand as hard as you can with your shovel."

Thebossorderedoneofhismentodigaholeeightfeetdeep.Afterthejob was completed, the boss returned and explained an error had been made and the hole wouldn't be needed. "Fill 'er up," he ordered.

The worker did as he'd been told. But he ran into a problem. He couldn't get all the dirt packed back into the hole without leaving a mound on top. He went to the office and explained his problem.

The boss snorted. "Honestly! The kind of help you get these days! There's obviously only one thing to do. You'll have to go back and dig that hole deeper so you can get all that dirt back in it!"

An old blacksmith realized he was soon going to quit working so hard. He picked out a strong young man to become his apprentice. The old man was crabby and exacting. "Don't ask me a lot of questions," he told the boy. "Just do exactly whatever I tell you to do."

One morning, the blacksmith took an iron out of the forge and laid it on the anvil. "Get the hammer over there," he said. "When I nod my head ... hit it good and hard."

Now the town is looking for a new blacksmith ...

A Southern lawyer purchased a box of very rare and expensive cigars, then insured them against fire, among other things. Within a month, he'd smoked his entire stockpile of these great cigars, and without yet having made even his first premium payment on the policy. The lawyer filed a claim against the insurance company. In his claim, he stated the cigars were lost "in a series of small fires."

The insurance company refused to pay, citing the obvious reason: that the man had consumed the cigars in the normal fashion.

The lawyer sued ... and won!

The Sense of Humor

In delivering the ruling the judge agreed with the insurance company that the claim was frivolous, however, the judge stated that the lawyer held a policy from the company in which it had warranted that the cigars were insurable and also guaranteed it would insure them against fire, without defining what is considered to be "unacceptable fire," and was obligated to pay the claim.

Rather than endure a lengthy and costly appeal process, the insurance company accepted the ruling and paid fifteen thousand dollars to the lawyer for his loss of the rare cigars lost in the "fires."

Now for the best part. After the lawyer cashed the check, the insurance company had him arrested on twenty-four counts of *arson*!

With his own insurance claim, and testimony from the previous case being used against him, the lawyer was convicted of intentionally burning his insured property and was sentenced to twenty-four months in jail and a twenty-four thousand dollars fine.

RELATIONSHIPS HUMOR

Two satellite dishes meet on a roof, fall in love and get married. The ceremony wasn't much, but the reception was excellent.

A ninety-three-year-old woman visited the pastor to make her final arrangements.

"I don't want any men carrying me out of the church," she said.

"No men? But why?"

"Because. They wouldn't take me out while I was alive … they're not gonna do it when I'm dead!" she grumbled.

A skycap loaded down with suitcases followed a couple to the airline check-in counter. As they approached the line, the husband glanced at the pile of luggage and said to his wife, "Why didn't you bring the piano, too?"

In a nasty mood she snapped back "Are you trying to be funny?"

"No, not really, I just wish you had" he sighed. "I left the tickets on it."

A man was driving home late one night when he picked up a hitchhiker.

As they rode along, he became suspicious of his passenger. He checked to see if his wallet was safe in the pocket of his coat that was on the seat between them, but it wasn't there!

So he slammed on the brakes, ordered the hitchhiker out, and said, "Hand over the wallet immediately!" The frightened hitchhiker handed over a billfold, and the man drove off.

When he arrived home, he began telling his wife about what happened, but she interrupted him, saying, "Before I forget, did you know you left your wallet on the kitchen table this morning?"

A couple went to breakfast at a restaurant where the special was two eggs, bacon, hash browns and toast for $5.99. "Sounds good," the wife said. "But I don't want the eggs."

"Then I'll have to charge you more because you're ordering a la carte," the waitress warned her.

"You mean I'd have to pay for *not* having the eggs?" the woman asked. "Then I'll take the special."

"How do you want your eggs?"

"Raw and in the shell."

She took the two eggs home.

Glenn was trying to sell his old car. He was having a lot of problems selling it because the car had almost two hundred thirty thousand miles on it. One day he told his problem to his friend, Bob.

Bob said, "There might be a way to make the car easier to sell, but it's not legal."

"That doesn't matter," Glenn said, "if I can only sell the thing."

"Okay," Bob said, "Here's the address of a friend of mine. He owns a repair shop. Tell him I sent you, and he will 'fix it'. Then you should have no problem selling your car."

The next weekend, Glenn made the trip to the mechanic.

The Sense of Humor

About one month later, Bob asked him, "Did you sell your car?"

"No," Glenn said, "Why should I? Now it only has fifty thousand miles on it!"

While attending a marriage seminar on communication, a man and his wife listened as the instructor said, "It's critical that husbands and wives know the things that are important to each other." The instructor asked the man, "Can you describe your wife's favorite flower?"

He leaned over, touched his wife's arm gently and whispered, "Pillsbury All-Purpose, isn't it?"

An eighty-year-old gentleman, retired to Florida after his wife of fifty-eight years had passed away. He was quite alone in the world and longed for companionship. One day, as he was walking through a public park, he spied what he considered to be a very pretty, silver-haired lady sitting alone on a park bench. Getting his nerve up, he approached the woman and asked graciously, "Pardon me, ma'am, but may I sit here with you."

She looked up to see a distinguished looking white-haired gentleman and replied, "Why certainly," and scooted over gently to give him room to sit down.

For the next two hours, the two sat and talked about everything. They discovered that they came from the same part of the country, liked the same kind of music, voted for the same presidential candidates, had had long happy marriages, lost their spouses in the last year and, in general, agreed about almost everything.

Finally, the old gentleman cleared his throat and asked sheepishly, "Ma'am, may I ask you two questions?"

With great anticipation she replied, "Of course!"

The old gentleman removed a handkerchief from his coat pocket and spread it out on the ground before her. He very gingerly got down on his one good knee and looked her softly in the eyes. "I know we've only known each other for a couple of hours, but we have so much in common. I feel I have known you all my life. Will you marry me and be my wife?"

She grabbed at his hands and said, "Why, yes, I will marry you! You've made me so very happy!" She reached over and kissed him gently on the cheek. Then she said, "You said you had two questions to ask me. What is the second question?"

With a sheepish grin he said, "Will you help me get back up?"

A wife went to the police station with her next-door neighbor to report that her husband was missing. The policeman asked for a description. She said, "He's thirty-four years old, six foot three, dark eyes, dark hair, an athletic build, weighs one hundred eight-five pounds, is soft-spoken and is good to the children."

Her neighbor protested, "Your husband is five foot four inches, chubby, fat, has a big mouth and is mean to your kids."

The wife replied, "Yeah, but who wants *him* back?"

A single guy is dining in an upscale restaurant where there is a beautiful woman sitting at the next table. He'd noticed her since he sat down, but lacks the nerve to talk with her.

Suddenly, she sneezes and her glass eye goes flying out of its socket towards the man.

Without thinking, he reaches up, grabs it out of the air, and hands it back.

"Oh my, I am so sorry," the woman says as she pops her eye back in place. "Let me buy your dinner to make it up to you," she says.

They enjoy a wonderful dinner together, and afterwards they go to the theater. They talk, they laugh, she shares her deepest dreams and he shares his. She listens intently.

After paying for everything, she asks him if she'll see him again. A few dates later, he said, "You know, you are the perfect woman. Are you this nice to every guy you meet?"

"No," she said. "You just happened to catch my eye."

A man was in his front yard mowing the grass when his neighbor came out of the house and went straight to her mailbox. She opened it, then slammed it shut and stormed back in the house. A little later she came out of her house again, went to the mailbox, opened it, and slammed it shut again. Angrily, back into the house she stormed. As the man was getting ready to edge the lawn, here she came again, marched to the mail box, opened it and then slammed it closed harder than ever.

Puzzled by her actions the man asked her, "Is something wrong?"

To which she replied, "There sure is! I just got a new computer and the dumb thing keeps saying, 'You've got mail."

Two hunters paid a pilot to fly them to Canada to go moose hunting. They got five of them. As they started loading the plane to fly back home, the pilot said his plane could only take four moose. The hunters complained, "Last year we shot five and the pilot let us take all of them, and he had the same plane as you do." So he let them continue loading. But, even with full power, the small plane couldn't handle the load. It went down shortly after takeoff.

As they climbed out of the wreckage, one hunter asked the other, "You got any idea where we are?"

The second hunter looked around for a moment, and said, "Yeah. I think we're pretty close to where we crashed the last time.

At the end of the first few of dates, the couple comes back to her house. He decides to try for that all important first kiss. Filled with confidence, he leans with his hand against the wall and smiles. "How 'bout a good night kiss?"

Embarrassed, she replies, "I couldn't do that. My parents might see us!"

"Oh, come on! Who's gonna see us? It's late"

"No, please. I would just die if someone saw us."

"There's nobody around. Besides, they're probably all asleep!"

"No. I can't!"

"Oh, please, please, please?"

"No. I like you, but I just can't!"

"Oh, yes, you can. Please?"

"No! I can't."

"Pleeeeease?"

Suddenly the porch light comes on and the girl's sister opens the door in her pajamas. In a sleepy voice she says, "Dad said to go ahead and give him a kiss. Or I can do it. Or he'll come down here and do it himself. But would you please tell that guy to take his hand off the intercom button!"

Two retirement center groups charter a double-decker bus for a weekend of site seeing. One group is in the bottom section of the bus, and the other group is in the top. The people down below are making a lot of noise and having a great time until one of them notices he doesn't hear anything from the people up above. He walks up the stairs, and up there, all the people are clutching the seats in front of them, and they're terrified!

So he asks, "What's the matter with you people? We're down here having a wonderful time."

The Sense of Humor

One of the guys from the second group says, "Oh, sure, but you guys have a *driver* down there."

A cowboy came riding around a bend in the trail and saw an Indian on the ground. His head was tilted with his ear to the ground.

When he saw the cowboy he said, "Three men, large wagon, four horses."

The cowboy is amazed. "You can tell all that just by listening to the ground?"

"No," said the Indian, "that's what just ran over me."

A soldier is stationed overseas, far from home, when he gets a "Dear John" letter from his girlfriend, breaking off their engagement. And, to make it even worse, she asks him to return her picture. So he goes around collecting all the unwanted pictures of other girls from several of his friends, sits down, and writes her a letter saying, "Regret I can't remember which one is you ... please keep your picture and return the rest."

An elderly widow and widower were dating for about five years. The man finally decided to ask her to marry him. She immediately said, "Yes." The next morning when he woke up, he couldn't remember what her answer was! *Was she happy? I think so, no, wait, she looked at me funny.* After about an hour of trying to remember, he got on the telephone and gave her a call. Embarrassed, he admitted that he didn't remember her answer to the marriage proposal.

"Oh," she said, "I'm so glad you called. I remembered saying 'yes' to someone, but I couldn't remember who."

Two bachelors are talking when one of them says, "I got a new cookbook last Christmas, but I could never use it."

"What, too many complicated recipes?" the other asked.

"No kidding. Every one of them starts out the same way. It says, "Take a clean dish and …"

A young married couple is back from their honeymoon for only a couple weeks when the husband comes home and tells his wife he has invited three of his friends from the office, and their wives, home for dinner on Friday.

Since this is their first dinner party, and his wife hasn't done much cooking, the husband suggests they order out for Chinese food and she could bake a cake for dessert. She agrees, but on Friday afternoon, she calls her husband in tears.

"The only recipe I can find is for a cake that will feed four," she says.

"Why don't you just double the recipe?" her husband asks.

Just before quitting time the husband gets another call from his wife, and this time she is hysterical.

"I just can't do it," she says. "It's impossible. I doubled everything, just like you said, and it's ready to go in the oven."

"Then what's the problem?" he asks.

His wife sobs, "I've doubled everything, and the book says the cake has to be baked at 350 degrees. I checked the oven and it doesn't go up to 700!"

A rich Texas oilman calls his equally rich buddy and tells him to step outside his house for a minute. The friend walks out the door and there's his wealthy buddy standing next to a pickup truck.

"Lookee here," says the oilman. "I've bought the coffin I want to be buried in when my time comes."

His friend takes a look in the back of the pickup and there is a magnificent coffin. It's top-grade mahogany, hand-carved with ivory inlays and has silver fasteners and pure gold handles.

"How much did this cost?" his friend asks.

"Forty-five thousand dollars," the oilman says very proudly.

"Well then you ain't so smart," says his friend. "For a few thousand more, you could be buried in a Cadillac."

Parents should tell their daughters to marry an archaeologist because the older she gets, the more interested he will be in her.

A stranger entered the building and asked a boy standing in the lobby, "Can you tell me where Mr. Smith lives?"

The boy smiled and said, "I can do better than that, I'll show you."

They walked up six flights of stairs and the boy pointed out the room that belonged to Mr. Smith.

The man pounded on the door repeatedly, but when there was no response, said, "I guess he's not here."

"Oh, no, sir," said the boy. "Mr. Smith is downstairs waiting in the lobby."

A very cheap man was looking for a gift for his friend. Everything was too expensive, except for a broken glass vase he could buy for almost nothing. He asked the store to mail it for him, hoping his friend would think it had been broken on the way.

A few days later he got a thank you note from his friend.

"Thanks for the beautiful vase. It was so thoughtful of you to wrap each piece separately."

"If you'll make the toast and pour the juice, Sweetheart," said the newlywed bride, "breakfast will be ready."

"Good. What are we having for breakfast?" asked her new husband.
"Toast and juice."

A man was showing some friends his new apartment. One of them asked, "What's that big brass basin for?"

"It's a talking clock," he said.

"A talking clock?"

"Sure, watch this." He hit it with a hammer making an ear splitting sound.

A voice on the other side of the wall yelled out, "Hey, knock it off, don't you know it's two o'clock in the morning!"

While traveling through New England, a motorist stopped for gas in a tiny village.

"What's this place called?" he asked the station attendant.

"All depends," the native drawled. "Do you mean what's it called by them that has to live in this crummy, moth-eaten, dust-covered dump, or by them that's merely enjoying its quaint and picturesque rustic charms for a short spell?"

A woman brought an old picture of her dead husband wearing a hat to the photographer and asked if he could remove the hat from the picture.

He convinced her he could easily do that, but he wanted to know on what side of his head he had parted his hair.

"I forget," she said. "But when you take off his hat, I'm sure you can see that for yourself."

Howard was a bird lover. Every night he stood in the backyard, hooting like an old owl. Then one night, an owl called back to him. For a year, the man and his feathered friend hooted back and forth for hours. He even kept a log of their conversations. Then one day his wife was talking with her next-door neighbor.

"My husband spends his nights ... calling out to an owl," she said.

"Isn't that interesting?" the neighbor said. "Mine does, too."

Two friends—one an optimist and the other a pessimist—could never agree on anything. One day, the optimist decided he had found a way to pull his friend out of his pessimistic thinking.

The optimist had a huntin' dog that could walk on water. His plan? Take the pessimist and the dog out duck hunting in his boat.

They went way out into the middle of the lake and right away the optimist brought down a duck. His dog jumped out of the boat, scampered across the water, retrieved the duck and dropped it in the boat.

The optimist looked at his pessimist friend and said, "What do you think about that?"

The pessimist said, "So what's the problem? Your dog can't swim?

An older couple was driving on a long trip and stopped for lunch at a restaurant. The woman left her reading glasses on the table, but she didn't miss them until they were back on the highway. By then, it took them a long time to turn around and go back. All the way, the old man fussed and complained. Finally they pulled into the parking lot, and as the old woman got out of the car, the old man said, "While you're in there, you might as well get my hat, too."

A man is driving down a steep, narrow mountain road. A woman is driving up the same road. As they pass each other, the woman leans out of her window and yells "Pig!"

The man immediately leans out his window and screams, "Witch!"

They each continue on their way, but when he rounds the next corner, *wham*, he smacks into a pig right in the middle of the road.

A married couple was enjoying their new fishing boat together, but it was the husband who was always behind the wheel. He was concerned about what might happen in an emergency. So one day, he said to his wife, "Please take the wheel, dear. Pretend that I am having a heart attack, and you have to get the boat safely back to the dock."

So she drove the boat back to the dock with no trouble.

Later that evening, his wife walked into the living room where her husband was watching TV. She sat down next to him, switched the channel, and said, "Please go into the kitchen, dear. Pretend I'm having a heart attack and you have to set the table, cook dinner and do the dishes."

A couple was having some trouble, so they went to a marriage counselor. After a few sessions, and a lot of questions and listening, the counselor said he had a solution. He got up, went over to the woman and gave her a big hug. Then he looked at the husband and said, "This is what your wife needs, at least once a day!"

The man thought for a minute and said, "All right, if you say so. What time should I have her back here tomorrow?"

A man, who had lived in the desert his whole life, comes to visit a friend. He'd never seen a train before or the tracks they run on. While he was standing there in the middle of the railroad tracks, he hears this whistle—*Whooee Whooee!*—but he has no idea what it is.

Just then he gets hit, and is thrown to the side of the tracks. It was only a glancing blow, but he still had internal injuries, a few broken bones, and some bruises.

The Sense of Humor

He gets out of the hospital and is finally at his friend's house. In the kitchen, the teakettle starts whistling. So he grabs a baseball bat, sneaks in and smashes it to smithereens.

His friend runs into the kitchen and asks, "What in the world did you do that for?"

The desert man said, "Believe me. You gotta kill those things when they're little."

A woman arrives in London on a rainy day. She wakes up the next day and it's raining. It rains the day after that, and the day after that. And the day after that it's still raining.

On her way out to lunch, she sees a little boy and asks, "Hey kid! Does it ever stop raining around here?"

He says, "How should I know? I'm only five."

A woman was talking to her friends about her husband who had recently passed away.

When he was on his deathbed, he told her there were three envelopes in his desk drawer that would "take care" of everything. After he died she opened the drawer and there were three envelopes, just like he'd said.

On the first envelope he wrote, "For the casket." Five thousand dollars was in that envelope. So she bought him a very nice casket.

The second envelope said, "For the expenses," and had four thousand dollars in it. So, she paid all the bills from the funeral.

The third envelope said, "For a nice stone," and had three thousand dollars in it. She held her hand out so her friends could see and said, "Isn't it beautiful!"

Two friends were standing in a bank when a pair of robbers came in. Not only did the thieves clean out all the cash drawers, but they also walked around with bags and ordered everyone to drop in their valuables. Just as the robbers got to the pair of friends, one turned to the other and as he passed him a bill, said, "By the way, here's that twenty bucks I owe you."

A guy bought his wife a beautiful diamond ring for Christmas.

His friend said, "I thought she wanted an SUV."

"She did," he said, "but where in the world was I going to find an imitation Jeep?"

Long ago a thin man insulted a large man. The large man challenged his tormentor to a duel with pistols.

On the day of the duel, the large man complained about the unfair advantage held by the thin man because he was a much smaller target. Finally, the thin man came up with an idea.

"Let the outline of my figure be chalked upon your body," he said to his opponent, "and any shots of mine that hit outside the chalk lines won't count."

A man was having trouble getting a neighbor to keep his chickens fenced in. The neighbor kept talking about chickens being God's creatures, and they had the right to go where they pleased.

The man was having no success keeping the chickens out of his flowerbeds, and he had tried everything.

"Two weeks later, on a visit, I noticed his yard was doing great, and the flowers were beginning to bloom. So I asked him, 'How did you get your neighbor to keep his hens in his own yard?'"

"One night I hid half a dozen eggs under a bush by my flower bed and, the next day, I let my neighbor see me gathering them. That took care of the problem."

The Sense of Humor

One day a man drove his secretary home after she got sick at the office. Although this was an innocent gesture, he decided not to mention it to his wife, because she tended to get jealous.

Later that night, the man and his wife were driving to a restaurant.

He looked down and saw a high-heel shoe half hidden under the passenger seat. He pointed to something out his wife's window and, while she was looking, he scooped up the shoe and tossed it out his side of the car.

When they pulled into the restaurant parking lot, his wife asked, "Honey, have you seen my other shoe?"

A young husband wanted to get his wife something nice for their first anniversary. So, he bought her a cell phone.

The next day, her phone rings and it's her husband. "Hi, Hon," he says. "How do you like your new phone?"

"Oh, I just love it. It's so cool and your voice is as clear as a bell. But there's one thing I don't understand. How did you know I was at the beauty shop?"

Two elderly women were driving in a large car; both could barely see over the dashboard. As they cruised along, they came to an intersection. The light was red but they just plowed right on through.

The woman in the passenger seat thought to herself, *I must be losing my mind, I'm positive we just went through a red light.*

A few minutes later, they came to another intersection. The light was red again, and once more they went right on through. This time the woman in the passenger seat was certain that light had been red.

She was getting nervous and decided to pay very close attention to the next intersection and see what was going on.

At that intersection, sure enough, the light was definitely red and they went right on through it. Finally she turned to woman driving and said, "Mildred! Did you know we just ran through three red lights in a row? You could have killed us!"

Mildred turned back to her and said, "Oh, dear, am I driving?"

An elderly woman decided to have her portrait painted.

She told the artist, "I want you to paint me with diamond earrings, a diamond necklace, an emerald bracelet, a ruby broach, and a gold Rolex."

"But you aren't wearing any of those things."

"I know," she said, "but in case I should die before my husband, I'm sure he'll remarry, and I want his new wife to go crazy looking for all the jewelry."

Two men were out hunting, and they decided to separate to have a better chance of getting something.

The first man said, "If you get lost, fire three shots in the air every hour. That way I can pinpoint your position and find you."

After about three hours, the second man found he was really lost. So he fired three shots into the air just as the first man had told him. He then waited an hour and did it again. He continued until he ran out of ammo.

The next morning, the first man finds the second with the help of forest rangers. He asked his friend if he did what he told him to do.

The man said, "Yes. I fired three shots into the air every hour on the hour ... until I ran out of arrows."

"Joe. Lean out the window and tell me if my turn signal is working."
Joe looked out and said, "Uhhh ...Yes ... No ... Yes ... No ...Yes ..."

The Sense of Humor

"I see," said the blind man to his deaf wife as he stuck his wooden leg out the window to see if it was raining.

Two men have been fishing all week but haven't caught a thing. They decide to spend the last day sleeping and letting the boat drift with the current. Suddenly, the first man feels a jerk on his line and, sure enough, there's a huge fish on the other end. The same thing happens to the second and before they knew it, they'd caught more fish than they could imagine. As the sun sets, they turn the boat around and head for shore; happy about their good fortune.

About halfway home, the first man turned to the second and sadly said, "That was the best place to fish, but how are we ever gonna find it again in the morning?"

"Don't worry," said the second man. "While you were pulling in that last fish, I painted a big X on the side of the boat!"

"How stupid can you be?" his friend said. "What if we can't rent the same boat tomorrow?"

Two men went into a diner and sat down at the counter. They ordered two iced teas, took sandwiches out of their packs and started eating.

The owner saw what was going on and said, "Hey, you can't eat your own sandwiches in here." The two men stopped, looked at each other and then swapped sandwiches.

Two guys go on a fishing trip. They spend a fortune renting all the equipment: the reels, the rods, the wading suits, the boat, the car, and even a cabin in the woods.

The first day they go fishing, but don't catch anything. The same thing happens on the second day and the third day. It goes on like this until finally, on the last day of their vacation, one of the men catches a fish.

259

As they're driving home, they're really depressed. One guy turns to the other and says, "Do you realize that this one lousy fish we caught cost us fifteen hundred dollars?"

The other guy says, "Wow! It's a good thing we didn't catch any more!"

What happens when you play a country song backwards?
You get your dog back, your truck back and your girlfriend back!!!

Two guys are out hiking. All of a sudden, a bear starts chasing them. They hurry to climb a tree, but the bear climbs up after them. The first guy gets his running shoes out of his backpack and starts putting them on.

The second guy asks, "What are you doing?"

"I figure when the bear gets close to us, we can jump down and make a run for it."

The second guy says, "Are you crazy? You can't outrun a bear."

The first guy says, "I don't have to outrun the bear ... I just have to outrun you."

A man left work one Friday afternoon, but it was payday so, instead of going home, he stayed out the entire weekend with the boys and spent all his money. When he finally did get home, Sunday night, his wife questioned him for two hours. Finally she stopped nagging him and simply said,

"How would *you* like it if you didn't see me for two or three days?"

To which he said, "That would be just fine with me."

So Monday went by and he didn't see his wife. Tuesday and Wednesday came and went, and he still didn't see her. By Thursday, the swelling went down enough in one eye so he could see her just a little bit.

The Sense of Humor

A little boy was in the garden filling in a big hole when his neighbor looked over the fence and saw him. "What are you up to there?"

With tears in his eyes the little boy said, "My goldfish died, and I've just buried him."

"That's an awfully big hole for a little goldfish, isn't it?"

The boy looked at him and said, "That's because he's inside *your* cat!"

After much arguing, a man went to his lawyer and had his will written. He took it home to his wife and asked her to read it for corrections or suggestions.

She only had one. "Are you real sure, you want to have your funeral at two a.m.?"

"You bet I do. I'd like to find out, once and for all, how many friends we really have."

So, what's the matter?" asked one woman of her friend over coffee. "I thought you just got back from a nice relaxing fishing trip with your husband."

"Oh, everything went wrong," the second woman answered. "First, he said I talked so loud I scared the fish. Next, he said I was using the wrong bait. And then, he told me I was reeling in too soon. All that might have been okay but then, to make matters worse, I ended up catching the most fish!"

A man became very emotional about certain times and dates. "Today," he said, "is a very special anniversary for me because on this day, over nine hundred years ago, William Tell was born. When I was just a boy, William Tell was my hero. I would get my best friend, who

261

lived next door, to go with me into the back yard. Every day, he used to put an apple on his head and, every day, I used to shoot it off with my bow and arrow."

Then the man started to cry, "He would have been thirty-nine tomorrow."

The groom-to-be ordered two-dozen roses for his fiancée for her twenty-fourth birthday. The card read, "One beautiful red rose for every wonderful year of your life."

Since he was such a good customer at the flower shop, the florist added another dozen roses.

The wedding was called off.

One friend said to the other, "She told me that you told her the secret that I told you not to tell her."

"That's terrible," said the friend. "I told her to promise not to tell you I told her."

"Well then make sure you don't tell her I told you she told me."

There were only two pieces of pie left on the plate, and both Tom and David wanted one. Since Tom decided to show his good manners, he let his friend choose first.

Without hesitation, David reached out and took the biggest piece.

"Didn't your mother ever teach you good manners?" Tom asked. "If you had offered them to me, I would have taken the smaller piece."

"Well, then, that's exactly what you got, so what's the problem?"

A couple of West Virginia hunters are out in the woods when one of them falls to the ground. He doesn't seem to be breathing. His eyes are rolled back in his head. The other guy whips out his cell phone and

The Sense of Humor

calls 911. He gasps to the operator, "I think my friend is dead! What can I do?"

The operator, in a calm soothing voice says, "Just take it easy. I can help. First, let's make sure he's dead."

There is a silence and then a shot is heard. The guy's voice comes back on the line. He says, "Okay, now what?"

A woman's husband had been slipping in and out of a coma for several months, yet she had stayed by his bedside every single day. One day, when he came to, he motioned for her to come nearer. As she sat by him, he whispered, eyes full of tears, "My dearest. You have been with me all through the bad times. When I got fired, you were there to support me. When my business failed, you were there. When I got shot, you were by my side. When we lost the house, you stayed right here. When my health started failing, you were still by my side. You know what?"

"What is it dear?" she gently asked, smiling as her heart began to fill with warmth.

"I think you're bad luck."

Two ladies are at the grocery store after not seeing each other for some time. One asked how the other's husband was doing.

"Oh! Roger died last week. He went out to the garden to dig up a cabbage for dinner, had a heart attack and dropped dead right there in the vegetable patch."

"Oh, dear, I'm sorry," replied her friend, "What did you do?"

"Opened a can of peas instead."

A foursome hadn't missed their Saturday tee-time for as long as any of them could remember. During one such round, a golfer was about to tee up his ball when he noticed a funeral procession winding down the road just off the fairway. He stopped what he was doing, removed his cap, and held it over his heart until the procession had passed.

"My, my," said one of his golfing buddies, "I never realized you had such respect for the dead."

"I felt I had to," said the other as he teed up his ball. "After all, I was married to her for forty-three years."

A Texas oilman hit a gusher and decided to celebrate by buying a souped-up European sports car. He took it for a test drive and eased the car up to seventy, then eighty, and then eighty-five, at which time he noticed a police car in his rearview mirror with its siren blaring. In response, the oilman edged forward another twenty miles per hour, but the patrolman followed closely behind. Finally, the oilman pulled over to the side of the road and looked up to see the furious uniformed patrolman bearing down on him.

"Didn't you see me and hear the siren?"

"Yes, sir, but I have a good explanation."

The patrolman took off his glasses, "This had better be good."

"Well, officer, about three weeks ago my wife ran off with a good-looking state trooper, just like you. When I saw your car, I thought you were him … bringing her back."

A mild mannered man is tired of his wife always bossing him around, so he decides to go to a psychiatrist.

The doctor tells him he has to develop self-esteem and gives him a booklet on assertiveness training. He reads it on the way home.

When he walks through the door and his wife comes to greet him, he tells her, "From now on I'm the man of this house and my word is law. When I come home from work, I want my dinner on the table. Now get

The Sense of Humor

upstairs and lay my clothes on the bed because I'm going out with the boys tonight. Then run my bath. When I get out of the tub, guess who is going to dress me and comb my hair?"

"The funeral director!" she shouted.

Two college roommates were talking, "How are things going with the banker's daughter? Have you popped the question yet?"

"I've asked her a couple times, but I think I'm wearing her down now."

"No kidding, how come?"

"Because last night she said she'd told me 'no' for the very last time."

In desperation the young man asked, "What do you mean you won't marry me? Is there someone else?"

"There has to be," she sighed.

A frustrated guy asked his friend, "How come my girlfriend closes her eyes every time I go to kiss her?

"Have you looked in the mirror lately?"

The newlyweds got tickets to a great concert as a wedding gift. The card, written in red ink, was simply marked, "Surprise!—Bet you can't guess who I am."

They tried and tried, but neither could come up with anyone. The night of the concert came, they went and had a wonderful time. When they got home, all their other gifts had been stolen. The note in the middle of the table, also written in red ink said, "Surprise!—I'm the creep who gave you those tickets."

A little old couple walked slowly into a family restaurant one winter evening. They looked out of place amid all the families and young couples eating there that night. Some of the customers looked

265

admiringly at them. You could tell what the admirers were thinking: *Look, there is a couple who has been through a lot together, probably for 60 years or more!*

The little old man walked right up to the cash register, placed his order with no hesitation, and then paid for their meal. They sat at a table, near the back wall, and started taking food off of the tray. There was one hamburger, one order of fries, and one drink. The little old man carefully unwrapped the plain hamburger and cut it in half. He counted the fries and placed half in front of his wife. He took a sip of the drink, then his wife took a sip, then set it between them.

The customers began to get restless. "That poor old couple," one woman whispered. "All they can afford is one meal for the two of them."

As the old man began eating a young man came to their table. He politely offered to buy another meal for them. The old man said they were fine and they were used to sharing everything. Then the customers noticed that the little old lady hadn't eaten a bite. She just sat there watching her husband eat, occasionally taking turns sipping the drink.

The young man came back and begged them to let him buy them another meal. This time the old lady explained that they were used to sharing everything.

After being politely refused again, he asked: "Ma'am, why aren't you eating? You said you share everything. What is it you're waiting for?"

She smiled and answered ... "The teeth."

An elderly couple—he, age ninety-five, she, age eight-seven—are all excited about their decision to get married. They go for a walk to discuss the wedding and on the way, pass a drugstore and decide to enter to look around.

The bridegroom says to the man behind the counter, "We're about to

The Sense of Humor

get married. Do you sell heart medication?"

Pharmacist: "Of course we do."

"How about medicine for poor circulation?"

Pharmacist: "All kinds."

"Medicine for rheumatism, scoliosis, arthritis?"

Pharmacist: "Certainly."

"What about vitamins, or sleeping pills?"

Pharmacist: "Of course."

"You sell wheelchairs and walkers?"

Pharmacist: "All speeds and sizes."

The man then says to the pharmacist, "We'd like to register here for wedding gifts, please."

A couple just started their Lamaze class, and they were given an activity requiring the husband to wear a bag of sand—to give him an idea of what it feels like to be pregnant. The husband stood up and shrugged saying, "This doesn't feel so bad."

The instructor then dropped a pen and asked the husband to pick it up.

"You want me to pick up the pen as if I were pregnant, the way my wife would do it?" the husband asked.

"Exactly," replied the instructor.

To the delight of the other husbands, he turned to his wife and said, "Honey, would you please pick up that pen for me."

Morris and his wife, Esther, went to the state fair every year and every year Morris would say, "Esther, I'd like to ride in that airplane."

Esther always replied, "I know, Morris, but the airplane ride costs fifty dollars, and fifty dollars is fifty dollars."

One year, Morris and Esther went to the fair and Morris said, "Esther,

267

I'm eighty-five years old. If I don't ride that airplane I might never get another chance."

Esther replied, "Morris, the airplane ride costs fifty dollars, and fifty is dollars is fifty dollars."

The pilot overheard them and said, "I'll make you a deal. I'll take you both up for a ride. If you can stay quiet for the entire ride and don't say one word, I won't charge you. But if you say one word, it's fifty dollars."

Morris and Esther agreed and up they went.

The pilot did all kinds of twists and turns, rolls and dives, but not a word was heard. He did all his tricks over again, but still not a sound.

When they landed, the pilot turned to Morris and said, "I did everything I could think of to get you to yell, but you didn't."

Morris replied, "Well, I was gonna say something when Esther fell out, but like she says, fifty dollars is fifty dollars."

A Police officer pulls over a speeding car. The officer says, "I clocked you at eighty miles per hour, sir."

The driver says, "I don't see how that could be, officer, I had it on cruise control at sixty. Maybe your radar needs calibrating."

Not looking up from her knitting his wife says sweetly, "Now don't be silly, dear, you know that this car doesn't have cruise control."

As the officer writes out the ticket, the driver looks over at his wife and growls, "Can't you keep your mouth shut for once?"

The wife smiles demurely and says, "You should be thankful your radar detector went off when it did, honey."

As the officer makes out the second ticket for the illegal radar detector, the man glares at his wife and says through clenched teeth, "Come on, woman, can't you keep your mouth shut!"

The officer frowns and says, "And I notice that you're not wearing your seatbelt, sir. That's an automatic one hundred dollars fine."

The driver says, "Yeah, well, you see, officer, I had it on but took it off when you pulled me over so I could get my license out of my back pocket."

The wife says, "Now dear, you know very well you didn't have your seat belt on. You never wear your seat belt when you're driving."

And as the police officer is writing out the third ticket the driver turns to his wife and barks, "Why don't you just be quiet?"

The officer looks over at the woman and asks, "Does your husband always talk to you this way, ma'am?"

"Oh, goodness no, officer," she sweetly replies, "only when he's been drinking."

A young wife said to her husband when he returned from work on Valentine's Day, "I have great news for you. Pretty soon we're going to be three in this house instead of two."

The husband started glowing with happiness and, kissing his wife, said, "Oh, sweetheart, I'm the happiest man in the world. What a wonderful Valentine present"

Then she said, "I'm glad that you feel that way because tomorrow morning, my mother is moving in with us."

MINISTRY HUMOR

A young preacher was asked to hold a grave-side service at a small local cemetery for someone with no family or friends. He got himself lost having made several wrong turns. Eventually, a half-hour late, he saw a backhoe and its crew, but the hearse was nowhere in sight, and the workmen were eating lunch.

The diligent young pastor went to the open grave and found the vault lid already in place.

Feeling guilty because of his tardiness, he preached an impassioned and lengthy service, sending the deceased to the great beyond in style.

As he was returning to his car, he overheard one of the workmen say: "I've been putting in septic tanks for a long time, and I ain't *never* seen nothin' like that."

A pastor, lawyer, and a doctor went deer hunting. A large buck appeared from the woods, and all three men took aim and fired. The game warden was called in to determine which man shot the deer first. The warden took one look at the buck and declared, "It's obvious the pastor shot him first. It went in one ear and out the other."

Two church members were going door to door and knocked on the door of a woman who wasn't happy to see them. She told them in no uncertain terms she did not want to hear what they had to say and slammed the door in their faces. To her surprise, the door didn't close and, in fact, bounced back open. She tried again, really put her back into it, and slammed the door, but the same thing happened … the door bounced back open. Convinced these rude people were sticking their foot in the door, she reared back to give it a slam that would really teach them a lesson.

Then one of them said, "Ma'am, before you do that again you need to remove your cat."

An archaeologist was digging in the desert in Israel and came upon a casket containing a mummy. After examining it, he called the curator of a prestigious natural history museum.

"I've just discovered a three-thousand-year-old mummy of a man who died of heart failure!" the excited scientist exclaimed.

The curator said, "Bring him in right away, we'll check it out."

A week later, the amazed curator called the archaeologist. "You were right about the mummy's age and cause of death. How in the world did you know?"

"Easy. There was a piece of paper in his hand that said, '10,000 shekels on Goliath'."

A Sunday school teacher asked her class, "What was Jesus' mother's name?"

One little girl answered, "Mary."

Then the teacher asked, "Can anyone tell me the name of Jesus' father?"

A little boy said, "Verge."

The Sense of Humor

The teacher asked, "Where did you get that name?"

And he said, "Well, you know they're always talking about The Verge 'n Mary."

A pastor was preoccupied with how he was going to ask the congregation to give more money than they were expecting for repairs to the church building. He was annoyed to find that the regular organist was sick and a substitute had been brought in at the last minute. The substitute didn't know what music to play.

"Here's a copy of the service," he said impatiently. "But you'll have to think of something on your own to play after I make my special announcement at the end of the service."

When the time came, the minister paused and said, "Brothers and sisters, we are in great difficulty. The roof repairs cost twice as much as we had expected, and we need another thirty thousand dollars. Anyone who can pledge one hundred dollars or more, please stand up."

Just then, the substitute organist started playing, "The Star Spangled Banner."

A minister who guarded his morning study time very carefully told the new maid that under no circumstances should he be interrupted … "except, of course, if it's a case of life and death."

About a half an hour later the she knocked at his door. "There's a gentleman to see you, sir."

"But I thought I told you …"

"Yes, and I told *him*," she said, "but he says it *is* a matter of life and death."

So he went downstairs … and who did he find? An insurance salesman!

A Sunday school teacher asked, "How many of you children would like to go to Heaven?"

They all raised their hands except little Tommy. The teacher asked, "Tommy, don't you want to go to Heaven, too?"

He said, "I'm sorry, teacher, but my mom told me to come straight home after Sunday school."

One beautiful Sunday morning, a minister announced to his congregation, "My good people, I have here in my hands three sermons ... a hundred-dollar sermon that lasts five minutes, a fifty-dollar sermon that lasts fifteen minutes, and a ten-dollar sermon that lasts a full hour.

"Now, let's take the collection and see which one I'll deliver."

Senators William B. Spong of Virginia and Hiram Fong of Hawaii sponsored a bill recommending the mass ringing of church bells to welcome the arrival in Hong Kong of the US Table Tennis Team after its tour of China.

The bill failed to pass, cheating the Senate out of passing the Spong-Fong Hong Kong Ping Pong Ding Dong Bell Bill.

A Sunday school teacher asked the children just before she dismissed them to go to church, "And why is it necessary to be quiet in church?"

Little replied, "Because people are sleeping?"

A new pastor was talking to the oldest member of his congregation. "I'm 90 years old, preacher, and I don't have an enemy in the world."

"That's an amazing accomplishment," the pastor said.

"Yes, sir, I'm happy to say I've outlived every last one of them."

After church, a lady was picking through frozen turkeys in the grocery store but couldn't find one big enough to feed her family. She asked the stock boy, "Do these turkeys get any bigger?"

He shook his head, "I don't think so, they're all dead."

The ninety-five-year old woman at the nursing home received a visit from one of her fellow church members.

"How are you feeling?" the visitor asked.

"Oh," said the lady, "I'm just worried sick!"

"What are you worried about, dear?" her friend asked. "You look like you're in good health. They're taking care of you, aren't they?"

"Yes, they're taking very good care of me."

"Are you in any pain?" she asked.

"No. I have never had a pain in my life."

"Well, what are you worried about?" her friend asked again.

The lady leaned back in her rocking chair and said with a sigh, "All of my friends have already died and gone on to Heaven. Now I'm afraid they're wondering where I went."

One Sunday, just as the minister was reaching the climax of the sermon, his own young son entered the church, ran to the center aisle, started making loud beeps and brrrmms like a car without a muffler, then zoomed right toward him.

The minister stopped his sermon, pointed at his son, and said, "Jimmy, park the car immediately beside your mother, turn off the ignition and hand her the keys."

The service continued after a good laugh by the congregation.

Little Abby, in church for the first time, watched as the ushers passed the offering plates.

When they neared the pew where her family sat, she said so everyone could hear, "You don't have to pay for me Daddy, I'm under five."

A pig and a chicken walked by a church where a fundraiser was going on. Getting caught up in the spirit of it all, the pig suggested to the chicken that they each make a contribution.

The chicken said, "Great idea, let's offer them ham and eggs?"

"Not so fast," said the pig. "For you, it's a contribution, but for me, that's a total commitment."

A teacher needed some supplies from a Sunday school cupboard that was seldom used and had a combination lock. The pastor offered to give it a try.

He placed his fingers on the lock's dial and raised his eyes heavenward for a moment, then confidently spun the dial and opened the lock. Seeing how impressed the teacher was with this demonstration of faith, he smiled, pointed and said, "The numbers are written up there on the ceiling."

After church one Sunday, a mother said, "The choir was awful this morning."

The father added, "The sermon was too long."

Little Olivia said, "You've got to admit, it was a pretty good show for a dollar."

After the dedication service of his baby brother in church, the older boy cried all the way home in the back seat of the car.

His dad asked him three times what was wrong.

Finally, the boy told him, "That preacher said he wanted us brought up in a Christian home, but I want to stay with you guys."

The Sense of Humor

The children were lined up for lunch in the cafeteria of a Christian school.

At the head of the table was a large pile of apples with a note that said, "Take just one. God is watching."

At the other end of the table was a large pile of chocolate chip cookies.

A boy wrote his own note, "Take as many as you want, God's watching the apples."

An elderly woman had just come home from church one evening when she was startled by a burglar. As she caught the man in the act of robbing her home, she yelled, "Stop! Acts 2:38!"

The burglar stopped dead in his tracks. The woman calmly called the police and explained what she had done.

As the officer cuffed the man to take him in, he asked the burglar, "Why did you just stand there? All the old lady did was yell a Bible reference at you."

"A Bible reference? She said she had an axe and two 38s!"

(Acts 3:28—*Turn from your sin ...*)

A pastor told an elderly neighbor that at his age, he should be giving some thought to the hereafter. The neighbor told the pastor that he thinks about it many times a day.

"That's very wise," the pastor said.

The neighbor explained that wisdom had nothing to do with it, "It's when I open a drawer or a closet and ask myself, 'Now what am I here after?'"

A pastor went to the hospital to visit a patient. On the elevator, a young man was passing around a photograph. Someone asked the weight and he said, "Six-and-a-half pounds."

"Congratulations," the pastor said, "Boy or girl?"

With a great big grin, he said, "Bass."

A country preacher was having trouble with his offering collections. So one Sunday, he announced from the pulpit, "Before we pass the collection plate, I would like to ask that whoever stole the chickens from Mr. Tyson's hen house please refrain from putting any money in the offering plate. The Lord doesn't want money from a thief."

The collection plate was passed around and, for the first time in months, everybody put something in.

Two "saints" were discussing which one of them was more spiritual.

"Huh," said the first guy, "I'll bet twenty dollars you can't even repeat the Lord's Prayer."

"You're on," said the second guy. He cleared his throat and started in.

"Now I lay me down to sleep. I pray the Lord my soul to keep. If I should die before I wake, I pray the Lord my soul to take."

The first guy is amazed. "Wow, I didn't think you could do it. Here's your twenty."

A good Quaker gentleman was awakened one night by noises downstairs in the living room. He realized there was an intruder in his house, so the Quaker took his hunting rifle, and standing at the top of the stairs, said, "Sir, I mean to do thee no harm, but where thou standest is where I am about to shoot."

A well-worn one-dollar bill and a similarly tattered hundred-dollar bill arrived at a Federal Reserve Bank to be retired.

The Sense of Humor

As they moved along the conveyor belt, the hundred-dollar bill began reminiscing about his travels all over the county. "I've had a pretty good life," the hundred said. "I've been to Vegas and Atlantic City, the finest restaurants in New York, Broadway shows—I even took a Caribbean cruise."

"Wow!" said the one-dollar bill. "You've really had an exciting life!"

"So tell me," said the hundred, "where have you been in your lifetime?"

The one-dollar bill said, "Oh, let's see, I've been to the Methodist Church, the Baptist Church, the Lutheran Church ..."

The hundred-dollar bill interrupted, "Wait a minute, what's a church?"

One Sunday, a preacher announced that he'd pass out miniature crosses made from palm leaves.

"Put a cross in the room in your house where your family argues the most. When you look at the cross, it will remind you that God is watching."

As people were leaving the church, a woman came up to the preacher, and said, "I'll take five of them."

A pastor went out on Saturday to visit with members of his church. At one house, it was obvious someone was home, but nobody came to the door even though the preacher knocked several times. Finally, he took out his card, wrote "Revelation 3:20" on the back of it and stuck it in the door.

Behold, I stand at the door and knock. If anyone hears my voice and opens the door, I will come in to him and dine with him, and he with me.—Rev 3:20.

The next day, his card turned up in the offering plate. Written below the pastor's note: *I heard your voice in the garden, and I was afraid because I was naked; and I hid myself.*—Genesis 3:10.

A young theologian named Fiddle
Refused to accept his degree.
He said, "It's bad enough being Fiddle,
Without being 'Fiddle, D.D.'"

A woman did lots of traveling for her business and often had to fly. Flying made her nervous, so she always took her Bible along to read and it helped her relax. One time, she was sitting next to a man. When he saw her pull out her Bible, he gave a little chuckle and went back to what he was doing.

After a while, he turned to her and asked, "You don't really believe all that stuff in there, do you?"

She said, "Of course, I do. It's the Bible."

He asked, "Well, what about that guy that was swallowed by the whale?"

She said, "Oh, Jonah. Yes, I believe that. It's in the Bible."

So he asked, "How do you suppose he survived all that time inside the whale?"

The woman said, "Well, I don't really know. I guess I'll have to ask him when I get to Heaven."

"What if he isn't in Heaven?" the man asked sarcastically.

"Well, then you can ask him."

A little boy was saying his bedtime prayers with his mother: "Lord, bless Mommy and Daddy, and God, *give me a new bicycle!*"

His mother said, "God's not deaf, son."

"I know, Mom, but Grandma's in the next room, and she doesn't

The Sense of Humor

hear so good.

A grandmother was mailing an old family Bible to her daughter in another part of the country.

"Is there anything breakable in here?" the postal clerk asked.

"Just the Ten Commandments."

The young couple invited their aged pastor for Sunday dinner. While they were in the kitchen preparing the meal, he asked their son what they were having.

"Goat," the little boy said.

"Goat?" asked the preacher. "Are you sure about that?"

"Yep," the boy said. "I heard Dad tell Mom, 'Might as well have the old goat for dinner today as any other day.'"

Brother John entered the "Monastery of Silence" and the Abbott said, "Brother, this is a silent monastery. You are welcome here as long as you wish, but you may not speak until I direct you to do so."

Brother John lived in the monastery for five years before the Abbott said to him, "Brother John, you have been here five years now. You may speak two words."

Brother John said, "Hard bed."

"I'm sorry to hear that," the Abbott said. "We will get you a better bed."

After another five years, Brother John was called by the Abbott.

"You may speak another two words."

"Cold food," Brother John said, and the Abbott assured him that the food would be better in the future.

On his fifteenth anniversary at the monastery, the Abbott again called Brother John into his office. "Two words you may say today."

281

"I quit!" said Brother John.

"It is probably for the best," the Abbott said. "You've done nothing but complain the whole time you've been here."

A pastor is walking down the street one day when he notices a very small boy trying to press a doorbell on a house across the street. But the boy is short and the doorbell is too high for him to reach.

After watching this for a little while, the pastor goes across the street, walks up behind the little boy, pats him on the head, reaches over and gives the doorbell a nice, long ring.

Then he leans down to the boy's level, and asks, "And now what?"

"Now we run!"

A funeral service is being held in a church for a woman who has just died. At the end of the service, the pallbearers are carrying her out when they accidentally bump into a wall jarring the casket. They hear a faint moan. They open the casket and find that the woman is actually still alive. She lives for almost ten more years and then she dies. A ceremony is again held at the same church and at the end of the service, as the pallbearers are carrying the casket, the husband calls out, "Watch out for the wall!"

A man has been in business for several years, but the business is going down the drain. He's seriously contemplating suicide. So he goes to his pastor for some advice. He tells the pastor about all his problems in the business and asks what he should do.

The pastor says, "Take a beach chair and a Bible, put them in your car and drive down to the ocean. Go to the water's edge. Take the beach chair out of the car, sit on it, take the Bible out and open it. The wind will blow the pages for a while and eventually, when it stops, the Bible will be open on a particular page. Read the first words your eyes fall on, and then do exactly what it says."

The man does as he's told. He puts a beach chair and a Bible in his car and drives down to the ocean. He sits in the chair by the water's edge and opens the Bible. Just as his pastor said, the wind blows the pages of the Bible and then stops. When he looks down, his eyes fall on the words that tell him what he has to do.

Three months later, the man and his family come back to see the pastor. The man is wearing a thousand-dollar suit, his wife is all decked out with jewels, and their child is dressed in the finest silk. The man hands the pastor a thick envelope full of cash and tells him that he wants to donate this money to the church in order to thank the pastor for his wonderful advice.

The pastor is delighted, and asks the man, "What words in the Bible brought you this good fortune?"

The man smiled and said: "Chapter 11."

"When I was a kid, I used to pray every night for a new bicycle. Then I realized God doesn't work that way, so I stole one and asked Him to forgive me."

There was this lady who was visiting a church one Sunday. The sermon seemed to go on and on forever, and many in the congregation fell asleep. After the service, she walked up to a very sleepy looking man and said, "Hello, I'm Gladys Dunn."

The man looked at her sleepily and said, "You're not the only one, I'm glad it's done too!"

A Sunday school teacher was talking to her class. "I have a question for you," she said, "Who has a fluffy tail, gray fur and eats nuts and bark?" The kids all sat silently. "I'll give you another hint," she said. "He climbs trees and sleeps in the winter." Still no one answered. The teacher was getting a little frustrated and asked them, "Can't you guess? He eats nuts, climbs trees, has a big fluffy tail … who could it be?" After a long pause, one little boy put his hand up and said, "I know it must be Jesus, but it sounds an awful lot like a squirrel."

A couple invited some people for dinner. At the table, the mother turned to her six-year-old daughter and said, "Would you like to say the blessing?"

"I wouldn't know what to say," the little girl said.

"Just use the words you've heard Mommy say."

So little Grace bowed her head, closed her eyes and said: "Oh Lord, why on earth did I invite all these people to dinner?"

Over the massive front doors of a church was inscribed "The Gate of Heaven." Below that was a small cardboard sign that said, "Please use other entrance."

A cowboy was telling his fellow cowboys, back at the ranch, about his first visit to a big-city church. "When I got there, they had me park my old truck in the corral," he began. "You mean the parking lot," interrupted Charlie.

"I walked up the trail to the door."

"The sidewalk to the door," Charlie corrected him.

"Inside the door, I was met by this dude."

"That would be the usher," Charlie explained.

"Well, the usher led me down the chute."

"You mean the aisle," Charlie said.

"Then, he took me to a stall and told me to sit there," the cowboy continued.

"Pew," Charlie corrected.

"Yeah," the cowboy answered. "That's exactly what that pretty lady said when I sat down beside her, 'Pew.'"

A pastor was asked by a politician, "Name something the government can do to help the church."

The pastor said, "Quit making the one-dollar bill."

At the first session of a church membership class, the preacher asked, "What must we do before we can expect forgiveness from sin?"

After a long silence, a man raised his hand and said, "Sin?"

A young pastor, in the first days at his new church, called on the widow of an eccentric man who had just died. Standing before the open casket and consoling the widow, he said, "I know this must be very difficult, but we have to remember that what we see here is like the husk only, the shell ... and the nut has gone on to Heaven."

Little Abby was in church with her mother when she started feeling sick.

"Mommy," she said, "can we leave now?"

"No," her mother scolded.

"Well, I think I have to throw up!"

"Then go out the front door and around to the back of the church. You can throw up in the bushes."

About two minutes later, Abby was back in her seat.

"Didn't you have to throw up?" her mother asked.

"Yes, I did."

"Well, how could you have gone all that way, and come back so fast?"

"I didn't need to go outside, Mommy. They have a real neat box right next to the front door that says, 'For the sick'."

A man drove past a nativity scene in a little country town. One small feature bothered him though. The three wise men were wearing firemen's helmets. He could not figure it out. At a convenience store on the edge of town, he asked the lady behind the counter about the helmets.

She asked him, "Don't you city people ever read the Bible!"

He told her he did, but couldn't recall anything about firemen in the Bible.

She took her Bible from behind the counter and shuffled through a few pages, and finally pointed to a particular passage. "See, it says right here, 'The three wise men came from a-*far*.'"

During the pastor's prayer one Sunday, there was a loud whistle from one of the back pews. The little boy's mother was horrified. She made him stop and, after church, asked, "Whatever made you do such a thing?"

The little boy told her: "I asked God to teach me how to whistle ... and just then He did!"

A six-year-old girl and her four-year-old brother were sitting together in church. The little boy giggled, sang and talked out loud. Finally, his big sister had had enough.

"You're not supposed to talk out loud in church."

"Why? Who's going to stop me?" he asked.

She pointed to the back of the church and said, "See those two men standing by the door? They're the hushers."

The Sense of Humor

Little Elizabeth opened the big, old family Bible and looked at the pages. Then something fell out, and she picked it up to take a closer look. It was an old leaf from a tree that had been pressed in between the pages.

"Momma, look what I found," she hollered.

"What have you got there?" she asked.

"I think it's Adam's suit!"

A pastor was called to a large church in Texas. He had just come from a middle-sized church in Minnesota and didn't know anything about the Southwest. He was greeted warmly and settled in. At his first official meeting, he told the deacons, "I'm interested in getting to know you better and, in order to do that, I want you to meet me here at the church Saturday morning. While I lived in Minnesota, I learned how to bungee jump, and I think it would be nice to go to that high bridge over the Medina River. I'll make a jump and show you how it's done."

Saturday morning, the leaders were all at the church, climbed into a van and headed to the bridge. Below the bridge, a family was having a reunion. The pastor said, "I don't think it'll be a problem, I know how far the cord stretches. I'll just tie it off so we won't disturb them."

He tied off the cord, put on his harness, climbed to the top of the handrail and jumped. As he got close to the bottom, a huge cloud of dust came up and there was a lot of laughing and shouting. As he bounced back up, he yelled, "Help!"

The church members reached out for him but they just missed. Again he went down and again there was a huge cloud of dust. Laughter and screams could be heard. As he came back up, all eight church members reached out and grabbed him. They pulled him back onto the bridge, but he had big welts all over his head.

He groaned, "Can anyone tell me … what's a piñata?"

287

A party of clergymen attended a Presbyterian conference in Scotland. Several of them set off to explore the district. Soon they came to a river spanned by a temporary bridge. Not seeing the notice that said it was unsafe, they began to walk across. The bridge keeper ran after them in protest.

"It's all right," the spokesman said, "we're Presbyterians from the conference."

"I'm no caring aboot that," he argued, "but if ye dinna get off the bridge, you'll soon be Baptists."

Prisoner: "As God is my Judge, my Lord, I am not guilty."

To which the judge replied tersely: "He's not, I am, you are, six months."

A lost and exhausted climber was walking across a snowy plateau when he suddenly became aware of a strong smell of fish and chips.

Through the mist ahead, he saw a Monastery with a priest and monk standing in the doorway.

"You must be the friar."

"No. He's the friar and I'm the chip monk."

A pastor had gone to see an elderly parishioner and she presented him with a jar of peaches saturated in brandy. He opened the jar, took a whiff and said, "Oh, my! You don't know how grateful I am for this."

"Really?" said the old lady. "It's only a small present."

"Yes, but it's not the present that counts, it's the spirit in which it is given."

When little Olivia was filling out a private girl's school questionnaire, she came to a box marked "Religion." After thinking about it for a while, she wrote "Baptist."

When the director noticed the entry, he called her into his office.

"Olivia," he said, "why did you write 'Baptist' under 'Religion'? Don't you know you're an Episcopalian?"

"Of course I do, but I couldn't spell Episcopalian."

In Sunday school, the teacher asked, "Can anyone give me a commandment with only four words in it?" A little boy raised his hand immediately.

"Yes?" the teacher said.

"Keep off the grass!"

The women's auxiliary was in favor of installing a new chandelier. A church conference was scheduled to discuss the matter.

An old deacon, representing a faction that opposed the proposal, said, "We are against this here chandelier for three reasons. In the first place, we can't even order one because nobody knows how to spell it! Second, there ain't anybody in our congregation that could play it. And third, what this church really needs is more light!"

An IRS agent asked a pastor, "One of your members has claimed on his tax return that he made a two-thousand-dollar contribution to your church. Do you know if that's true?"

"Don't worry," the pastor said, "if he didn't … he will."

Western Union officials claim this actually happened in the spring of 1899:

Deacon Shipsley went to Omaha to purchase a new sign to be hung in front of his church. He copied the motto and dimensions but, when he got to Omaha, he discovered he had left the drawing behind. He quickly wired his wife, "Send motto and dimensions."

An hour later, Miss Balsam, the new clerk who knew nothing of the previous message, returned from lunch. When the message came over the wire, she read it and fainted: "Unto Us A Child Is Born. six feet long, two inches wide."

A pastor was walking down a country road and sees a young farmer struggling to load hay back onto a wagon.

"You look hot, my son," the pastor said, "why don't you rest a moment, and I'll give you a hand."

"No thanks," the man said. "My father wouldn't like it."

"Don't be silly, everyone is entitled to a break. Come and have a drink of water."

Again the young man told him, "No thanks, my father wouldn't like it."

The pastor said, "Your father must be a real slave driver. Tell me, where I can find him and I'll give him a piece of my mind!"

"Well," the young farmer said, "he's under that load of hay."

A pastor told his congregation, "Next week, I plan to preach about the sin of lying. To help you understand my sermon, I want you all to read Mark 17."

The following Sunday, as he prepared to deliver his sermon, the preacher asked how many had read Mark 17. Every hand went up. The pastor smiled and said, "Mark has only sixteen chapters. And now, my sermon on the sin of lying."

A pastor went to a large seminar where there was a well-known motivational speaker who began his talk by saying, "The best years of my life were spent in the arms of a woman who was not my wife!"

The crowd was shocked until he said, "And that woman was my mother!" The audience burst into laughter and then he gave his speech, which went over well.

About a week later, one of the pastors at the seminar decided to use that joke in his sermon. Even though he had practiced, he wasn't sure if he could remember exactly how it went.

"The greatest years of my life were spent in the arms of another woman that was not my wife!" he announced.

His congregation sat in stunned silence. After standing there for what seemed like forever, and trying to recall the second half of the joke, he finally blurted out "...but now I can't remember who she was!"

A pastor was asked to dinner by a member of his church, who he knew was a poor housekeeper. When he sat down at the table, he noticed that the dishes were the dirtiest he had ever seen in his life. He ran his fingers over the grit and grime and asked his hostess, "Were these dishes ever washed?"

"Well, yes, they're as clean as soap and water could get them," she told him.

So he blessed the food anyway and started eating. The food was delicious and he said so, despite the dirty dishes.

When dinner was over, the hostess took the dishes outside and yelled, "Here Soap! Here Water!" and two of the biggest, ugliest slobbering dogs he'd ever seen came running over the hill.

After church, a little boy told his parents he needed to go and talk to the pastor right away. They agreed and the pastor greeted them.

"Pastor," the boy said, "I heard you say today that our bodies came from dust."

"That's right, I did," the pastor said.

"And I heard you say that when we die, we go back to dust."

"Yes, I'm glad you were listening. Why do you ask?"

"Well you'd better come over to our house right away, and look under my bed, 'cause there's somebody under there and he's either comin' or goin'!"

A burglar was cruising through an expensive suburb looking for a target of opportunity. At one house, he saw a truck delivering a big flat-screen TV, a stereo system, and speakers. They had to be worth thousands of dollars. He made a mental note and went on his way. The next day he was back in the same neighborhood. When he drove past the house where the electronics had been delivered, he saw an elderly couple loading suitcases into the trunk of their car. He could hardly wait. That night it was foggy, and there was no moon in the sky. He drove up to the house, rang the doorbell and when no one answered, he broke the lock on the kitchen door and went in. It was pitch black inside as he made his way through the kitchen, then the dining room, and finally into the den where he expected to find the all the loot.

"I see you and Jesus sees you," a voice said.

The burglar froze in his tracks.

"I see you and Jesus sees you," the voice said again.

When nothing more happened, the burglar took out his flashlight and shined it in the direction of the voice. All he saw was a parrot sitting on its perch.

"I see you and Jesus sees you."

The burglar threw back his head and laughed.

"It's just a dumb bird," he said.

The burglar closed the drapes before turning on a lamp and that's when he saw a big, mean looking Doberman Pincher sitting beneath the

The Sense of Humor

parrot's perch.

The parrot said, "Sic him, Jesus!"

The members of a church were accustomed to always answering with "And so with you" when the pastor said the prayer. But, one day, he was having problems with his microphone. It went like this:

Pastor: "God bless all those with a meek spirit."

Members: "And so with you."

Then a long silence as the pastor fumbled with the microphone to get it to work. The microphone started working just as the pastor said,

"This thing isn't working."

Members: "And so with you."

The old maid was explaining to her sister, who was visiting from a large city, "Our church is so small, when the preacher says, 'dearly beloved,' I just blush all over."

At work the next day, a man said to his friend, "I heard you skipped church yesterday and played golf."

"That's a lie," said the friend, "and I have the fish to prove it."

On a balmy day in the South Pacific, a navy ship spied smoke coming from one of three huts on an island they thought was deserted. Upon arriving at the shore they were met by a "survivor." He said, "I'm so glad you're here! I've been alone on this island for more than three years!"

The captain of the ship replied, "But we saw *three* huts."

The survivor said, "Oh. Well, I live in one, and go to church in another."

"What about the *third* hut?" asked the captain.

"That's where I *used* to go to church."

293

A little girl became restless as the preacher's sermon dragged on and on. Finally, she leaned over to her mother and whispered, "Mommy, if we give him the money now, will he let us go?"

The teacher asked her Sunday school class to draw pictures of their favorite Bible stories. She was puzzled by Steve's picture, which showed four people on an airplane. So she asked him which story it was meant to represent.

"The flight to Egypt," he said.

"I see. And that must be Mary, Joseph, and Baby Jesus," his teacher said. "But who's the fourth person?"

"Oh, that's Pontius-the Pilot."

When was medicine first mentioned in the Bible?
When Moses received the two tablets.

The pastor turns to the congregation, and points to a coffin in front of him.

"We gather here in the memory of the dearly departed. Is there anyone who wants to say anything about him?"

Silence

"I said, is there anyone who wants to say anything about him? Anything?"

Silence

"I said, is there anyone who wants to say anything about our dearly departed friend?"

A strong voice comes from the back of the church, "His brother was worse."

The Sense of Humor

Three little boys are bragging as only little boys can do.

"My dad's a lawyer," said the first. "Every time he goes to court, he comes home with over a thousand dollars."

"Big deal," the second one said. "My dad's a surgeon. Whenever he does an operation, he makes five thousand dollars."

"You guys make me laugh," the third boy said. "My dad's a preacher, and after he talks for a few minutes on Sunday, it takes six guys just to carry all the money."

Danny was a Baptist. He loved to sneak off to the racetrack. One day he was there betting on the horses and losing his shirt when he noticed a priest step out onto the track and blessed the forehead of one of the horses lining up for the fourth race. Lo and behold, this horse, a very long shot, won the race. Danny was most interested to see what the priest did before the next race.

Sure enough, he watched the priest step out onto the track as the horses lined up. Again he placed a blessing on the forehead of one of the horses. Danny made a mad dash for the betting window and placed a small bet on the horse. And again, even though another long shot, the horse the priest had blessed, won the race. Danny collected his winning and anxiously waited to see which horse the priest bestowed his blessing on for the next race.

The priest blessed a horse, Danny bet on it, and it won! Danny was so excited!

As the day went on, the priest continued blessing one of the horses, and it always came in first. Danny began to make some serious money, and by the last race, he knew his wildest dreams were about to come true. He made a quick stop at the ATM, withdrew all his money and awaited the priest's blessing that would tell him which horse to bet on.

True to his pattern, the priest stepped out onto the track before the last race and blessed the forehead, eyes, ears and hooves of one of the horses.

Danny bet everything he had and then watched as the horse come in dead last. He was bewildered.

He made his way to the track and when he found the priest, he asked, "What happened, Father? All day you blessed horses and they won. Then that last race, you blessed a horse and he finished last. I've lost everything, thanks to you!"

The priest nodded wisely and said, "That's the problem with you Protestants ... you can't tell the difference between a simple blessing and Last Rites."

Mildred, the church gossip and self-appointed supervisor of the church's morals, kept sticking her nose into other people's business. Several residents were unappreciative of her activities, but feared her enough to maintain their silence.

She made a mistake, however, when she accused Harold, a new member, of being an alcoholic, after she saw his pickup truck parked in front of the town's only bar one afternoon.

She commented to Harold and others that everyone seeing it there would know he was an alcoholic.

Harold, a man of few words, stared at her for a moment and just walked away.

He said nothing.

Later that night, Harold quietly parked his pickup in front of Mildred's house ... and left it there all night!

A Pastor was called to a local nursing home to perform a wedding. An anxious old man met him at the door.

The pastor sat down to counsel him, asking several questions "Do you love her?"

The old man replied, "I guess."

"Is she a good Christian woman?"

"I don't know for sure," the old man answered.

"Does she have lots of money?" asked the pastor.

"I doubt it."

"Then why are you marrying her?" the preacher asked.

"Because *she's* still allowed to drive at night," the old man said.

MISCELLANEOUS HUMOR

Two friends were talking. "Can you believe it? A candidate dropped out of the race because of the lack of campaign funds."

"Any politician who stops spending just because he's out of money doesn't belong in Washington anyway."

A crafty pirate was captured by cannibals.

"Plan to eat me, do ya now?" he asked.

He took a knife from his belt, cut off a piece of his leg and handed it to the chief. The cannibal tried as hard as he could to chew it, but finally had to give up.

"First time that old wooden leg has done me a bit of good," the pirate snickered.

One day the pilot of a Cherokee 180 was told by the tower to hold short of the runway while a MD80 landed. The MD80 landed, rolled out, turned around, and taxied back past the Cherokee. Some quick-witted comedian in the MD80 crew got on the radio and said, "What a cute little plane. Did you make it all by yourself?"

The Cherokee pilot, not about to let the insult go by, came back with: "I made it out of MD80 parts. Another landing like that and I'll have enough parts for another one."

A man was hitchhiking the other day, and a hearse stopped. He shook his head and said, "No thanks, I'm not going that far."

The traffic cop stopped the woman for a minor traffic violation. After examining her driver's license in silence for a moment he said, "You know something, this is one of the finest, most realistic pictures I've ever seen on a driver's license. I'm glad to see you aren't one of those vain women who have their photos retouched to remove all the lines in their face."

"Sir," she fumed, "that's my thumb-print."

A senator telephoned the British Embassy on George Washington's birthday. When the phone was answered, he kidded the embassy staff member: "You are working on one of our national holidays; I'm not sure our government would approve of that."

The Britisher replied: "My government expects me to be attentive to duty on *all* American holidays. By not being alert one July fourth, we lost some valuable real estate!"

During a heated World War Two battle, three GIs were captured by the Germans and held under guard in a farmhouse. After several days of detention, the three planned their escape. Breaking a board in the back of the building, they waited for the sentry to pass. When he did, the sergeant squeezed out, ran across a field and dived into some bushes.

The sentry heard a rustle, turned around and shouted, "Who goes?"

The sergeant thought for a moment, then replied, "Meow."

"Ah," the sentry murmured, "only za cat."

300

The Sense of Humor

The two remaining Americans waited for the sentry to pass again. As soon as he did, the corporal dived for the bushes. Hearing the rustle again, the sentry yelled, "Who goes?"

"Meow."

"Ah, only za cat," the sentry said again, resuming his march.

Finally, the private made a run for it and dived into the bushes. "Who goes?" demanded the sentry.

The private thought, then confidently replied, "Za cat."

A couple of mangy, small-town dogs wandered into the big city for the first time. As they roamed through the streets, they passed by a parking meter.

"Will you look at that," one said to the other, "a pay toilet!"

One day the zookeeper noticed the gorilla was reading two books … the Bible, and Darwin's Origin of Species.

So he asked the ape, "Why are you reading those two books?"

"Well," the gorilla said, "I can't decide if I'm my brother's keeper or my keeper's brother."

A man had a ticket to the theater but, after the usher seated him, he wanted to sit closer to the stage.

He whispered to the usher, "This is a mystery play. I can only watch a mystery close up. If you can find me a better seat, I'll give you a tip."

The usher finds a seat and moves him to the second row, but the man only hands the usher a dollar.

The usher is not happy. He looks at the dollar, then leans over and whispers, "The wife did it."

A man loved his old white convertible, but it was in terrible shape.

He refused to get rid of it and even had it insured as an antique. So when the old junker was stolen from his office parking lot, he called the police and his insurance company.

It was all the police officer could do to keep from laughing when he called to tell him, "We found your car less than a mile away. It had a note stuck to the cracked windshield that said, 'Thanks anyway, but I'd rather walk.'"

A tourist was admiring the necklace worn by an old Indian.

"What's it made of?" she asked.

"Alligator teeth," the Indian said.

"I suppose they mean as much to you as my pearls mean to me."

"Not really," he told her. "Anybody can pop open an oyster."

For the first time in many years, an old farmer went to the city to see a movie.

After buying his ticket he stopped at the concession stand to get some popcorn.

"The last time I went to a movie, popcorn was only twenty-five cents."

The kid behind the counter said, "Then you're really going to enjoy yourself because we have sound now."

A man approached a local person in a village he was visiting.

"What's the quickest way to New York?"

The local scratched his head. "Are you walking or driving?" he asked the stranger.

"I'm driving."

"Well that would be the quickest way!"

The Sense of Humor

Give a man a fish and he will eat for a day.

Teach a man to fish and he will go out and buy expensive fishing equipment, stupid looking clothes, a sports utility vehicle, travel a thousand miles to the "hottest" fishing spot and stand waist deep in cold water just so he can outsmart a fish.

A man was driving past a Texas ranch when he hit and killed a calf that was crossing the road. The driver went to the owner of the calf and explained what happened. He asked what the animal was worth.

"Now let me see, about two hundred dollars today," said the rancher. "But in six years, it would have been worth nine hundred dollars. So nine hundred dollars is what you owe me."

The driver sat down and wrote out a check and handed it to the farmer. "Here's a check for nine hundred dollars, but it's postdated for six years from now."

The policeman arrived at the scene of an accident to find that a car had struck a telephone pole. Searching for witnesses, he discovered a pale, nervous young man in work clothes who claimed he was an eyewitness.

"Exactly where were you at the time of the accident?" asked the officer.

"Mister," said the telephone lineman, "I was on top of the pole!"

As a jet flew over Arizona on a clear day, the pilot provided his passengers with a running commentary about landmarks over the intercom.

"Coming up on the right, you can see a large meteor crater, which is a major tourist attraction in northern Arizona. It was formed when a lump of nickel and iron, roughly one hundred fifty feet in diameter and weighing three hundred thousand tons, struck the earth at about forty thousand miles an hour, scattering white-hot debris for miles in every direction. The hole measures nearly a mile across and is five hundred seventy feet deep."

One of the passengers pointed and said, "Will you look at that. It just missed the highway!"

A tiny but dignified little old lady was looking at an art exhibition in a newly opened gallery when a contemporary painting caught her eye.

"What on earth is that supposed to be?" she asked the artist who was standing nearby.

He smiled condescendingly. "That, my dear lady, is supposed to be a mother and her child."

"Well, then, why isn't it?" she snapped.

(Veja du) The overwhelming feeling you've never been in this place before.

President Calvin Coolidge once invited friends from his hometown to dine at the White House. Worried about their table manners, the guests decided to do everything that Coolidge did. This strategy succeeded until coffee was served. The president poured his coffee into the saucer. The guests did the same. Coolidge added sugar and cream. His guests did that too. Then Coolidge bent over and put his saucer on the floor for the cat.

A sailor meets a pirate, and they take turns telling of their adventures on the sea. The sailor notices that the pirate has a peg leg, a hook, and an eye patch. "So how did you end up with the peg leg?"

The pirate said they were in a storm, he was washed overboard and,

The Sense of Humor

as they were pulling him out, a shark bit off his leg.

"Wow! And the hook?"

"Well" the pirate told him, "we were boarding an enemy ship. While we were battling the sailors with swords, one of them cut off my hand."

"Incredible!" the sailor said. "Then how did you get that eye patch?"

"A seagull dropping."

"You lost your eye to a seagull dropping?"

"Yea, but it was also my first day with the hook."

A string walks into a restaurant, sits down and orders a sandwich. The waitress says, "We don't serve strings here."

The string goes outside, ties himself in a knot, roughs up his head, goes back in the restaurant and orders another sandwich. The waitress says "Hey, aren't you the same string who was just in here?"

"No, I'm a frayed *knot*."

A man drove his car into a ditch in a desolate area. Luckily, a farmer came to help with his big strong horse named Prince. He hitched Prince up to the car and yelled, "Pull, Mage, pull!" Prince didn't move.

Then the farmer hollered, "Pull, Bess, pull!" Prince didn't budge.

Once more the farmer commanded, "Pull, Flash, pull!" Nothing happened.

Then the farmer calmly said, "Pull, Prince, pull!" And the horse easily dragged the car out of the ditch. The driver asked the farmer why he called his horse by the wrong name three times.

The farmer said, "Ol' Prince is blind and if he thought he was the only one pulling, he wouldn't even try."

What do you call three rabbits in a row, hopping backwards together? A receding hare line.

There's a guy with a Doberman Pinscher and a guy with a Chihuahua. The guy with the Doberman says to the guy with a Chihuahua, "Let's go over to that restaurant and get something to eat."

The guy with the Chihuahua says, "We can't go in there. We've got dogs with us."

The guy with the Doberman says, "Just follow my lead."

They walk over to the restaurant. The guy with the Doberman puts on a pair of dark glasses and starts to walk in.

A guy at the door says, "Sorry, Bud, no pets allowed."

The guy with the Doberman says, "You don't understand. This is my seeing-eye dog." The guy at the door says, "A Doberman Pinscher?"

He says, "Yes, they're using them now. They're very good."

The guy at the door says, "Okay, come on in."

The guy with the Chihuahua figures, "Well, why not?" So he puts on a pair of dark glasses and starts to walk in.

The guy at the door says, "Sorry, pal, no pets allowed."

The guy with the Chihuahua says, "You don't understand. This is my seeing-eye dog."

The guy at the door says, "A Chihuahua?"

The guy with the Chihuahua yells, "They gave me a *Chihuahua*?"

The metal strips used to band birds are inscribed: "Notify Fish and Wild Life Service, Washington, D.C."

They used to read Washington Biological Survey, abbreviated to "Wash. Biol. Surv."

This was changed after an Alberta farmer shot a crow and then angrily wrote the US government:

"Dear Sirs: I shot one of your pet crows by mistake the other day. I followed the instructions on the band, but the bird was tough and tasted

The Sense of Humor

terrible. You should stop trying to fool the people like this."

What's the difference between an accordion and an onion?
No one cries when you cut up an accordion.

Did you hear about the snail that got beat up by two turtles?
When the police asked him, "Did you get a good look at the turtles that did this?"
He said, "No, it all happened so fast."

A baby snake says to the mother snake, "Mommy, are we poisonous?"
The mother snake says, "Why do you ask?"
And the baby snake says, "Because I just bit my tongue."

On a cold, wintery day, an old man walked out onto a frozen lake, cut a hole in the ice, dropped in his fishing line, and waited patiently for a bite. He was there for almost an hour, without even a nibble, when a young boy walked out onto the ice and cut a hole right next to him. The young boy dropped in his fishing line and minutes later he hooked a Largemouth Bass.

The old man couldn't believe his eyes and chalked it up to beginners luck. But then the little boy pulled in another gigantic fish. The boy kept hauling in one big fish after another. Finally, the old man couldn't stand it any longer.

"Son, I've been fishing here for years and have never caught fish like you are. You've been out here only a few minutes and have caught a half-dozen big fish! How *do* you do it?"

The boy mumbled, "Roo raf roo reep ra rums rrarm."

"What was that?" the old man asked.

"Roo raf roo reep ra rums rarrm."

307

"I'm sorry, but my hearing isn't so good. I can't understand a word you're saying."

The boy spit into one hand and said, "You have to keep the worms warm!"

Police caught two stray dogs yesterday: one was drinking battery acid, and the other was eating fireworks. They charged one and set the other one off.

The tombstone is the only thing that can stand upright and lie on its face at the same time.

A collector of rare books was browsing at a garage sale when the owner struck up a conversation with him.

"I just got rid of an old Bible that had been in our family for generations," he said.

"It had Guten ... something printed on it."

"Not Gutenberg?" gasped the book collector.

"Yes, that was the name."

"Good grief. You've thrown away one of the first books ever printed. A copy just recently sold at auction for over two million dollars."

"Mine wouldn't have been worth near that much," the owner scoffed. "Some clown named Martin Luther had written all over inside it."

In a small village church, a poor widow put one dollar in the collection plate—twice her usual offering. So the pastor asked, "Why?"

"My grandchildren are visiting," she told him.

Two weeks later she put a five-dollar bill in the plate and said with a smile, "They just left."

The Sense of Humor

Before criticizing people, walk a mile in their shoes. Then at least you'll be a mile away and still have their shoes.

During the Middle Ages, probably one of the biggest mistakes was not putting on your armor because you were "just going down to the corner."

All his life, a man had dreamed of going to a Broadway show in New York City. Finally, the opportunity came, and he went to see his first play. But he returned home very disappointed. His friend asked how he enjoyed the performance.

He said, "I only got to see the first act."

"Why, what happened," his friend asked?

"Well, the program said, 'Act two … Three Years Later,' and there's no way I could afford to wait around that long, so I came home."

A farmer stood leaning against a fence post, at the edge of his field, when a flashy sports car roared over the top of the hill. It came to a stop in a cloud of dust right in front of where the farmer was standing.

The driver asked, "Do you know how I can get to Highway 15?"

After thinking for a little bit, the farmer said, "Nope."

"Well, then, can you tell me where the entrance is to the Interstate?"

Again the farmer said, "Nope."

"How about the town of Cherry Valley? Do you know how far that is from here?"

"Nope," the farmer said again.

Finally the driver said, "You don't know very much, do you?"

This time the farmer told him, "Nope, but I'm not the one that's lost, am I?"

A man escaped from the county jail one night and high-tailed it to the nearest farm where he planned to hide out until things cooled down. Close behind him were the sheriff, his deputies and two big bloodhounds. The dogs tracked the man straight down the lane and into the farmyard. Building by building, they looked for the fugitive. He wasn't in the machine shed, he wasn't in the barn, and he wasn't in the corncrib. But, the dogs continued to circle around, indicating they had found their man. Finally, they came to the chicken coop, and the dogs stopped. The sheriff opened the front door to the building, but could only see, hear, and smell chickens. He called out, "Anybody in here?"

A frightened voice answered, "Nobody in here but us chickens."

A duel was fought between Alexander Shott and John Nott. Nott was shot and Shott was not. In this case it is better to be Shott than Nott. Some said that Nott was not shot. But Shott says that he shot Nott. It may be that the shot Shott shot, shot Nott, or it may be possible that the shot Shott shot, shot Shott himself. We think, however, that the shot Shott shot, shot not Shott, but Nott. Anyway it is hard to tell which was shot and which was not.

A man in a rowboat was about to push off shore when a game warden walked up and greeted him. The boater invited the warden along, and the two of them set out on the water.

In the middle of the lake, the man stopped rowing and reached under his seat into a backpack. He pulled out a stick of dynamite, lit it and threw it into the lake.

"Ka-Boom!" went the dynamite. Several fish began to float to the surface, and the man started using his net to scoop them into the boat.

It was a full minute after the explosion, before the wide-eyed game warden recovered from his shock.

The Sense of Humor

"I … I … I can't believe you just did that," said the warden. "In all my life … I mean, you can't do that!"

"Shucks," said the man as he reached into his knapsack. He lit another stick of dynamite, handed it to the warden and asked, "You gonna talk, or you gonna fish?"

A man went into a pet shop and picked out the most colorful parrot he could find. The pet store owner, seeing that he had such good taste, commended him on his choice.

"If you would like, I could send you the bill next month," the owner offered.

"No, that's alright, I'd rather take the whole bird with me today."

A farmer had always wanted to go to the beach, but, unfortunately, he took a wrong turn and wound up in the desert. There was white sand everywhere. Along came an old prospector with his broken-down donkey as the farmer stripped down to his swimming trunks and began to smear on some suntan lotion.

"Whatcha doin'," asked the prospector?

"Goin swimming," said the farmer.

"Swimming?" grumbled the prospector. "The ocean is another nine hundred miles from here?"

"Wow," said the farmer, "this is *some* beach!"

A man was all excited about making his first parachute jump.

"Breathe deeply," coached his instructor, "and remember, if your first rip cord fails, just pull the emergency chute."

"Okay," the man yelled.

"One … two … three … jump," the instructor called out.

With that the man left the plane. He counted one … two … three

… four, until he reached the number ten. Then he pulled the cord … nothing happened. He fumbled around until he found the emergency cord and frantically gave that a yank. Again, nothing.

As he tumbled to earth like a sack of birdseed, he saw a farmer come flying up from the ground. He'd been removing stumps from a field.

"Hey!" he screamed to the farmer, "you know anything about parachutes?"

"No, I don't, but tell me, do you know anything about dynamite?" he asked as he flew out of sight.

Three men were shipwrecked on a small tropical island. One of them spotted a lamp in the sand, and picked it up. He began to polish the lamp when there was a puff of smoke, and out popped a genie.

"Master, I will grant you three wishes," the genie announced.

The first man missed his family, "I wish I could be back home," he sighed. Suddenly he was gone.

The second man said, "I wish I could be back with all my great friends," and like the first, he was gone.

The third man looked around for a minute, and said, "I sure do miss my two friends. I wish they were back here with me," and back they came.

A man had just sat down at the counter and ordered a large iced tea when there was a loud commotion in the street. He wanted to see what it was so he wrote a note, "I spit in this tea."

When he returned to his seat there was another note on the counter that said, "So did I."

A farmer crossed one of his cows with a pit bull. When a neighbor asked him what he got, he told him, "Don't rightly know. It's too ornery

The Sense of Humor

to milk."

Whenever the farmer wanted to know what time it was, he just asked his watch dog.

A farmer was getting tired of people stealing from his watermelon patch, so one day he put up a sign that said, "One of these melons has a roach in it."

Next day he went out to see if any watermelons had been stolen and was happy to see that they hadn't, until he noticed the sign had been changed to say, "Now two of these melons have roaches in them."

A man was so unlucky, when he crossed the street he was hit by a car, and it sent him flying fifteen feet in the air. When the police came, he got a ticket for leaving the scene of an accident.

As he crossed the street, an old man was cautioned by a police officer that a man is run over by a car every five minutes.

"How stupid could he be?" asked the old man.

"Didn't your family take a vacation in California this year?" young Sarah asked.

"Yes," said the little boy. "We went to San Jo Sey."

"Wait a minute. I have an aunt that lives there, and you're supposed to say it so the J sounds like H. She calls it 'San Hosey."

"I didn't know that, but we were only there at the end of Hune, and the first part of Huly."

The attractive young Peace Corps volunteer was speaking at a service club. She described her work in a small African country and told how

313

a native had informally adopted her as his daughter. One day a stranger asked for her hand in marriage. Adhering to custom, the adoptive father asked what livestock the stranger could give in return. When the man said four cows, the father refused, saying that for such a fair young woman the price should be ten cows.

As she concluded her remarks and was returning to her chair, a young man in the audience stood up and asked enthusiastically, "Are you still single?"

Perplexed, she answered, "Yes."

"Great!" he announced. "*I've* got ten cows."

A woman was driving down the highway at about seventy-five miles an hour when she noticed a motorcycle policeman following her. Instead of slowing down, she picked up speed. When she looked back again, there were two motorcycles following her. She shot up to ninety miles an hour. The next time she looked around, there were three cops following her. Suddenly, she spotted a gas station just ahead. She screeched to a stop and ran into the lady's room. Ten minutes later, she innocently walked out. The three cops were standing there waiting for her. Without batting an eye, she said innocently, "I'll bet none of you thought I would make it."

A prisoner at a large maximum-security prison, doing fifty years to life, started training a large fly to do tricks. For years and years, day and night, for thousands of hours, he worked with the tiny insect. After five years, he taught it to walk across a miniature high wire. Another five years passed, and he taught it to ride a tiny one-wheel bike, balance on a pair of stilts and sing songs from "Phantom of the Opera."

"When you and I get out of here," the jailbird said to the fly, "we're gonna tour the night-spots and make a fortune."

Finally the day arrived. With the fly safely tucked away in his pocket

The Sense of Humor

(inside its matchbox home), the ex-con made his way to a local diner for his first meal and to show off his talented friend. Once seated, he brought out his trick fly and placed him on the counter. On cue, it started moon-walking.

The man called to the waiter, "Did you see this fly?"

In one swift motion, the waiter reached for an extra menu, rolled it up and smashed the fly with a mighty swipe. "Glad you told me," muttered the waiter. "Those pesky things are everywhere."

A man was driving to work when a truck ran a stop sign, hit his car broadside and knocked him out cold. A police officer arrived on the scene almost immediately, pulled him from the wreck and revived him. He began to put up a terrific struggle and had to be tranquilized by the paramedics. Later, when he was calm, the cop asked him why he struggled so much.

He said, "I remember the impact, then nothing. I woke up on a concrete slab in front of a huge, flashing 'Shell' sign. And somebody was standing right in front of the S."

A big-city counterfeiter, recently released from prison, decided the best place to pass off his phony $18 bills would be in some small Texas town. So, he got into his new car and off he went. He found a tiny town with a single store.

He entered the store and handed one of the bogus bills to the man behind the counter. "Can you change this for me, please?" he said.

The store clerk looked at the $18 bill a short time, then smiled and told the man, "Ah reckon so, Mister. Ya'll want two nines or three sixes?"

Slim, not the sharpest knife in the drawer, walked into the local post office and noticed a new sign on the wall. Word for word he slowly read out loud, "Man Wanted for Robbery in California."

"Wow," he said. "If that there job was only around here, I'd apply fer it."

A young man was strolling down a street in south London. As he passed a large building with a fence around it, he heard a group of people chanting "Thirteen, thirteen, thirteen, thirteen" over and over again.

Curious, he tried to see over the fence, but couldn't. Then he spotted a knot in the wood, and put his eye to the hole. He managed to spy some old people sitting in deckchairs chanting, just as a thumb came out of nowhere and poked him in the eye.

As he staggered backward, the old people started chanting, "Fourteen, fourteen, fourteen, fourteen ..."

A rich man was riding in the back of his limousine when he saw another man eating grass by the side of the road. He ordered his driver to stop and he got out to investigate.

"Why are you eating grass?" he asked the man.

"I don't have any money for food," the poor man said.

"Oh, please come to my house!"

"But sir, I have a wife and four children."

"Bring them along!" the rich man said. They all climbed into the limo.

Once underway, the poor fellow said, "Sir, you are too kind. Thank you for taking all of us in."

The rich man replied, "No, you don't understand. The grass at my house is over three feet tall!"

Three men are sitting in the sauna. Suddenly there is a beeping sound. The first man presses his forearm and the beeping stops. The others look at him questioningly.

The Sense of Humor

"That's my pager," he says. "I have a microchip under the skin of my arm."

A few minutes later, a phone rings. The second man lifts up his palm to his ear. When he finishes, he explains, "That's my cell phone. I have a microchip in my hand."

The third man, feeling decidedly low-tech, steps out of the sauna. In a few minutes, he returns with a piece of toilet paper hanging from his nose. The others raise their eyebrows.

"I'm getting a fax."

From a passenger ship, everyone can see a bearded man on a small island who is shouting and desperately waving his hands.

"Who is it?" a passenger asks the captain.

"I've no idea. Every year when we pass by, the guy just goes nuts like that."

A fishing club in Minnesota challenged a fishing club from Florida to an ice-fishing tournament. On February 1st, they met on a frozen lake, then went off to find the best spots.

After the first day, the Minnesota team caught fifty fish, and the Florida team caught none.

On the second day the Minnesota team caught a hundred fish, and the Florida team again caught nothing. So the leader of the Florida team chose one of his members to dress up like the Minnesota team to go see if they were following the rules.

When he came back the president asked, "So what did you find? Were they cheating?"

"They sure were. Those guys are cuttin' holes in the ice!"

"The human race has only one really effective weapon, and that is laughter."—Mark Twain

I like long walks ... especially when they are taken by other people who annoy me.

If you are going to try cross-country skiing, start with a small country.

Fifteen minutes into a flight from Kansas City to Toronto, the Captain announced, "Ladies and gentlemen, one of our engines has failed but there is nothing to worry about. Our flight will take an hour longer than scheduled but we still have three engines left."

Thirty minutes later the Captain announced, "One more engine has failed and the flight will take an additional two hours but don't worry, we can fly just fine on two engines."

An hour later the Captain announced, "One more engine has failed and our arrival will be delayed another three hours but don't worry, we still have one engine left."

A young novice passenger turned to the man in the next seat and said, "If we lose one more engine, we'll be up here all day!"

A long New Orleans style funeral procession passes by, but instead of a jazz; band, it's lead by a man walking a lion. Behind the coffin, at least 300 people followed.

A bystander asks the man, "What's going on?"

"My lion ate my lawyer, and this is his funeral," is the reply.

"Could I borrow your lion?" asks the bystander. "I've got a lawyer I'd like to have eaten."

"Sorry," said the man, pointing to the three hundred people following the coffin, "but you'll have to get at the end of that line,"

The Sense of Humor

Two robins were sitting in a tree.

"I'm really hungry," said the first one.

"Me too," said the second. "Let's fly down and find some lunch."

They flew to the ground and found a nice plot of newly plowed ground bursting with juicy worms. They ate and ate and ate and ate until they couldn't eat any more.

"I'm so full I don't think I can fly back up into the tree," said the first one.

"Me neither. Let's just lay here and bask in the warm sun," said the second.

"Okay," said the first.

They plopped down, basking in the sun. No sooner than they had fallen asleep than a big fat farm cat snuck in and gobbled them up.

As he sat there picking feathers from his teeth, he thought to himself, *I really do love baskin' robins.*

A boy walks up to his friends in the playground, holds out his hand and says,

"Did you know my dad can't move these two fingers?"

"Why," his friends ask.

"Because they're mine"

A tourist in Vienna is going through a graveyard when all of a sudden he hears music. No one is around, so he starts searching for the source. He finally locates the origin and finds it is coming from a grave with a headstone that reads: Ludwig van Beethoven, 1770-1827.

Then he realizes that the music is the Ninth Symphony and is being played backwards! Puzzled, he leaves the graveyard and persuades a friend to return with him. By the time they arrive back at the grave, the music has changed. This time it is the Seventh Symphony but like the previous piece, it is also being played backwards. Curious, the men agree to consult a music scholar. When they return with the expert, the Fifth Symphony is now playing—again backwards. The expert notices too the symphonies are all being played in the reverse order in which they were composed. By the next day, the word has spread and a throng has gathered around the grave. They are all listening, as the Second Symphony is being played backward. Just then the graveyard's caretaker ambles up to the group. Someone asked him if he had an explanation for the music.

"Don't you get it?" the caretaker said, "he is de-composing."

Three men were waiting for a cab. The next guy in line let the others push past him into the only two cabs that stopped.

While he was left standing there, a stranger at the bus stop asked, "Why did you do that? Those were the last cabs for the night."

"That's just great," the man said. "Now I'm going to miss my assertiveness training class."

A type-A, hard-charging, corporate ladder-climbing executive was waiting for the circus parade to go past, and he was already late for an appointment. He saw a banner that said, "See our 40 Magnificent Elephants."

Not being the best at math, he started counting as they passed, only he was off by one, "Thirty-eight, thirty-nine, forty."

Then he stomped on the gas. Bam! He ran right into the last elephant in line and killed it instantly.

About a week later he got a bill for five-million dollars. Being a high-pressured kind of a guy, he nearly blew up. "How can one stinking elephant possibly be worth that much money?" he asked his lawyer.

"Well, it's true you only killed one elephant, but you yanked the trunks and tails off of thirty-nine others.

Two Englishmen were sharing the same compartment as their train climbed through the Swiss Mountains. Since it was time for tea, they had just been served. As one of the men raised the cup to his lips and took his first sip, the train roared into a tunnel.

"I say Nigel, have you tasted your tea yet?"

"Not yet, Geoffery, why?"

"I wouldn't recommend it."

"No tea, but why not?"

"Because I just took a sip of mine and went completely blind."

Two women were at the beauty shop when one said to the other, "It's already February, and we're still clearing out after Christmas."

"You are?" asked the other.

"Yes. Last month we cleared out our checking account and, this month, we'll have to clear out our savings."

A man told his friend, "I went to the store the other day. I was only in there for about three minutes but, when I came out, there was a meter maid writing a parking ticket. So I went up to her and said, "Come on, give a guy a break?" She ignored me and continued writing the ticket. So I called her a name. She glared at me and started writing another ticket for having bald tires! So I started arguing with her. She finished the second ticket and put it on the car with the first. Then she wrote a third ticket! This went on for about twenty minutes. The more I abused her, the more tickets she wrote."

"So what did you do?" his friend asked.

"It didn't really matter to me,"

"How come?"

"Because, my car was parked around the corner."

A salesman is driving down a country road when he sees a young boy in front of a barn. On the barn were several targets with arrows in the bull's eye of each target.

Screeching to a stop, he runs out to the boy amazed that this kid could shoot so well.

"Son," he says, "how did you hit all those bulls eyes?"

"Well, sir," the boy replied, "I take the arrow and lick my fingers like this, then I take my fingers and straighten the feathers like this, take aim with my hand against my cheek and let go. Where ever the arrow hits I draw a bull's eye on the barn."

This guy sees a sign in front of a house: "Talking Dog for Sale." He rings the bell and the owner tells him the dog is in the back yard. The guy goes into the back yard and sees a mutt sitting there.

"You talk?" he asks.

"Sure do," the dog replies.

"So, what's your story?"

The mutt looks up and says, "Well, I discovered this gift pretty young and I wanted to help the government, so I told the CIA about my gift. In no time, they had me jetting from country to country, sitting in rooms with spies and world leaders, 'cause no one figured a dog would be eavesdropping. I was one of their most valuable spies eight years running. But the jetting around really tired me out, I knew I wasn't getting any younger and I wanted to settle down. So, I signed up for a job at the airport to do some undercover security work, mostly wandering near suspicious characters and listening in. I uncovered some incredible dealings there and was awarded a batch of medals. Had a wife, a mess of puppies and now I'm just retired."

The Sense of Humor

The man is amazed. He goes back in and asks the owner what he wants for the dog.

The owner says "Ten dollars."

The man says he'll buy him but asks the owner, "This dog is amazing. Why on earth are you selling him?"

The owner replies, "Because he's such a big fat liar."

A little boy was attending his first wedding. After the service, his cousin asked him, "How many women can a man marry?"

"Sixteen," the boy said.

His cousin is amazed that he had an answer so quickly. "How do you know that?"

"Easy," the little boy said. "All you have to do is add it up, like the preacher said: four better, four worse, four richer, four poorer."

Leonard and Ralph built a skating rink in the middle of a pasture. One-day a shepherd, leading his flock, decided to take a shortcut across the rink.

The sheep, however, were afraid of the ice and wouldn't cross it.

Desperate, the shepherd began tugging them to the other side.

"Look at that," Leonard said to Ralph.

"That guy is trying to pull the wool over our ice!"

An immigrant was taking an oral exam applying for US citizenship. He was asked to spell "cultivate". He spelled it correctly. Next he was asked to use the word in a sentence.

He brightened up and said, "Last vinter on a very cold day, I vas vaiting

for a bus, but it vas too cultivate, so I took the subvay home."

He passed.

Three old veterans were bragging about the heroic exploits of their ancestors one afternoon down at the VFW hall.

"My great grandfather, at age thirteen," one declared proudly, "was a drummer boy at Shiloh."

"Mine," boasts another, "went down with Custer at the Battle of Little Big Horn."

"I'm the only soldier in my family," confessed vet number three. "But if my great grandfather was living today he'd be the most famous man in the world."

"Really? What'd he do?" his friends wanted to know.

"Nothing really. But he'd be a hundred and sixty-five years old."

VINTAGE HUMOR

He: I can't marry you, Hannah, we ain't of the same religion.

She: "Oh, that's all right, you can sleep in your church and I'll sleep in mine."

"Can you tell by your husband's face if he's lying?"
"Yes. If his lips are moving, he is."

"I was sorry for your wife in church this morning when she had her coughing attack and everyone turned to look at her.

"Oh, don't worry, she was wearing her new spring hat."

Depression or no depression, a manicurist can make money hand over fist.

On a voyage of one of the Cunard liners from New York to Liverpool, a Major H. Reynolds of London was registered on the passenger list. The purser, running over the names, found he was assigned to the same stateroom as fellow travelers, Major Reynolds and a husky stockman from the Panhandle of Texas.

A little later the cattleman, ignoring the purser, hunted up the skipper.

"Look here, Cap," he demanded, "What kind of a joker is this here head clerk of yours? I can't travel in the same stateroom with that there Major Reynolds. I can't and I won't! So far as that goes, neither of us likes the idea."

"What complaint have you?" asked the skipper. "Do you object to an army officer for a traveling companion?"

"Not generally," stated the Texan, "only this happens to be the Salvation Army. That there major's other name is Henrietta."

When D. L. Moody was on a journey in the western part of Massachusetts, he called on a brother in the ministry on a Saturday, to spend the Sabbath with him. He offered to preach, but his friend objected on account of his congregation having got into the habit of going out before the meeting was closed.

"If that's all, I must and will stop and preach for you," was Moody's reply. When Mr. Moody had opened the meeting and named his text, he looked around on the assembly and said, "My hearers, I am going to speak to two sorts of folks today—saints and sinners! Sinners, I'm going to give you your portion first and would have you give good attention." When he had preached to them as long as he thought best, he paused and said, "There, sinners, I have done with you now. You may take your hats and go out of the meeting house as soon as you please." But all tarried and heard him through.

The reason I wanted to be Adam is, if I pulled a joke, no one could say, "I heard that one before."

A foreign pianist was engaged to act as accompanist for an aspiring amateur singer. The amateur was a lady. She had bounding ambitions, but her technique was faulty. This defect became manifest at the first rehearsal.

After the poor woman had flatted and flatted until she had flatted practically all of her notes, the accompanist waved her to silence.

"Madam," he said mournfully, "it is no use. I gif up der chob. I blay der black keys, I blay der white keys, und always you sing in der cracks.

"Who shined my shoes last night?"

"I did."

"One is black and the other one is brown."

"What a coincidence."

"What do you mean—coincidence?"

"A man got off at the last station complaining of the same thing."

"Did you meet your son at the station?"

"No, I've known him for years."

The conductor, making his rounds on the train, was surprised to find a little old man rolled up under one of the seats.

Caught in his hideout, the little man pleaded, "I'm a poor old man and haven't got the money for a ticket. But my daughter is being married in another town, and I simply must get there for the wedding. Please let me stay here. I promise to be very quiet and not disturb any of the passengers."

The conductor was a kindly man and agreed. But under the very next seat, he found another little old gent huddled up and looking badly frightened. "And where are you going?" he asked.

The man answered, "I'm the groom."

There was an unhappy mountaineer whose son was marched off to school by the truant officer.

"Larnin'!" mocked the mountaineer. "Fiddlesticks! Why, they're teachin' my poor boy to spell 'taters with a P!"

The train was so crowded, a man had to sleep in an upper berth. It was so small, he stuck his feet out the window and in the morning, he found two mail bags on them.

The meditative Hollander delivered a monologue to his dog:

"You vas only a dog, but I vish I vas you. Ven you go your bed in, you shust turn round dree times and lie down; ven I go de bed in, I haf to lock up the blace, and vind up de clock, and put out de cat, and undress myself, and my vife vakes up and scolds, and den de baby vakes and cries and I haf to valk him de house around, and den maybe I get myself to bed in time to get up again.

Ven you get up, you shust stretch yourself, dig your neck a little, and you vas up. I haf to light de fire, put on de kiddle, scrap some vit my vife and get myself breakfast. You be lays round all day and haf blenty of fun. I haf to vork all day and have blenty of drubble. Ven you die, you vas dead; ven I die, I haf to go somewhere again."

"The conductor threw my suitcase out the window because I didn't have a ticket, but my little brother brought it back."

"How did your brother do that?"

"He was in the suitcase."

"How much is a room?"

"Six dollars a week."

"Could you make it a little cheaper?"

"Since it's you, I'll make it one dollar a night."

The Sense of Humor

Little Evelyn ran into the cottage in the North Woods where she was spending the summer with her parents.

"Oh, Mama," she cried, "Where is the bottle of Listerine!"

"What do you want with Listerine?" asked her mother.

"For halitosis," said Evelyn, whose family read the advertisements in magazines and believed what the advertisements said.

"Who has halitosis?" asked her mother.

"A kitty cat, that's who. I want to make friends with her."

"A kitty cat?"

"Yessum. I just now found a lovely strange kitty cat out in the woods. She's nice and tame and she's an awfully pretty kitty with a big bushy tail and white and black stripes down her back and the cunningest black eyes. But, Mama, she has a perfect terrible breath!"

Woman: "Can you give me a room and bath?"

Clerk: "I can give you a room, madam, but you'll have to take your own bath."

This boy came into the grocery store to buy some Wisk.

The grocer reminded him his mother didn't use Wisk, she used Tide. They had an argument over it. Finally, the boy told him he was getting the Wisk so he could wash his canary. The grocer warned him the Wisk could kill the canary, but sold it to him anyway A few days later, the boy was back in the store, and the grocer asked him, "How's your canary?"

"My canary is dead, if you must know."

The grocer said, "I told you that you'd kill the canary, washing it in Wisk."

"The Wisk didn't kill him," the boy said. "It was the wringer."

"Pa got a telegram."

"Bad news?"

"Yes, it came collect, but he can't open it until later."

"Why not?"

"It's a night letter."

"Laughter is free, legal, has no calories, no cholesterol, no preservatives, no artificial ingredients, and it's absolutely safe."

—Dale Irvin